Critical Praise for
Expert Investing on the Net

"Online investing is the wave of the future. It offers low commissions, fast executions, and elimination of the psychological impediments to decision-making that comes from having to go through middlemen. The hard part is navigation, and Paul Farrell is an accomplished guide."

> —Robert R. Prechter, Jr., President
> Elliott Wave International

"Paul Farrell carefully moves an investor through the principles of investing and financial planning and then how to make use of an amazing array of services on the Internet. This is a book for both novices and sophisticated investors. It is absolutely complete."

> —Richard Mogey, Executive Director
> Foundation for the Study of Cycles

"Farrell has done a wonderful job of creating user-friendly text that helps ferret out the best spots on the Net for investors who want to maximize the resources available in cyberspace. Investors should not venture into cyberspace without this guide."

> —Charles Carlson, Editor
> *Dow Theory Forecasts*

"There's a ton of tools on-line to help every investor, but how do you find them? Better yet, are they worth their cost? Paul Farrell provides readers with that ever-so-valuable resource—knowledge—to help investors select those important tools."

> —Ted Kunzog, Editor
> *The Asset Allocator*

"*Expert Investing on the Net* is a well-organized overview of what's out there on the internet for the individual investor; it brings order to the chaos of tens of thousands of investment-related web sites and tells us which are most useful to the investor, and why."

> —Harry Rood, Webmaster
> Investment Special Interest Group,
> Capital PC User Group

"Paul Farrell has articulated the recurring promise of the Net for the individual investor: empowerment. *Expert Investing on the Net* is a must-read for all who want to be empowered."

> —Rohit Shukla, Executive Director
> Los Angeles Regional Technology Alliance

Also by Paul B. Farrell

**The Investor's Guide to the Net:
Making Money Online**

Expert Investing on the Net

Profit from the Top-25 Online Money Makers

Paul B. Farrell, J.D., Ph.D.

John Wiley & Sons, Inc.

NEW YORK • CHICHESTER • BRISBANE • TORONTO • SINGAPORE

This text is printed on acid-free paper.

Copyright © 1996 by Paul B. Farrell
Published by John Wiley & Sons, Inc.

This publication is designed to provide accurate and authoritative information in regard to the subject matter covered. It is sold with the understanding that the publisher is not engaged in rendering legal, accounting, or other professional services. If legal advice or other expert assistance is required, the services of a competent professional person should be sought.

Library of Congress Cataloging-in-Publication Data:
Farrell, Paul B.
    Expert investing on the Net : profit from the top-25 online money makers / Paul B. Farrell.
      p.   cm.
    Includes index.
    ISBN 0-471-15867-4 (pbk. : alk. paper)
    1. Investments—Computer networks. 2. Investments—United States—Computer network resources. 3. Internet (Computer network). 4. World Wide Web (Information retrieval system). I. Title.
HG4515.95.F37   1996
332.6'0285'467—dc20   96-28611

Printed in the United States of America
10 9 8 7 6 5 4 3 2 1

Welcome to the
Do-It-Yourself Cyberspace Revolution

The telecommunications revolution will enlarge the role of the individual with more access to information, greater speed of execution, and greater ability to communicate to anyone or to great numbers anywhere, anytime. *All trends are in the direction of making the smallest player in the global economy more and more powerful.*

—John Naisbitt, *Global Paradox*

Independence. . . . You need to do your own thinking. Don't get caught up in mass hysteria . . . by the time a story is making the cover of the national periodicals, the trend is probably near an end. . . . Never listen to the opinions of others.

—Jack Schwager, *The New Market Wizards*

Take all advice with a grain of salt. . . . In the final analysis, if you are going to be an independent investor, the decision is yours.

—Charles Schwab, *How To Be Your Own Stockbroker*

Think like an amateur as frequently as possible. . . . You don't have to invest like an institution. If you invest like an institution, you're doomed to perform like one, which in many cases isn't very well. . . . If you're a surfer, a trucker, a high school dropout, or an eccentric retiree, then you've got an edge already.

—Peter Lynch, *One Up On Wall Street*

Most of us believe that money-making is a game that is played with forces outside of ourselves, forces such as the economy, the stock market, interest rates, the Fed, government policies, employment statistics and the like. But as you move along the spiritual path and begin to get a taste of the power of your invisible self, you discover that money-making is merely a game that you play with yourself.

—Wayne W. Dyer, *Real Magic*

ACKNOWLEDGMENTS

A special note of thanks to so many friends who made this book a reality:

- ❏ The Wiley publishing team—especially my editors, Myles Thompson and Jacque Urinyi, along with Andrea Abbott, Karin Mihkels, Jeff DeMarrais, Michael Detweiler, and Jennifer Pincott. They are one of those rare gifts every writer dreams of.

- ❏ Three Internet pioneers for helping me get up on the World Wide Web when it was brand new: Michael Strangelove for his insights in *How to Advertise on the Internet;* Howard Harawitz for his HTML editing software; John Celestian and his partners at Internet Media Services for getting my Website online.

- ❏ The North Market Street Graphics team, Ginny Carroll, Chris Furry, and all the staff for converting the raw manuscript into an attractive book design.

- ❏ Netcom Communications for helping to make my mailing list, Wall-Street-News, the largest on its network, and for its NetCruiser browser.

- ❏ All my special friends at the organizations reviewed here, in corporate communications, publicity, and media relations, as well as many journalists, for sharing their insights, software, news articles, analytical reports, financial statements, and many other essential research materials.

- ❏ Mike Blodgett, author, friend, and coach, for his bottom-line wisdom over the years, beginning with such simple truths as write three pages a day and you'll have a book in three months.

- ❏ Steve Wendel, president of StockPro Technologies, for his friendship at each step along the path, and for his brainstorming, nudging, editing, and pep talks.

- ❏ My wife and dearest friend, Dorothy, for many wonderful years of encouragement, faith, and unconditional love.

- ❏ And a Higher Power who's always there with me, no matter what, trudging the road of happy destiny.

Contents

Chapter 4. The Seven Steps of Successful Cyberspace Investing

PART TWO: THE INVESTOR'S TOP-25 NAVIGATORS ONLINE AND ON THE INTERNET

Section One: Online and Internet Services for Cyberspace Investors

1 America Online: Personal Finance Center

2 CompuServe: Global Network for Cyber-Investors

3 Prodigy: The Informed Investor Online and on the Web

4 Reuters Money Network and WealthBuilder

5 Dow Jones News/Retrieval and the New Digital Dow

6 Telescan Investor's Platform, TIPnet, and Wall Street City

Section Two: *Mutual Fund Investing in Cyberspace*

Section Three: *Discount Brokers Online and on the Web*

Do-It-Yourself Investors and the Wall Street Cyberspace Revolution

By the year 2001 virtually all individual shareholders will be cyberspace investors, online and on the Internet—all 52 million stockholders and all 43 million mutual fund shareholders. Impossible? Not at current growth rates.

The high-tech cyberspace revolution is rapidly transforming not only traditional Wall Street, but the investment community worldwide. In sheer numbers alone, this dramatic growth represents a significant shift of power from the large Wall Street institutions into the hands of the Main Street investor.

TODAY'S INVESTORS ARE COMPUTER SAVVY AND VERY INDEPENDENT

A new breed of investor is emerging: an independent, do-it-yourself individual investor armed with high-tech cyberspace power tools. Beardstown Ladies and Generation Xers, Market Wizards and Motley Fools.

Today there are about 25 million computers online and on the World Wide Web. Many are owned by investors. By 2001 they will expand several times over, to 100 million, and probably as high as 250 million.

Branch offices for brokers and banks will soon be obsolete. Computers, modems, and telecommunications will be the primary links connecting you to the new global investment community—nonstop, round-the-clock, to Tokyo, Singapore, Zurich—everywhere, every exchange, every money center—instant real-time information.

In cyberspace, money never sleeps . . . nor do investment opportunities.

You'll hook into this global network without leaving your home or office. Or link up from your cellular phone at a vacation cabin in the mountains. You can handle all of your financial transactions in cyberspace: investing and trading, budgeting and bill paying, online banking and commercial transactions.

As a cyberspace investor, you're hooked into a powerful worldwide network, anytime and anywhere investment decisions are being made.

THE POWER IS SHIFTING TO DO-IT-YOURSELF INVESTORS

The cyberspace revolution is creating a dramatic shift in the balance of power. Wall Street institutions created financial cyberspace 20 years ago, before the personal computer even existed. Until recently, institutional investors had all the power tools; today the playing field is virtually level, thanks to two powerful new weapons for the individual investor: supercharged personal computers and the exploding cyberspace technologies.

Armed with today's powerful new personal computers and the vast resources on the Net, the individual investor can now compete effectively against the big Wall Street institutions. More important, the individual investor can now achieve the goal of financial independence. The financial cyberspace playing field is indeed leveling, and the power is shifting to the new individual NET*investor.

THE INVESTOR'S BIGGEST PROBLEM . . . INFORMATION OVERLOAD

As the financial cyberspace revolution accelerates in the next few years, millions of individual investors will be rapidly tooling up for online and on-the-Net transactions—investing, trading, buying, selling, exchanging, online banking, even shopping and telecommuting.

What will the cyberspace investor discover out there? *Mega-resources!*

Fortunately, there is an enormous selection of products and services available all over the Internet and the Web, as well as the commercial online services, software developers, financial data vendors, newswires, electronic publishers, exchanges, government, cable, and the telecommunication networks. The Net is awesome and exhausting.

In fact, there's too much information out there!

Most cyberspace investors—both newcomers and old-timers—quickly discover that cyberspace is becoming too much of a good thing. In the *Investor's Guide to the Net* we identified well over a thousand key resources for cyberspace investors, online and on the Internet. We also discovered that the number of resources was *multiplying at an accelerating rate,* as the Web continues to double every four months. In fact, from the investor's perspective, the system often appears on the edge of a massive information overload, about to spin out of control and into a meltdown.

Fortunately, there's a solution to managing all this cyberspace information.

THE SOLUTION: PICK ONE OF THE TOP-25 INVESTOR'S NAVIGATIONAL SYSTEMS

Here's the biggest test you'll face in cyberspace: learning how to manage this overwhelming, free-floating global information Net so you can build a winning investment portfolio.

And for that task, you'll need an *investor's NET*navigator*—a central control system, a package of high-tech tools, an operating platform, something to pull together all the *relevant* information into a workable whole, so you can make intelligent investment decisions.

Most investors are quite capable of making their own decisions, *once they have the right information.* In this book we'll give you the facts about the available systems, so you can make your own decisions. With that objective in mind, we've divided the book into two parts.

Part One: Basic Training for the New Cyberspace Investor

The first four chapters are an introduction to the basic tools of cyberspace investing. They describe the environment surrounding your all-important choice of the best navigational system for you as an investor.

These first four chapters are a practical outline of the principles, steps, resources, and processes essential to successful online investing. They're designed to help you stay focused on the goal of financial independence, show you how to prepare a personal financial plan, and guide you through the seven basic steps of cyberspace investing.

Part Two: Top Navigational Systems for Do-It-Yourself Investors

Successful online investing requires a NET*navigator designed specifically for investing, a special cyberspace navigational tool to help you organize, centralize, and control your financial decision-making processes, whether online, offline, or on the Internet.

In Part Two we identify the first 15 NET*navigators, the ones *already in operation* and being used by today's cyberspace investors. They are *tested and proven,* online and on the Internet. We will review and evaluate their key features. These 15 navigational systems are:

Commercial Online Services:

1. America Online: Personal Finance Menu
2. CompuServe: Personal Financial Center
3. Prodigy: Informed Investor

New Online Competitors:

4. Reuters Money Network
5. Dow Jones News/Retrieval
6. Telescan Investor Platform

Mutual Fund Resources:

7. Fidelity Investments
8. Vanguard Group
9. NETworth Internet Investor Network
10. *Mutual Funds* Magazine Online

Discount Brokers Online:

11. The New Cyber-Brokers
12. Charles Schwab & Company
13. PAWWS Financial Network
14. K. Aufhauser's WealthWEB
15. Lombard Internet Securities Trading

Review each of these 15 NET*navigators, without giving any particular weight to their rank on this list. The needs of individual investors vary quite a bit, depending on personality, style of investing, and a host of other factors. What works for one may be quite inappropriate for another. How *you* rank them is all that matters.

Besides, at this early stage of development, most cyberspace investors will be using more than one system. Also included in Part Two is a simple checklist intended to help you evaluate and rate the systems according to your own personal needs and investment style.

The Next Generation of Cyberspace Navigational Systems for Investors

The remainder of the book is a survey of the new, competing systems emerging in this cyberspace arena. Some of the best of this next generation of NET*navigators are already in operation. Compared to the first 15 reviewed, however, these 10 are newer and relatively unseasoned.

The next generation is emerging from within 10 reasonably well-known sectors of the economy. Several systems already appear promising—for example, Quicken's Investor Insight, the AT&T Business Network, and D. E. Shaw's FarSight. As a group, however, this next generation needs further seasoning under operating conditions. Among this group of navigational systems for investors are:

16. **Commercial Banks:** Quicken's Online Banking
17. **Corporate America:** DRIPs and No-Load Stocks
18. **Telecommunications:** AT&T Business Network
19. **Electronic Publishers:** Time Warner's Pathfinder
20. **Financial Television Broadcasters:** CNBC and CNNfn
21. **Quote and Market Data Vendors:** DBC and Quote.Com
22. **World Wide Web Directories:** Classified Yellow Pages
23. **Software Developers:** Microsoft, Sun, and Netscape
24. **Securities Exchanges:** U.S. and Global Financial Networks
25. **Investment Bankers:** Institutions and Rocket Scientists

Again, the order of these 10 groups of NET*navigators is not intended as a rating system. As already mentioned, the needs and decision-making styles of cyberspace investors vary so much that what may rank number one with you, may not work at all for another investor. *The real question is: What fits your unique style of investing?*

THE TOP-25 SYSTEMS: POWER FOR TODAY AND THE FUTURE

Financial cyberspace can be overwhelming. The purpose of this book is to help investors sidestep the problem by simplifying the process. We'll help you identify the 25 major competitors, give you the key facts about their systems, and show you a simple method you can use to rate and select the system best suited for you.

We know that by the year 2001, not only will all investors be in cyberspace, virtually *all cyberspace investment decisions will be made by using one of these Top-25 NET*navigators.* A few new systems will surface, and some existing systems will vanish as consolidation occurs.

However, even with the unpredictability of cyberspace technologies, there's a high probability that the bulk of these Top-25 systems will still be around well into the next century. Therefore, it's real important that the new cyberspace investor get to know all about the top navigational systems available.

A NEW LANGUAGE FOR CYBERSPACE INVESTORS

The field of cyberspace investing is so new, so revolutionary, and so unpredictable that there is no definitive dictionary to describe this emerging technology. Here's a guide to several of the terms we use:

❏ **Wall Street cyberspace:** Terms such as *Wall Street cyberspace, Wall Street Net,* and *financial cyberspace* include all technologies and networks linked to the new electronic investment world. Wall Street cyberspace is not *physically* located in New York City. In fact, today's Wall Street cyberspace is more of a global state of mind that simultaneously ties together all of the world's electronic investors, institutional and individual, while encouraging *independent* decision making.

❏ **The Net is bigger than the Internet:** The Internet is often referred to loosely as "the Net." Actually, *the Net* is the larger information superhighway, including all online services, IntraNets, offline analytics, electronic databases, telecommunication networks, and more.

❏ **NET*Investor:** *Online investor, cyberspace investor,* and *NET*investor* are used interchangeably to describe the new computer-savvy, network-focused investors.

❏ **The NET*investing process:** *Cyberspace investing, Wall Street cyberspace investing,* and *NET*investing* are used interchangeably and refer to your unique investment decision-making thought processes, aided by an online service, the Internet, electronic databases, and/or offline analytics software.

❏ **An Investor's NET*Navigator:** At times we'll combine the term *NET*navigator* with *platform, system,* or *package,* referring to any integrated, one-stop/total-service computerized system investors use to focus, control, and manage their own investment decision-making processes. A NET*navigator is not a Web browser, although one may be a part of your whole system.

Bottom line: Cyberspace is a moving target, and so are the new terms used by the cyberspace investor. The elusiveness of this new cyberspace language is a necessary and even welcomed expression of the dynamic nature of investing in Wall Street cyberspace, a sign that it is healthy and growing rapidly.

In the 1962 classic, *The Structure of Scientific Revolutions,* Thomas Kuhn warned that during periods of major transformations, the language of the old paradigm is inadequate, and the new one is evolving. The same warning applies here with the Wall Street cyberspace revolution.

PART I

Basic Training
for Online Investors

CHAPTER 1

Profile of the New Cyberspace Investor

DISCOVERING FINANCIAL INDEPENDENCE IN CYBERSPACE

You are an individual investor. You make your own investment decisions. It's your money: every dollar earned, every dollar saved. You do the searching for new investments. You're the one analyzing opportunities. You make the buy and sell decisions. You are your own best analyst, your own broker.

It's your portfolio, and the bottom line is yours. Today you are using an online service and some offline analytics to make the job easier. Possibly you're active in an investment club or you subscribe to advisory news-letters. Whether a new investor or an old salt, whether a beginner or an expert with computerized investing, when the chips are down, the bottom line is yours. And that's the way you want it.

Win, lose, or draw, the responsibility and the rewards are yours. You are an independent investor. You enjoy the freedom.

TODAY'S INDEPENDENT INVESTOR IS A CYBERSPACE INVESTOR

You are also a cyberspace investor. Most of today's independent investors are keenly aware that they are on the leading edge of the Wall Street cyberspace revolution. At your command is an enormous arsenal of new, advanced technological firepower. And you have the confidence and ability to use that power.

CYBERSPACE IS NOW "THE INVESTOR'S NEW EDGE"

"Welcome to the sober side of cyberspace. Online services and the World Wide Web have tons of useful resources for do-it-yourself investors. . . . If you want to track the value of your portfolio, buy 100 shares of stock, talk shop with other investors, or find a mutual fund that will help put your kids through college, you can do it with a personal computer and a modem. . . . In fact, financial research is fast becoming one of the main reasons people log on to cyberspace."

SOURCE: Michael Himowitz, "Cyberspace: The Investor's New Edge," *Fortune* (December 25, 1995).

You also are in uncharted territory, although not for long. *Soon all investors will be in cyberspace,* competing for position and profits.

Successful cyberspace investing depends on having state-of-the-art technology. In fact, your choice of technological systems and equipment will be at least as critical as your investment strategies and methods.

CYBERSPACE INVESTING—WALL STREET TOP GUNS VERSUS MAIN STREET DO-IT-YOURSELF

Today you're playing a very competitive, high-stakes game. The big guns on Wall Street have been in cyberspace investing for over two decades. This battlefield is familiar ground to them. In fact, the Merrill Lynches and Smith Barneys have been through *several generations* of high-tech, real-time computer systems playing in their own private cyberspace networks.

If you are going to compete as an independent investor, you need the best possible power tools. Fortunately, the technology is now available for you to compete effectively in Wall Street cyberspace. Everything you need—to beat the street, beat the indexes, and beat the big institutional investors—is *out there*. And we'll help you find all of it.

CYBERSPACE INVESTORS NEED POWERFUL NAVIGATIONAL SYSTEMS

In the *Investor's Guide to the Net* we identified over a thousand separate online/on-Net resources for investors—everything from Internet browsers and CD-ROM technology, to commercial online services and offline software developers, and database search engines and systems platforms from the new Wall Street rocket scientists.

NAVY JET NAVIGATOR DISCOVERS NEW CYBERSPACE NAVIGATOR

"For three years, Kevin Furr watched his retirement savings go next to nowhere in a mutual fund. Then the Navy jet navigator discovered the Motley Fool, an America Online investment club. . . .

"Within a few weeks, Furr, who'd never bought a share of stock in his life, had taken charge of his own IRA. Less than nine months later, he'd more than doubled his nest egg, learning a lot about securities markets in the process. . . .

"He is among a growing group of new and experienced investors who are turning to the Internet and on-line services to trade, learn and generally schmooze about stocks and other securities. . . .

"These proverbial 'little guys' are acquiring genuine market muscle in a *quiet revolution* that is attracting the attention of the financial community, publicly held companies and regulators."

SOURCE: Yardena Arar and Dawn Yoshitake, "On-line Investing, The Wall Street Revolution," *Los Angeles Daily News* (January 14, 1996).

Here, we're focusing more specifically on the Top-25 systems that you can use as operating platforms for your cyberspace investing, rather than surveying *all* of the emerging new Wall Street cyberspace technologies. Now we're getting behind the wheel of the Formula 500 race car, commanding the bridge of the *Enterprise,* a Top Gun pilot.

We're talking about the technology that comes alive when serious investors fire up their computers in the morning, when they log online, check the news, review their portfolios, analyze funds, get quotes on hot stocks, make trades, and fire off E-mail. This demand for new technologies is creating intense competition and the development of one-stop/total-service systems for the new cyberspace investors.

SIX KEY COMPONENTS OF EVERY NET*NAVIGATIONAL SYSTEM

First let's take a quick look at the six basic modules that make up every one of these new high-tech investing systems. *Ideally, all six modules should work together as a single package, although few systems do yet.* The basic functions that every one of these top NET*navigators have in common are:

1. **Your personal computer:**   For over a decade Scott McNealy, founder and CEO of Sun Microsystems, has been telling us that the "network is the computer." Translated, that means that today your computer is actually more powerful than just your hard drive, your central processing unit, and the software at your workstation. Through the Internet and online services, you can now tap into remote databases, temporarily download software, or have somebody else's computer handle a special program application—you don't need everything at your workstation. *The Net is now your computer.*

2. **Online connections:**   Your modem is the key that unlocks all your electronic links and hookups to commercial online services and other private, members-only IntraNets, as well as that powerful new public utility, the Internet. Through your modem you are, in effect, adding modules to your computer, increasing its power.

3. **Offline analytical tools:**   These are all the software tools and databases you prefer to use to search and screen securities, do research on companies and funds, run diagnostic checks and forecasts on price patterns, and so forth. You'll also find many of these analytical functions online and on the Net. In addition, many of the best tools are offline software packages and CD-ROM databases. They offer bigger databases and also help minimize online connection costs and delays.

4. **Financial news updates:**   The cyberspace investor needs services that provide current news and information updates about the markets and companies, which are delivered today by many different electronic publishers—online, on-air, on the Internet, and from private IntraNet resources.

5. **Historical databases:**   Your investment decisions build on past performance and historical information. The facts may come from databases on your hard drive, but in today's new world of cyberspace investing, *they're likely stored somewhere other than your computer,* possi-

bly on a CD-ROM, or somewhere *out there* on the Internet, on somebody else's system, or an online service.

6. **Electronic brokerage:** Your electronic brokerage connection links you with the securities exchanges for your trading, buying, selling, and exchanges. For most new independent cyberspace investors, no live broker contact is necessary; it's all online by modem. Some of these network connections also include the growing number of private systems permitting you to exchange shares within a members-only network.

   For example, Reuter's Instinet, Schwab's OneSource, and Fidelity FundsNetwork, as well as your online modem, hook up to one of the many new electronic discount brokers for a simple stock purchase. Someday soon AT&T may provide a direct link to the securities exchange of your choice, bypassing the online brokers and possibly even extending you credit on margin to buy securities.

BOTTOM LINE: ONE-STOP/TOTAL-SERVICE NAVIGATIONAL SYSTEMS

Today the new cyberspace investor has available many services that package *everything* you need to support your NET*investing process. This trend is guaranteed to continue, and, in the process, you will see more leveling of the playing field as the new cyberspace NET*investor is armed with increased power to compete with the big institutional investors.

The new Wall Street cyberspace, new electronic Wall Street, the WallStreetNET—whatever you want to call this exciting phenomenon—is creating an enormous demand for these one-stop/total-service NET*navigational systems. As a result, the new do-it-yourself cyberspace investor now has all the power tools necessary to become financially independent.

HOW TO TURN $5,000 INTO $22 MILLION: 10 STEPS USED BY ONE SUCCESSFUL INDIVIDUAL INVESTOR

"In the depths of the Depression, when she was already 38 years old and earning little more than $3,000 a year, Anne Schreiber invested a major portion of her life savings in stocks. . . . Few investors, including the best-known professionals of our age, have matched her record. Her return works out to 22.1%, above the performance of the venerable John Neff (13.9%), better than pioneering securities analyst Benjamin Graham (17.4%), and just below Warren Buffett (22.7%) and Fidelity Magellan's Peter Lynch (29.2%).

"*What's more, Anne's basic time-tested investing style can be adapted by any small investor.* . . . What are the lessons of Anne Schreiber's story? Here are eight investment tips—plus two concluding thoughts.

1. Invest in leading brands.
2. Favor firms with growing earnings.
3. Capitalize on your interests.
4. Invest in small bites.
5. Reinvest your dividends.
6. Never sell.
7. Keep informed.
8. Save with tax-exempt bonds.
9. Give back something.
10. And finally, enjoy your money."

SOURCE: Frank Lalli, "10 Secrets From The Investor Who Turned $5,000 into $22 Million," *Money* (January 1996).

If you want to test your skills as a new cyberspace investor, see how quickly you can research and locate the full text of Lalli's article. Try *Money* magazine's archives at Time Warner's Pathfinder Website, discussed in Chapter 23. Also see p. 94 in this book.

CHAPTER 2

Financial Planning Basics for Cyberspace Investors

HOW TO DEVELOP A SUCCESSFUL FINANCIAL PLAN

When it comes to developing a financial plan, any computerized planning system has a definite edge over the old-fashioned pencil, paper, and calculator method. You may eventually decide to hire a financial planning consultant, but before you do, you are likely to find what you're looking for in cyberspace, with some of the excellent financial planning systems pretested by the top experts in the field. For example:

❑ Reuters Money Network's WealthBuilder has Jonathan Pond.
❑ Managing Your Money has Andrew Tobias.
❑ Quicken's Financial Planner has tutorials by well-known financial columnist Jane Bryant Quinn.

In fact, with all of the new online and Internet-based systems out there, it couldn't be easier for you to begin taking charge of your financial future *right now.* Whether you're in your early 20s and starting your first job or cashing in on a successful life and retiring near your favorite golf course, you'll need a financial plan to target the path to your goal. Fortunately, most financial planning systems are integrated into some larger programs

---

HOW YOU CAN SAVE 15 PERCENT . . . AND STILL LIVE IT UP!

"Face it. Most Americans today need to pump up their savings. But take heart: You can be a supersaver and have a great life too. Here's how.

1. Choose your goals, and then put yourself on a savings diet, but leave room for a few treats . . .
2. Sock away your extra, invisible income: bonuses, gifts, raises, refunds . . .
3. Don't pay your bills until you put money in your own savings account . . .
4. Shield your savings from the tax man, and watch your savings swell . . .
5. Make a few small sacrifices to save big bucks, like cut out Domino's deliveries, take vacations near home, brown bag lunch occasionally . . .
6. Shop around until your expenses drop . . . everything including mortgage refinancing, Price Club, insurance, grocery coupons and volume discounts."

SOURCE: Adapted from Penelope Wang, "Save 15% and Still Live It Up," *Money* (December 1995)

---

and will be reviewed later as part of a one-stop/total-service system for NET*investors.

In this chapter our main goal is simply to introduce you to some basic concepts and steps necessary for financial planning today. Anyone can buy stocks, bonds, and mutual funds before formalizing their personal financial plan—especially when there's some extra cash at the end of the month or when a nice bonus arrives. For many investors, however, preparing a personal financial plan is an essential first step to selecting specific securities and designing an investing program that is right for their objectives.

Luckily, there are several excellent personal financial planners in existence that can be used with the investment systems recommended and discussed throughout this book. New programs have been developed by experts in several different disciplines, including discount brokers, accounting firms, mutual fund families, software developers, newswire agencies, and other disciplines.

Many others continue to appear online and on the Net. Once you discover the right time-saving financial planning system for you and start using it on a regular basis, you'll probably toss out all your old reference books and wonder why you didn't get into this online investing game earlier. With all your records right there on your computer, the power for accurate analysis, quick access to the same databases the big guns use, and an online electronic link to your commercial bank and discount trader, you will be on your way to financial independence.

So let's begin with a simple overview of personal financial planning from a recognized expert.

TEN STEPS TO FINANCIAL PROSPERITY

Before you start evaluating computerized NET*investor systems, check out Bill Griffeth's *Ten Steps to Financial Prosperity*. It is one of the best references you can use to get started. Griffeth is an experienced anchor on CNBC-TV and one of the nation's most respected and best-recognized financial journalists. His book is a no-nonsense plan for financial independence, and it is extremely useful if you need to consult a solid print reference on personal financial planning.

The book is an excellent overview because Griffeth is a gifted teacher and knows how to keep it simple. Since the early '80s, Griffeth has displayed a rare talent for presenting complex financial issues in an easy-to-understand, user-friendly manner. It's one reference you'll turn to frequently.

The book's all about saving and investing. Here's a for-instance reinforcing our basic emphasis on disciplined savings. Griffeth's seventh step is about your home and real estate investment. The analogy he draws hits home quickly and simply: "If only we could save for retirement the way we pay for our homes: equal payments every month for up to 30 years. That's how you pay a mortgage, and that's exactly how you should save for retirement, one payment at a time."

Solid advice. Apply it to any financial goal, apply it to the entire process of developing and maintaining your personal financial plan, and you'll come out a winner. Whether you set aside twenty-five bucks a month or a thousand, start now and watch the nest egg grow.

Successful Budgeting: Expenses Past, Present, and Future

Budgeting is necessary for successful financial planning, and the best way to do it is to keep it as simple as possible. Griffeth simplifies budgeting by dividing income into three easy-to-remember categories:

BILL GRIFFETH'S TEN KEY STEPS TO FINANCIAL PROSPERITY

1. **Take Control of Your Money.**
   Set financial goals for yourself.
2. **Budget-ize Yourself.**
   Control every dollar you earn.
3. **Create Your Own Lifetime Investment Plan.**
   Risks, returns, and asset allocations.
4. **Let Mutual Funds Be Your Vehicle to Prosperity.**
   The short course on the perfect investment.
5. **Learn to Manage Your Debt.**
   Turn Deficit Dollars into Prosperity Dollars.
6. **Develop a Do-It-Yourself Retirement Plan.**
   Savings and tax-deferred opportunities.
7. **Make Your Home a Financial Nest Egg.**
   Ten things to maximize your values.
8. **Let Insurance Be Your Prosperity's Safety Net.**
   Contingency protection and planning.
9. **Make Your Estate Planning Fun.**
   Responsible wills and living trusts.
10. **Start Your Children on the Road to Prosperity.**
    Instill financial values; save for college.

SOURCE: Adapted from Bill Griffeth, *Ten Steps to Financial Prosperity* (Chicago: Probus, 1994).

You are strongly encouraged to purchase this book, read it, *and work through each of these steps.* Many of these steps, while beyond the scope of our book, are nevertheless essential to solid personal financial planning.

1. **Budget dollars** (*today's bills*):   Regular monthly bills for rent or home mortgages, utilities, phone, groceries, clothes, and other necessities; payments that come right off the top of the paycheck.

2. **Deficit dollars** (*yesterday's bills*):   Money for short-term installment loans, all your credit cards, auto loans, and line of credit; payments that also demand near-term settlement, but cover past expenditures.

3. **Prosperity dollars** (*tomorrow's bills*):   Moneys set aside for the future, often for specific goals and contingencies, retirement, children's college funds, big-ticket purchases, and unplanned events, both emergencies and opportunities. All too often this is where people fall short on their

budgeting commitments, satisfying these needs only if there's money left over. Unfortunately, if you don't consciously plan, there's nothing left over. Not at the end of the month. And not when you decide to retire. So plan now, save, and invest wisely.

Budgeting is actually very simple using the structure described here. And from your prosperity dollars you will use a percentage of your savings to begin investing toward your personal financial goals.

Risk Tolerance Controls Your Asset Allocations

Griffeth also simplifies investment planning in terms of your tolerance for risk by defining the three primary types of investors, how they react to risk, and their likely asset allocations:

1. **The Speculator:** Is comfortable with investment risks; leans toward heavy stocks.
2. **The Investor:** Accepts a moderate tolerance for risk taking; strives for balance.
3. **The Saver:** Minimizes investment risks; aims for capital preservation.

According to Griffeth, all three investor types seek to allocate portfolio assets to include securities that satisfy a mixture of investor goals—primarily growth, income, and capital preservation. In addition, these allocations will change as a person approaches retirement, although the speculator will almost consistently go for a higher number of growth investments with higher risks. The saver, on the other hand, will typically opt for capital preservation and lower-risk securities. Neither is better. It's merely a matter of knowing yourself and your investment objectives, as well as understanding which investments best fit your tolerance for risk.

Griffeth's personal financial planning book, *Ten Steps to Financial Prosperity,* is one of the best in print. Buy it for your reference bookshelf. We'll also be looking at a number of excellent planning systems—online, offline, and on the Net. Of course, none of them is likely to be your sole resource. The state of the art hasn't evolved sufficiently to eliminate print publications—and it probably never will in our lifetime. So you're well advised to supplement your online system with some solid books for references.

FOUR FUNDAMENTAL STEPS IN ALL FINANCIAL PLANNING

The process of financial planning really isn't all that complex today, simply because the new high-powered software systems do all the number crunching for you. In fact, most of these new programs give you the best of both worlds: lightning-fast calculations that allow you to test as many scenarios as you want, plus the built-in advice of the experienced professional planners who designed the programs.

The process of these new systems is almost as good as a visit with a professional planner, except as you gain experience *you become your own financial planner*. The opening screen of the Fidelity Retirement Planner says: "*At Fidelity, we believe that given the proper tools and information, individual investors like you make their own best investment decisions.*" The giant of the mutual fund industry knows today's investors are taking charge of their own financial futures.

Bottom line: Financial planning is not a complicated process. Virtually every personal financial planner is structured to address these four issues:

1. **Current portfolio:**   How much do you have today?
2. **New savings:**   How much do you plan to save regularly, until you need the money?
3. **Risk and asset allocation:**   What's the best way to invest my savings so they grow enough to satisfy my future goals?
4. **Making up the shortfall:**   What do you do about not having enough either now or later, through more savings and debt management?

For example, if you have $100,000 in savings now and you expect to add $10,000 annually for the next 25 years, you'll have $350,000 in today's dollars and possibly close to a million bucks when you consider future dollars and the returns on wise investments. Depending on your desired income in retirement, your portfolio may well return what you need.

BOTTOM LINE: THE BIG SECRET TO SUCCESSFUL FINANCIAL PLANNING . . . JUST DO IT

If you have trouble with planning and budgeting, remember that you're not alone. Most people experience similar difficulties with savings and investment planning tasks, not because they can't understand the planning process, but for any number of reasons. It happens to the best of us.

The message is loud and clear. Most people fail to plan for the future; they never even begin saving. Remember, it takes money to make money.

The key to financial independence is action. Analysis is essential and planning is important, but the secret is getting into action—*just do it!*

Here's a simple solution. Forget about all the fancy planning and use this one rule of thumb: *Just set aside 5 to 10 percent of your income in one of your savings or investment accounts every month, without fail.* Don't ever touch it, except to invest it. And reinvest the earnings. Get in the habit of saving, and the investment decisions will follow along naturally.

SOFTWARE AND BOOKS ON FINANCIAL PLANNING

Here are some great books on personal financial planning, investment strategies, and asset allocations that can be used with the following planning software:

- ❑ **CA/Your Money:** Daniel Kehrer, *Kiplinger's 12 Steps to Worry-Free Retirement* (Kiplinger's Books, 1993).
- ❑ **FundMap:** Charles R. Schwab, *How to Be Your Own Stockbroker* (Dell Publishing, 1984).
- ❑ **Managing Your Money:** Andrew Tobias, *Still the Only Investment Guide You'll Ever Need* (Harcourt Brace Jovanovich, 1987).
- ❑ **Plan Ahead:** Douglas Sease and John Prestbo, *Barron's Guide to Making Investment Decisions* (Prentice Hall, 1994).
- ❑ **Plan Ahead:** Kenneth Morris and Alan Siegel, The Wall Street Journal's *Guide to Planning Your Financial Future* (Lightbulb Press, 1995).
- ❑ **Prosper:** Ernst & Young Accountants, *Personal Financial Planning Guide* (Wiley, 1995).
- ❑ **Quicken's Financial Planner:** Jane Bryant Quinn, *Making the Most of Your Money* (Simon & Schuster, 1991).
- ❑ **Reuter's WealthBuilder:** Jonathan D. Pond, *The Family Money Book* (Dell, 1993).

Most of these experts are prolific authors, with several books to their credit. Spend a couple hours in the business and investing section of your favorite bookstore. Compare several of these books on financial planning . . . then buy one.

CHAPTER **3**

Financial Planning Online: The Power Tools

THE NEW BREED OF COMPUTERIZED FINANCIAL PLANNERS

Let's check out one of the new breed of cyberspace planners, as an example of the quality of the products now available to help NET*investors. We've looked at some of the basic principles; here's one of the many new, first-class, computerized packages available for personal financial planning.

Charles Schwab is one of the true pioneers in Wall Street cyberspace; he is clearly a leader offline, online, on the Net—you name it. Their cyber-

---

TODAY'S NEW SOFTWARE MAKES FINANCIAL PLANNING EASY!

"Time was when trying to develop a long-term financial strategy meant dealing with a professional planner who might charge steep fees or steer you toward those investment products that would pay big commissions.

"But thanks to the revolution that's underway in personal computing, there's another option: A proliferation of new software programs can help you prepare for retirement, funding your children's education, and reach other major financial goals."

SOURCE: Amy Dunkin, "Set Yourself Free from Financial-Planning Phobia," *Business Week* (May 29, 1995).

---

space investing systems are "killer apps," as an experienced Netsurfer might call them. Schwab has several products worth the close attention of every cyberspace investor, if for no other reason than as detailed examples of the high quality of the products available for both beginners and seasoned investors.

A FIRST-CLASS FINANCIAL PLANNER FOR CYBER-INVESTORS

One of Schwab's more interesting cyberproducts is FundMap. You'll get it free if you have an account with them; otherwise, it's a modest $25. Check Schwab's Website for instructions. FundMap is a solid, basic personal financial planner and a great starting place for the cyberspace investor. Schwab developed the structure and content with a leading accounting firm, Deloitte & Touche, plus the extensive market statistics of Ibbotson & Associates.

FundMap is both sophisticated and user-friendly. All you have to do is answer questions and make the decisions; all the complex calculations are done for you. It's almost as easy as a Nintendo game. FundMap is a perfect guide for any investor who wants an overview of an investment portfolio

FINANCIAL PLANNING SYSTEMS: OFFLINE, ONLINE, AND ON THE NET

Financial Planner	Cyberspace Developer	Contacts
Fidelity Retirement Planner	Fidelity Investments	(800) 544-0246
FundMap	Charles Schwab & Co.	(800) 435-4000
Kiplinger's Simply Money	Computer Associates	(800) 225-5224
Managing Your Money	MECA Software	(800) 537-9993
MS-Money	Microsoft	(800) 426-9400
Plan Ahead	Dow Jones News/Retrieval	(800) 815-5100
Portfolio Manager	Telescan, Inc.	(800) 324-8246
Prosper	Ernst & Young	(800) 277-6773
Quant IX & Pulse	CompuServe	(800) 848-8990
Quicken Financial Planner	Intuit	(800) 964-1040
Retirement Planner	Vanguard Group	(800) 662-7447
Retirement Planning Kit	T. Rowe Price	(800) 541-4041
WealthBuilder	Reuters Money Network	(800) 346-2024

as it interfaces with your online investment strategies. It's a solid tool for the college graduate just beginning to invest, as well as for the more experienced investor with a sizable portfolio. And it is a prerequisite to full-scale NET*investing.

The name "FundMap" is a bit misleading, as you'll discover is the case with many other tools for cyberspace investing. FundMap is actually much more than a map to navigating the world of mutual funds. Yes, you do end up with a fund selection module that emphasizes Schwab funds, along with hundreds of other funds. However, FundMap maintains a high level of professionalism in offering many other funds.

Actually, FundMap is a basic retirement planner, and an excellent one at that. It deserves a close look by every NET*investor. In fact, Schwab may soon put this planner on the Web as an interactive service for all investors. It would quickly become a major cyberspace attraction and a super marketing tool for Schwab's discount brokerage business.

The FundMap planning process has four main steps to help plan your future:

Step 1. Investing Basics: This is a short course on key concepts and terms for independent investors.

Step 2. Savings & Retirement: These 26 questions are designed to help you estimate your savings goals and retirement income. This is a flexible system, so you can go back, change assumptions, check alternative scenarios, and quickly develop your personal financial plan.

Step 3. Asset Allocations: This should help you decide on the right mix of stocks, bonds, and mutual funds, based on your risk profile, current financial position, projections of future needs, and targeted goals. FundMap's eight questions are designed to reveal your risk tolerance.

Step 4. Fund Selection: This process is quite democratic. It features Schwab's funds, plus it includes many other excellent investment opportunities, which are screened for you.

In less than an hour you'll work through some thought-provoking questions and input some key facts about yourself and your financial picture, and—zip—out comes a financial plan, complete with a set of financial goals, a savings plan, asset allocations recommendations, plus some specific mutual fund suggestions.

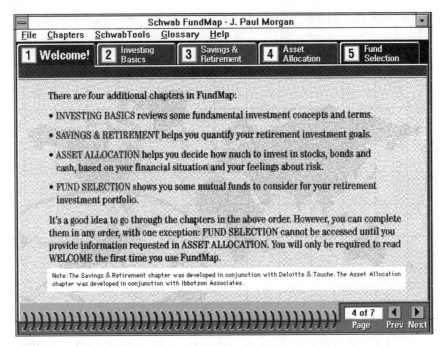

Figure 3.1   FundMap's four modules of financial planning.

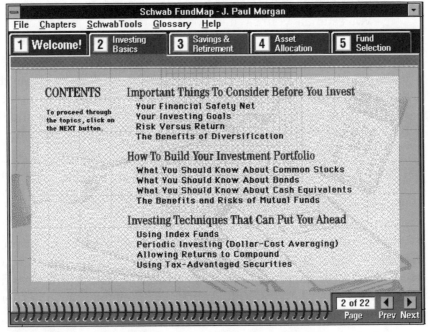

Figure 3.2   The FundMap outline of investing basics.

Step One: Reviewing Basic Investment Terms and Concepts

The FundMap section on Investing Basics is an excellent refresher for any investor. Here's its no-nonsense summary of the essentials of making money online:

❐ **Safety Net:** How much you need in the event of an emergency.

❐ **Investment Goals and Age:** How the number of years to retirement affects your investment goals and asset allocation strategies.

❐ **Risk/Return:** Balancing your risk tolerance and return expectations.

❐ **Portfolio Diversification:** The benefits of diversifying your investments.

❐ **Basic Characteristics:** Stocks, bonds, mutual funds, and cash equivalents.

❐ **Investing Techniques:** A review of key investor strategies and tools, such as index funds, periodic dollar-cost averaging, compounding through reinvesting, and use of tax-advantaged securities.

FundMap provides a great start for the independent investor tooling up for the new electronic Wall Street, online and on the Net. The Investing Basics section of FundMap is 22 pages of one to three brief paragraphs each, plus a glossary of key terms for investors. If you want more details, you may want a more comprehensive guide to financial planning, such as Reuters' WealthBuilder or the Quicken Financial Planner.

However, FundMap's Investing Basics are exactly what you need for this purpose, just enough of a lead-in to the next few working sections of the program. This section is really all you need to get you in the right thinking mood about the financial planning process you're going through.

Step Two: How to Set Financial Goals and Create Savings

This next section of FundMap includes a complete inventory of your current situation, 26 key variables in the form of questions, and data you must input. It assumes you have certain basic information about your financial health. And the great thing is that if anything's missing, you have a checklist of necessary information and decisions to be made.

In fact, if you are serious about becoming a fully digitized electronic investor, this brilliantly conceived software will structure your thinking

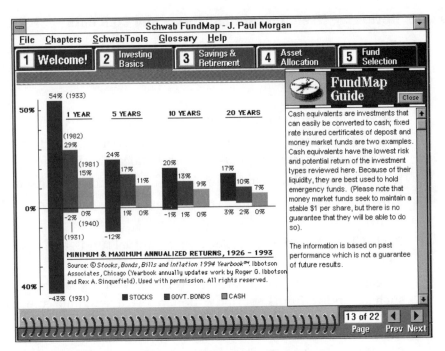

Figure 3.3   Risk vs. returns: stocks and bonds vs. cash.

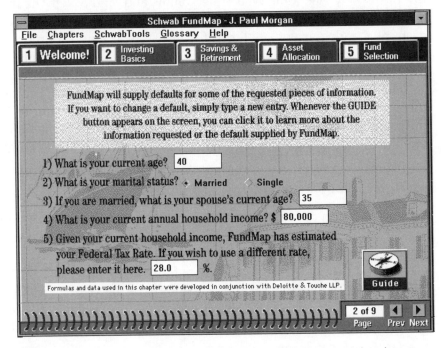

Figure 3.4   Sample questions: your savings and retirement planning.

26 KEY VARIABLES FOR ONLINE FINANCIAL PLANNING

All of FundMap's variables are included here in some detail to show you the scope and levels of complexity and sophistication of one of these financial planning programs. FundMap, like several of the other more advanced systems, simplifies an otherwise quite complex process by eliminating an endlessly boring series of calculations.

1. **Your age**
2. **Marital status**
3. **Spouse's age**
4. **Annual household income**
5. **Federal tax rate** (input or calculated)
6. State of **primary residency**
7. **State tax rates**
8. Estimated **inflation rate**
9. Anticipated **changes in your annual income**
10. **Total savings** now in **tax-deferred accounts,** such as IRAs, 401(k)s, employee profit sharing, or stock ownership
11. **Annual savings** you will **add to that plan** (percent or actual)
12. **Amount the company will be adding** to your plan.
13. Total **other taxable investments** set aside for retirement
14. **Amount you expect to add annually** to taxable investments
15. **Estimated return** on investments **before retirement**
16. Expected **return after retirement**
17. **Age** at which you expect to **retire**
18. Your **life expectancy**
19. Desired annual **income during retirement**
20. **Tax rate during retirement** (input or calculated)
21. State where you'll be **living when you retire**
22. **State tax during retirement**
23. Projected **Social Security benefits**
24. **Pension benefits** during retirement, amount, and start date
25. **Other incomes** during retirement, amounts, and start dates
26. Expected **one-time payments** of money, amount, and start date

SOURCE: Adapted from Charles Schwab's FundMap program, developed in conjunction with Deloitte & Touche.

and handle the calculations with such ease you'll want to move right into Schwab's more advanced trading programs, StreetSmart and e.Schwab, and start investing online immediately.

This section of FundMap is for the serious investor. After you answer the 26 questions and input the necessary data, you can print out a summary of your projected income and investments for retirement along with a summary of your savings rates and amounts, both taxable and tax-deferred.

The advantage of these computerized financial planning systems is their speed. A program like FundMap is designed by professional planners who know the right questions to ask. Furthermore, FundMap has structured a user-friendly way to input what would otherwise require a 100-page workbook for the pencil, paper, and calculator planners.

Schwab's FundMap and its competitors have developed computer software to handle all the calculations instantly. All you have to do is make decisions. It takes less than an hour. Moreover, FundMap gives you total

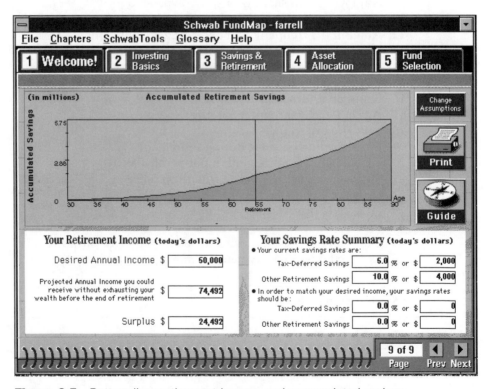

Figure 3.5   Bottom line: retirement income and accumulated savings.

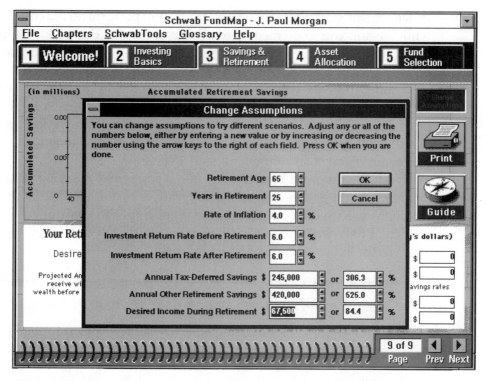

Figure 3.6 Testing your alternatives: flexibility in changing assumptions.

flexibility to vary your assumptions so you can test some alternatives instantly. And the results are displayed in easy-to-read graphics and spreadsheet forms.

You zip through your savings and retirement plan, enjoying the process and chomping at the bit to get on to investing the money you didn't realize you had or to savings you know you really need as a responsible investor.

Step Three: Analyze Your Risk Tolerance and Allocate Assets

Now that you know how much you have to save, you're ready to start making the next level of decisions about *where* to invest the hard-earned dollars currently in your savings plan. And please note at this point a subtle, but crucial, point.

Whether you use FundMap or some other combination of online and offline programs, *these systems will organize your thinking processes with structures that are professionally tested.* They will perform all the calculations, while freeing you to do the real tough job of making decisions and getting into action. Becoming an electronic investor gives you the freedom to focus on your goal of financial independence.

FundMap helps you make your asset allocation decision. A series of eight multiple-choice questions focuses on the major elements of sound portfolio asset allocation. Experience has proven these are the key elements necessary to developing a solid strategy for your investment portfolio—one you can adjust as your circumstances change.

Next, the program bottom-lines into a suggested portfolio, which, for example, might be "moderately conservative." Your answers to the eight questions are used to calculate the type of portfolio best suited for your particular near- and long-term financial needs and your tolerance for risk, a key factor in the asset mix and its returns.

KEEP-IT-SIMPLE FORMULAS FOR DO-IT-YOURSELF INVESTORS

"One rule of thumb for deciding what investments to make: add a percentage sign in front of your age. You should have no more than that percentage of your money in fixed income investments like bonds or CDs. The rest should be in stocks."

SOURCE: Kenneth Morris and Alan Siegel, The Wall Street Journal's *Guide to Planning Your Financial Future* (Lightbulb Press, 1995).

Stephen Wendel, president of StockPro Technologies, uses a very basic rule of thumb with his clients. Simply subtract your age from 100 and invest that amount as a percentage of your portfolio in stocks and stock funds. For example, a 30-year-old would have 70 percent of the portfolio in stocks, while a 70-year-old retiree may have 70 percent in lower-risk, fixed-income securities.

FundMap also guides you in selecting different asset allocation mixes, if you want to quickly test the assumptions. The five basic portfolios or asset allocations created by FundMap are:

1. **Conservative:**   Income, stability, and short term; 55 percent bonds and 25 percent cash, with only 20 percent in stocks.

2. **Moderately conservative:**   Current income and some appreciation; 45 percent bonds and 15 percent cash, with 40 percent in stocks.

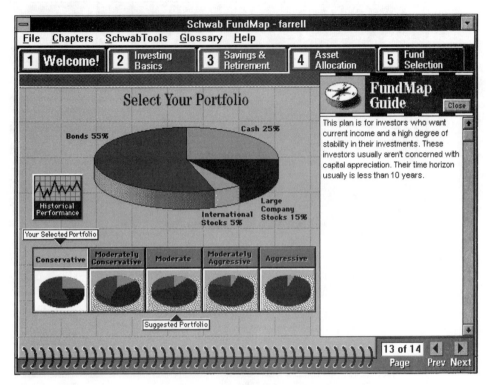

Figure 3.7   Asset allocation #1: conservative portfolio.

3. **Moderate:**   Longer-term capital appreciation and modest risk; 60 percent stocks and 10 percent cash, with only 30 percent in bonds.

4. **Moderately aggressive:**   Good growth, longer term, risk takers; 75 percent stocks, with small cap and 40 percent international, 20 percent in bonds.

5. **Aggressive:**   Long term, capital growth, high risks and returns; 95 percent stocks, only 5 percent cash.

Keep in mind, however, that going for higher returns (potential gains) is likely to create higher risks (potential losses).

In addition, the FundMap system gives you a graphic summary of the historical performance of all five basic portfolios, along with a chart showing the likely growth of each allocation over the long term. That way you can compare the portfolio recommended for you with the major alternatives. You also have the freedom to select one of the other portfolio asset allocations and work with it if you prefer. And in the process you'll learn

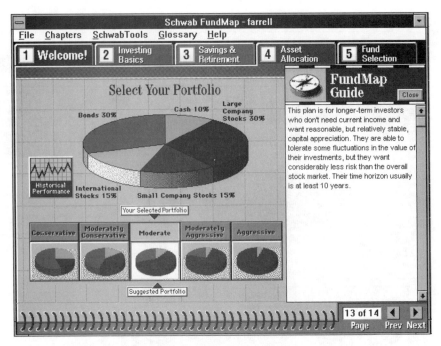

Figure 3.8 Asset allocation #3: moderate portfolio.

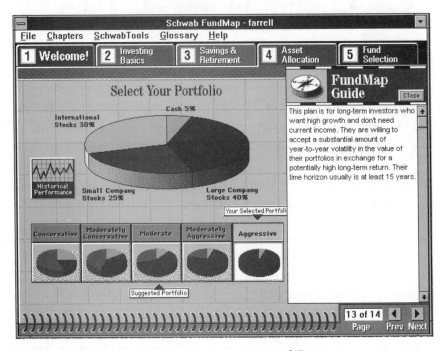

Figure 3.9 Asset allocation #5: aggressive portfolio.

more about yourself and the risks and returns necessary to achieve your financial goals.

Each of the more popular financial planning programs has a range of portfolios—usually three of five—that will fit the needs of almost every cyberspace investor from one end of the spectrum to the other, from the more aggressive stock investors to the more conservative investors seeking income, minimum risk, and capital appreciation.

Step Four: Picking Mutual Funds to Fit Your Portfolio

FundMap was designed for the large majority of investors—over 40 million of them—who are making investments in mutual funds. If you want to invest in stocks, bonds, and other securities, you'll have to move on to Schwab's StreetSmart system or one of the others in this NET*investing guidebook—for example, Reuters Money Network, Telescan, or Quicken's

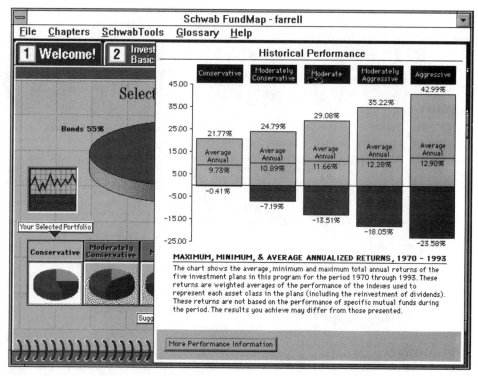

Figure 3.10 Performance comparison of FundMap's five portfolios.

Investor Insight—many of which are specifically designed to interface with each other.

Although FundMap does emphasize Schwab's own funds, the system is objective and balanced. FundMap does have an extensive selection of many other mutual funds sold by other leading fund managers. You can choose from several in each of the primary categories, including high performers from well-known fund families, such as Benham, Crabbe Huson, Dreyfus, Twentieth Century, and Warburg.

Moreover, when you examine other Schwab services, such as the Schwab OneSource system, you can directly access over 1,000 of the most popular and most successful mutual funds in the United States. Another service is Schwab's Mutual Fund Select List of the top 50 performers with outstanding five-year track records. We'll have much more to say about these and other excellent features in later chapters dealing with the online mutual funds and discount brokerage systems.

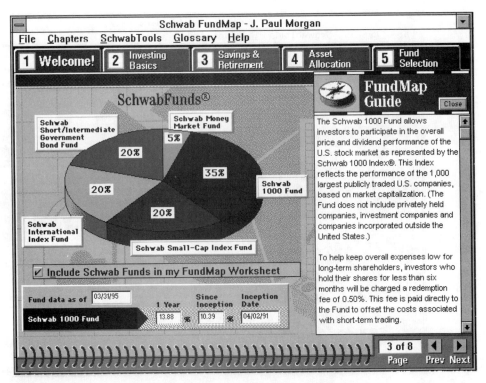

Figure 3.11 Using Schwab's funds for your asset allocations.

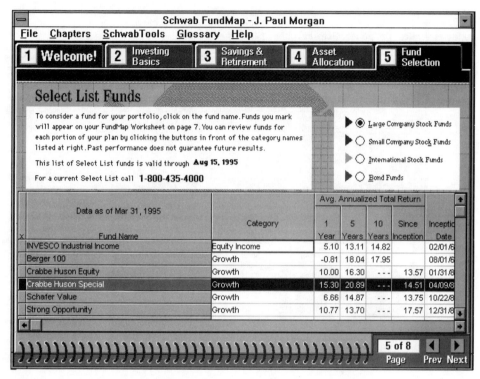

Figure 3.12   Selecting other top funds to build your portfolio.

BOTTOM LINE: BUILD A SUCCESSFUL PORTFOLIO IN CYBERSPACE

FundMap is discussed here as one of many examples of the high-quality, high-tech computerized financial planners now available for the cyber-space investor. *We highly recommend you test and compare at least three before making a decision* on which to use on a continuing basis. Do your homework; check with AAII and NAIC bulletin boards on CompuServe and America Online, or the Internet Usenet newsgroups; get recommendations. Actually load and test the systems.

Despite its potentially misleading name, FundMap is an excellent personal financial planner for both the new online investor or a Wall Street cyberspace old-timer. You may want something more like Quicken Deluxe if you're looking for detailed family budgeting, financial management, and online banking, but when it comes to the business of long-term planning for investors, this is the perfect system to get anyone going. Moreover,

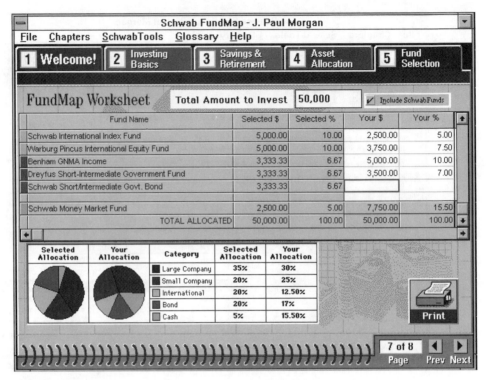

Figure 3.13 Bottom line: portfolio allocations to specific funds.

Schwab's wealth-building strategies are consistent with those of most investors, who lean to the conservative side and invest for the long haul.

Like many of these software planners, the FundMap program is an invaluable self-teaching tool, as well as a planning and decision-making tool. You should take this opportunity to go through and complete the worksheet at the end of the FundMap program. After all, that's the logical conclusion of this personal financial planning process: a sound investment program leading to financial independence.

In this process you will have an opportunity to allocate assets between a number of specific, recommended funds in five categories, including large company equities, small companies, bonds, money markets, and international funds. Moreover, FundMap spells out the data essential to your decision making, fund objectives, performance, risk, management, expenses, and fees.

Even if you defer the actual buy decisions until later or buy a different software package, the FundMap decision-making process will help you hone your investment skills and prepare you for your next step. In addition, review the coverage of Schwab's StreetSmart and e.Schwab programs in this book, as you go to the next step in building your investment portfolio.

YES, YOU CAN BEAT WALL STREET'S BIG MONEY MANAGERS

"Fund managers' records aren't all that impressive: fewer than 30% of all U.S. diversified equity funds beat Standard & Poor's 500-stock index, the best measure of large-stock performance, over the past year. . . . When you become your own portfolio manager, you're in control and can take satisfaction in your investing prowess."

SOURCE: Gregory Spears, *Kiplinger's Personal Finance Magazine* (November 1995).

Given the state of today's technology for cyberspace investors, most of the more powerful financial planning takes place offline using software on your computer at home. As the Internet improves in the next couple years, with encryption, interactive processing, higher speeds, and other advances, we definitely anticipate that more financial planning programs will be directly accessible on the Web and as online services, as well as through these offline software programs.

For the near future, you will need to purchase one of the more popular software programs on disk or CD-ROM to do the job on your home computer. Get one and start using it today. *If you've got one, test another.* There are some great new products that have come out in the past year.

CHAPTER 4

The Seven Steps of Successful Cyberspace Investing

Our primary goal here is to review and illustrate the general principles and the process of cyberspace investing, focusing on the seven key steps that any cyberspace investor will make to build a solid investment portfolio.

These seven key steps involve the following decisions. However, they are often made rapidly and in somewhat less than the clear-cut, logical sequence suggested here (as any investor who's had to react in timely fashion to some critical political or economic news that's redirecting market trends must know).

We will use the Internet as one example of the Top-25 NET*navigators available to cyberspace investors. However, this is merely to demonstrate the seven-step process. Combinations of the Internet—plus private networks, IntraNets, commercial online services, CD-ROMs, and offline analytics—are also extremely important, as discussed in later chapters.

Nevertheless, we focus on the Internet here because it is becoming one of the primary resource tools used by individual investors throughout the world. The Internet will certainly become one of the most important communication links in your cyberspace investing arsenal.

Of course, you will need other products and services—offline analytic software, CD-ROMs filled with data, and access to private networks or IntraNets—to complete your NET*investing system. But the Internet itself

SEVEN KEY STEPS OF INVESTING ONLINE AND ON THE NET

☐ **Step 1:   Input the results of your financial plan:** How much to invest, allocating assets.

☐ **Step 2:   Search databases for new investments:** Picking the right databases for your plan.

☐ **Step 3:   Screen securities using your criteria:** Using the right criteria and screening tools.

☐ **Step 4:   Select specific securities:** Narrowing the decision, pulling the trigger.

☐ **Step 5:   Execute trades with online brokers:** Working with an easy-to-understand system.

☐ **Step 6:   Manage ongoing investment portfolio:** Ongoing news, alerts, and strategic information.

☐ **Step 7:   Handle disposition:** Timing the sales of your securities; economic, tax, and life-cycle considerations.

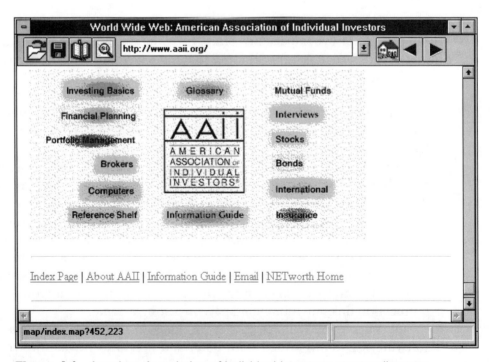

Figure 4.1 American Association of Individual Investors: master directory.

may well become your system's focal point, the NET*navigator's central processing unit or command module.

So before we launch into the other Top-25 NET*investing systems, all of which will probably become linked to the Internet in time, we begin with the concept that *the Internet is your computer.*

THE INTERNET: A NAVIGATIONAL TOOL FOR INVESTORS

The Internet is the single most important development in the history of communication. By the year 2000 the Internet will be the primary NET*navigator for millions of cyberspace investors. In fact, it is quite probable that the Internet's impact will far outstrip the combined historical effects of the printing press, telephones, television, personal computers, satellites, faxes, and all other telecommunications technologies. And even that may be an understatement.

Why? Because the Internet has the potential of combining *all* forms of communication: printing, audio/visual messaging, television broadcasting, news and entertainment, commercial transactions, data transmission, and a lot more. If anything, the reality of the Internet will prove much greater than the promise and more than anyone can imagine. *For the investor, this is a gold rush—the whole Internet is your computer!*

This is an important concept for every cyberspace investor to understand *before* continuing. Networking is in. Whether the Internet or IntraNets, the information revolution and the new telecommunications technologies are transforming Wall Street. The result is a paradigm shift: a new way of thinking, a new state of mind, and a new way of investing. It's time to get on the bandwagon, get online, *get on the Net.*

Think of it this way: In this new era of cyberspace investing, your computer is not just your 486 or Pentium with a 500MB or 1 GB hard drive. Today, the whole Internet itself has become an extension of the hard drive in your PC, substantially increasing its power—and your personal power.

Remember, the Internet is connected to the hard drives of tens of thousands of other hard drives on computers all over the Net. They are accessible to you. In cyberspace you are already connected to countless databases loaded with enormous data, information, and analytical firepower.

You don't need to install bigger and bigger hard drives to store ever-increasing amounts of data. Why duplicate what's already out there on the Internet? Today, you can use the whole Internet as your new computer.

BUSINESSWEEK DISCOVERS THE POWER OF NET*INVESTING!

Investing on the Net requires an Indiana Jones–style spirit of adventure. Consider the following paragraph which actually filled the entire front cover of *BusinessWeek* magazine, in large type without graphics, and served as the lead-in to an excellent, lengthy feature article by editor Gary Weiss:

> Online Investing, A Personal Account of The Pitfalls And Payoffs of Investing on The Internet . . . I have just emerged from a long exploration of the frontiers of online investing. It was worth it. What I found is a new, unique, and potentially very powerful source of investor information and interaction. It is largely shunned by the established powers on Wall Street. The online world is unruly and anarchic—unfettered by conventional wisdom. It is a world where small investors dominate, and where facts—not the Street's agenda—are paramount.

BusinessWeek has done an exceptional job of reporting on the Wall Street cyberspace revolution. Their cover stories and special issues are well worth review, especially "How the Internet Will Change the Way You Do Business" (11/14/94), "Cyberspace" (2/27/95), "The Technology Paradox" (3/6/95), "The Software Revolution" (12/4/95), and a special issue on "The Information Revolution" (7/12/95). Other related *Business-Week* cover stories worth a look are "The Technology Payoff," "ReThinking The Computer," "Hot Money," and "Portable Executive." Find them through various databases including BusinessWeek Online on the Web at *http://www.businessweek.com* and with other cyberspace search tools.

The Internet is rapidly evolving as an essential tool for cyberspace investing and the #1 high-tech tool for many cyber-investors. Okay, so it does have a way to go in its development before it becomes the vehicle of choice for the majority of investors, even for the majority of dedicated cyberspace investors.

But, *in combination with one of the other Top-25 NET*investing systems* that are emerging as delivery systems for financial information, the Internet has to be the major contender. This will be even more the case when the following transactions-based technologies are operational:

❐ **Secured commercial transactions** for trading stocks and mutual funds

❐ **Online banking** transactions that also work through the Internet

❐ **Centralized credit** transactions for quick, impulse purchases of information

Figure 4.2 *BusinessWeek* on the World Wide Web: hot IntraNets.

The Internet already is a major resource for many individual investors. And once these new technologies are in place—facilitated by the commercial banking system, with the help of Intuit, Microsoft, Oracle, Sun, and other software developers—the Internet will become the ultimate free marketplace. As that progresses, competitive pressures from discounters will drive financial information costs down, making the Internet even more exciting and inviting to the new individual investor who uses it.

HOW THE INTERNET FITS INTO THE SEVEN-STEP PROCESS

If you are using the Internet as your launchpad into cyberspace, you start by logging on to your Internet access provider. And once you're hyperlinked to the Net, you have access to all the data, information, interactivity, and analytics on all the hard drives out there everywhere in that enormous Internet of networks. Out there in cyberspace, on the Internet, is where you can begin this exploration of how to become a full-fledged cyberspace investor.

Figure 4.3 NetGuide: Money and Investments Website.

A word of caution: The Internet is one road on the information super-highway that's definitely incomplete. Don't expect the same easy maneuvering that you're used to at your commercial online service. But it sure beats telephoning brokers, making trips to the library, and waiting for the mails. So hang in there—the technology's catching up to the demand even while you're sleeping tonight.

Your first stops on the Internet are likely to be some of your favorite Weblists, those cyberspace yellow pages *out there* on the Web. Most likely, you already have several listed on your browser's directory of bookmarks (because you put them there sometime in the past when you found some good ones). In addition, here are several Internet Website directories of business, financial, and investing resources. We've included a set for you. Bookmark them on your Web browser, if you haven't already done so.

These directories are your links to the other key resources on investing, finance, and business in cyberspace; cyberports for investor information; and navigators filled with high-speed point-and-click links to specific information you'll need for investing. These cyberports attract other Web-

---

ELEVEN FREE INTERNET WEB DIRECTORIES FOR INVESTORS

American Association of Individual Investors
http://www.aaii.org

Briefing: Concise Market Analysis
http://briefing.com

CPCUG's Investment Special Interest Group
http://cpcug.org/user/invest

FINWeb with the University of Texas
http://www.finweb.com

Innovation's Financial Roadmap
http://www.euro.net/innovation

NetGuide: Money & Investments Directory
http://www.ypn.com

OSU Financial Data Finder
http://www.cob.ohio-state.edu/dept/fin/osudata.htm

Pathfinder: Time Warner Publishing
htp://www.pathfinder.com

PAWWS: Portfolio Accounting WorldWide
http://pawws.secapl.com

Quote.Com: First in Financial Information
http://www.quote.com

Yahoo's Business and Investing Directory
http://www.yahoo.com

---

sites that want the exposure of being listed on these directories, because they're known for high-volume cybertraffic. They are invaluable.

Fortunately, there are new directories being added every day. You will soon discover many others on your own that are better suited to your style of investing. And other Websites, such as Mutual Funds Online, Money & Investing Update, and Quote.Com, will have the kind of specific information you'll need for your investment decisions.

Nevertheless, you have to visit the Internet regularly to stay ahead of the curve on the Internet. That means periodically returning to check these yellow-page directories for new information and updates and bookmarking new discoveries. In short, you must start building your own special collection of Website directories if you're going to compete in this exciting new cyberspace investing arena.

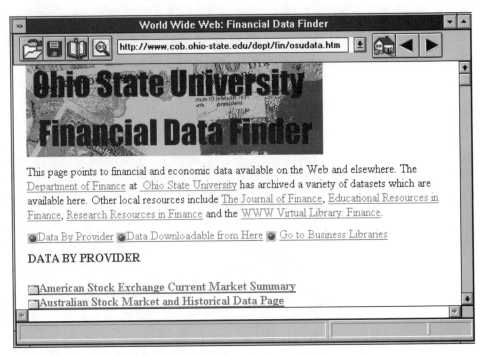

Figure 4.4   Ohio State University's Financial Data Finder.

Step One: Financial Planning—Your Savings and Asset Strategies

Every successful cyberspace investor begins with a personal financial plan, which includes personal financial goals, a savings plan, asset allocations, investment strategies, and so forth. That way the anxieties of anxiously chasing hot tips and rumors are avoided.

Hopefully you already prepared your plan, using one of the new computerized planning systems, such as FundMap, Prosper, WealthBuilder, or Quicken's Financial Planner. And from your plan, you know how much to set aside in savings accounts every month as you build your investment portfolio. If you're on track, you are probably saving and investing at least 5 percent to 10 percent of your income.

In addition, if you're serious about your personal financial planning, you will have an asset allocation strategy that comfortably fits your personality—especially your tolerance for market and investment risks. And you will also have some ideas about where to put those savings—what mixture of stocks, bonds, and mutual funds is suitable.

> ### HOW TO NAVIGATE CYBERSPACE: START WITH A FLIGHT PLAN
>
> "Venturing into cyberspace without a plan is like trying to get from New York to California without a roadmap. You might enjoy the scenery, but until you find the right highway and get on it, you'll never reach your destination.
>
> "Similarly, you can wander all over the information superhighway and have a perfectly grand time trying out all the tools, but unless you have a plan and a procedure for implementing it, you will never accomplish your mission."
>
> SOURCE: David L. Brown, *Cyber-Investing* (Wiley, 1995). (Brown is the CEO of Telescan, Inc., one of our Top-25 investor's NET*navigators.)

If you've passed over this planning process, we can recommend a short course out there in cyberspace, a quick Web version of our financial planning step and one that will help get you in the swing of the NET*investing process. Even if you already have a plan, it's a good idea to review and double-check your investor profile, while practicing with these new cyberspace resources for investing. This simple exercise will give you an opportunity to work through a cyberspace questionnaire designed to help you develop a workable asset allocation strategy, while giving you an opportunity to test out the Internet as an investment tool.

Later you'll discover other, perhaps more sophisticated, planning questionnaires. But for now, Fidelity's FundMatch questionnaire is an excellent way to make the transition into the planning process and kick-start your entry into this new world of cyberspace investing. Like Schwab's FundMap, the name is a bit misleading since it does more than "match funds." You can use it as a self-diagnosis tool to help you develop a preliminary asset allocation strategy.

Here's a preview of the 12 simple but telling questions included on the FundMatch portfolio-building questionnaire. It takes less than 15 minutes—all you have to do is give some straightforward, thoughtful answers. Just point-and-click your answers onto a cyberspace electronic form, and the math is all done for you, instantly. FundMatch does all the numbers-crunching, and produces an asset allocation strategy so you can proceed to convert your hard-earned savings into investment. All your answers are inputted right there in cyberspace with your trusty mouse, in less than 15 minutes, thanks to the magic of the new Internet technology.

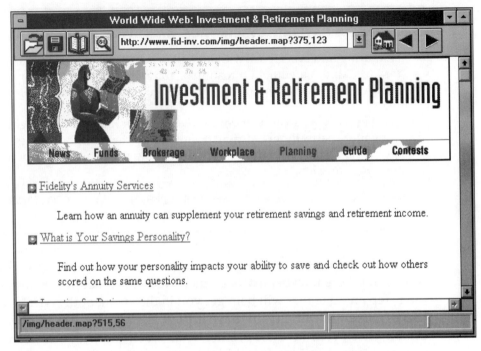

Figure 4.5 Fidelity Investment's Financial Planning on the Web.

Later you can buy a more complicated system such as Quicken or WealthBuilder to help you integrate and manage your day-to-day personal finances along with your investment portfolio. You'll see some of the better ones among the Top-25 systems throughout our book.

Once you complete FundMatch you've got clearance from mission control for liftoff into cyberspace investing!

Step Two: Searching—Start with the Right Databases

Now you're ready to make the transition from personal financial planning to cyberspace investing. Now you know about how much you need to invest over the years in order to meet your planning goals. You also know how much you actually decided you can save and invest on a regular monthly basis, or perhaps you have a lump sum to invest (from a bonus or inheritance, for example).

From here on, the game of cyberspace investing starts getting *real*. Why? Hard money. Now you're planning with real, hard-earned money,

FIDELITY'S FUNDMATCH: FREE FINANCIAL PLANNING ON THE WEB

A. *How does this investment fit into your overall plans?*

1. The savings you are investing are what percent of your total assets?
2. How will your earnings compare to inflation over the next five years?
3. What percent of your monthly income pays down installment debt?
4. How many dependents do you have?

B. *Do you have savings in place for other purposes?*

5. Do you have savings to cover a six-month emergency?
6. If you have other major expenses, do you also have savings?

C. *What's your tolerance and attitude toward risks?*

7. Have you ever invested in bond or bond funds?
8. Have you previously invested in stocks or stock funds?
9. Rate your feelings about increasing risk to get higher returns.
10. How much risk would you take with all or part of your portfolio?

D. *How long will the money be tied up?*

11. How many years before you need this new investment?
12. Will you be using more than a third of the money within ten years?

SOURCE: *Fidelity Investments Website, http://www.fid-inv.com.*

THE THREE S's OF INVESTING: SEARCH, SCREEN, AND SELECT

Here's a simple way to remember the guts of this investment process. The crucial three steps start with the letter S and they are:

Search: Limit to databases fitting your asset allocations.
Screen: Narrow to a few securities that meet your criteria.
Select: Make your decision based on timing factors.

Remember the three S's: search, screen, and select. Focus on databases that match your asset allocations, narrow the decision to securities that fit your criteria, particularly risk/return. Pick the one that feels right.

not the hypothetical portfolio you may have been "trading" on the Contests and Games menu at Fidelity or some other Website.

Now you have to start searching cyberspace for new investment opportunities that match the basic criteria spelled out by your asset allocation model. But which stocks, or bonds, or mutual funds? There are over 6,500 stocks and 7,000 mutual funds to choose from. How do you search through this universe of securities before narrowing down your choice to a specific security?

Remember the inputs from your financial planning process. You actually began your initial search right there. For example, there were five suggested portfolios from the Fidelity Website. Each one of the five had an asset allocation strategy. We're going to review those five portfolios here, to make an important point, both for simplifying the investment process as well as making the critical transition from the asset allocations in your personal financial plan into the actual investment process.

The five basic suggested portfolios are:

❐ **Short-term portfolio:** 100 percent money markets and short-term investments.

❐ **Capital preservation portfolio:** 50 percent money markets, 30 percent bonds, and 20 percent stocks.

❐ **Moderate-risk portfolio:** 20 percent money markets, 40 percent bonds, and 40 percent stocks.

❐ **Wealth-building portfolio:** 5 percent short term, 30 percent bonds, and 65 percent stocks.

❐ **Aggressive stock portfolio:** 100 percent invested in stocks (or stock funds).

Focus. Search databases that will help you discover real investment opportunities, and ignore the rest—the ones that won't fit anyway. After all, with over 6,500 stocks and over 2,500 stock mutual funds, you don't need to look at all of them.

Now you can see why your financial planning and your asset allocation is crucial. Not only is it essential as a prerequisite to financial independence, it is also a valuable initial screening tool. If you're looking for low-risk, short-term investments, ignore the international emerging market funds. If your plan calls for high returns, you might focus on growth stocks, and fewer fixed-income bonds or money market funds.

Use your asset allocation strategy wisely and it'll help you immediately narrow your search to 5 percent to 15 percent of the total universe of securities out there. Fortunately, the Internet's Web has many databases for both stocks and mutual funds that you can access. One of the best places to start is the Website of the Capital PC User Group Investment Special Interest Group (cpcup.org/user/invest), which is building a truly exceptional directory of resources for NET*investors. They will also link you to other sites.

As the Internet's Web continues, however, most of the databases that were originally free are rapidly converting to fee-paid services, including Quote.Com, InterQuote, PC Quote, and PAWWS, although limited free delayed quotes typically remain as marketing teasers. NETworth, *Mutual Funds* Magazine Online, and IDD/Nestegg all offer mutual fund data. However, using their free services is often a limiting and slow process. On the other hand, their fee-paid services and others you'll find are quite reasonable. Any one of them may be a bargain fitting your particular needs. In fact, you can easily get by at $10 to $20 a month for the basic services; no more than $30 for real-time information.

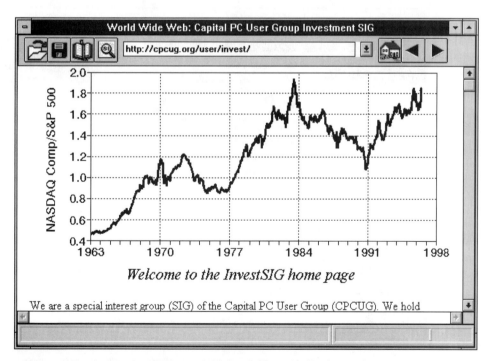

Figure 4.6 Master directory of InvestSIG on the Web.

BEAT THE MARKET WITH ZACKS ANALYST WATCH ON THE WEB

"The most powerful force driving any stock's price is revisions in earnings estimates by the 2,700 analysts employed by all 230 U.S. brokerage firms. *As analysts revise their estimates up or down, this represents new information not yet accounted for in the stock's price.*

"Every day, Chicago-based Zacks Investment Research gathers and analyzes every earnings estimate revision, and every change in brokerage firm buy/hold/sell recommendations by all 2,700 Wall Street analysts. . . .

"From this unending torrent of stock market intelligence, Zacks continuously updates a database of 5,400 stocks and maintains a stock rating system. . . .

"Since 1980, Zacks' top-ranked stocks show gains averaging 34.8% per year. At that rate of return, a $10,000 starting portfolio would grow to $1,189,430. In contrast, a $10,000 investment in the S&P 500 would have grown to $108,060 over the same 16-year period—less than one-tenth of Zacks' return."

SOURCE: Zacks Analyst Watch ad, *Telescan News* (First Quarter, 1996), and on the Web at: *www.zacks.com.*

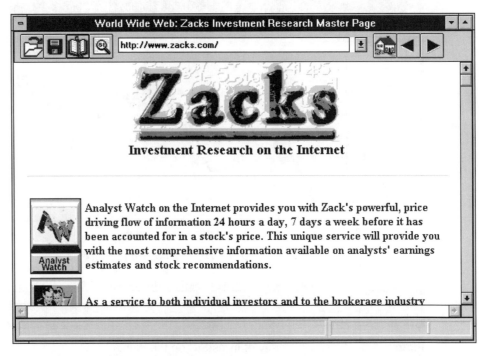

Figure 4.7 Zacks Analyst Watch on the Internet.

You should also consider the quote systems that are included as part of the package with commercial online services such as AOL, Prodigy, and CompuServe. Overall, they may be cheaper and less of a hassle when you add in all the other services they include.

Step Three: Screening Securities—Your Analytical Criteria

Now let's move on to screening the specific databases that match the asset allocations in your financial plan. Obviously, you need a set of criteria—and a screening program—to help you screen through the database. Here's where you must rely on your own skills. Today you are not likely to find many securities-screening tools on the Internet *for free.*

In fact, even the more sophisticated, private, online subscriber-based systems, such as Reuters Money Network, CompuServe, and Telescan, are designed to permit all or substantially all of the analytics *offline,* rather than wasting time while logged online. Reuters, for example, lets you make your update requests on a menu, then the program automatically dials, logs on, downloads the updated information, and goes offline, where you can manipulate the new data.

In other words, it is highly unlikely that you'll use only the Internet. Most NET*investing alternatives work in combination with *offline* analytics. That's true for the best ones with stocks, bonds, and mutual funds. Moreover, there are very few "free lunches" when screening securities on the Internet, which is why it's becoming important to use one of the new Top-25 NET*investing systems in conjunction with the Internet—that's what we mean by the *InternetPLUS.*

Let's look at one of the most respected stock-screening tools available used by hundreds of thousands of investors throughout the world: William O'Neil's CANSLIM analysis. O'Neil is the publisher of *The Wall Street Journal's* biggest competitor, *Investor's Business Daily,* and author of *How to Make Money in Stocks.* His time-honored CANSLIM system is designed to help you pick winners in the stock market.

Fortunately, most of the online services will provide you with a CANSLIM screening tool to use with their databases. You'll find it on AOL, CompuServe, and Prodigy online services. Later, you will also discover many other workable screening tools for stocks and mutual funds on these commercial online services. And in the process, you'll discover the one that works best for you.

For example, one of the more sophisticated, Top-25 systems, Telescan's ProSearch, has 207 screening criteria from which to select. Using them, you

A WINNING STOCK FORMULA FROM *INVESTOR'S BUSINESS DAILY*

C = **Current quarterly earnings:** Shoot for 18 percent to 20 percent earnings.

A = **Annual earnings increases:** Look for five years of solid growth.

N = **New products, management, changes:** Look for winners making new highs.

S = **Shares outstanding:** Small capitalization with volume demand.

L = **Leader or laggard in sector:** Stick with the sector front runners.

I = **Institutional sponsorship:** Plus better-than-average performance.

M = **Market direction:** Ride price/volume trends in the general market.

can quickly sift through thousands of stocks and isolate the ones that match your criteria. Of course, you can also use super-sophisticated offline analytic programs such as MetaStock, SuperCharts, and Windows on Wall-Street. In all probability, however, 98 percent of the new breed of NET*investors will find their needs met by one of the Top-25 cyberspace investment systems discussed here.

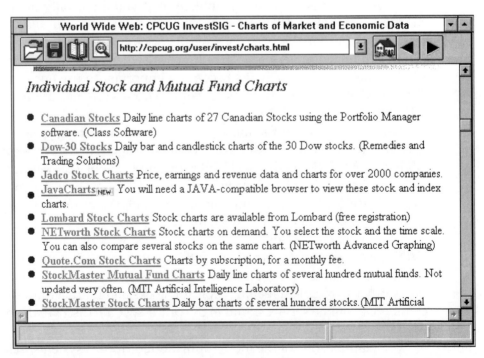

Figure 4.8 InvestSIG's Web directory: Individual Stock and Mutual Fund Charts.

Figure 4.9 Charts by CPCUG InvestSIG.

Bottom line: When you're screening stocks and mutual funds on the Internet, be prepared to use your favorite screening tools—either offline analytical software on your hard drive or from a private online service.

Which methods are best for you? Only time and firsthand experience will tell. In the earlier stages of your discovery, lean on a proven method, such as CANSLIM, Graham/Dodd, Lynch's One Up On Wall Street, or one of the other five methods preprogrammed on Prodigy's Stock Hunter. Later, you can get a more sophisticated one or even invent your own hybrid.

Through personal experience, you'll discover *over time* what specific system works for your particular portfolio-building style, what best helps you pick winners, and what feels right to you as an individual investor headed for financial independence.

Step Four: Selecting Specific Securities and Building a Portfolio

Now you're getting down to the nitty-gritty. Any strategy for picking securities involves a series of steps that successively narrow down the number you're researching. By way of review, here's the narrowing-down process again:

☐ **Search:** Your asset allocation strategy focused on money market funds or emerging international stocks, municipal bonds, or whatever developed in your financial plan, taking you from thousands of stocks or funds, down to a few hundred possibilities.

☐ **Screening:** You then further narrow the list of choices of, for example, growth stocks. Based on your screening criteria, you come up with perhaps 5 to 25, then you start narrowing that list based on other criteria.

☐ **Selection:** Finally, if you're lucky, you will be in the enviable position of having two or three excellent alternatives, each, of course, with a slightly different profile, so they're not exactly equal candidates.

At this point, no system—Internet, IntraNet, or otherwise—can make the decision for you. You have to pull the trigger.

And don't be concerned if you go through the process one day and don't find *anything* that fits your portfolio criteria or if you find some prospects that statistically fit, but still don't feel right in your gut. Trust that instinct. Investors usually go through the process many times before a gem surfaces *and feels right*.

Passing on opportunities is very common in investing—everyone does it. In fact, you're likely to run through one of these processes 20, maybe even 100, times, before you actually purchase a security.

HIGH-TECH POWER TOOLS VERSUS EXPERIENCE AND GUT INSTINCTS

Consider, for example, that you may have your choices narrowed down to these three essentially evenly matched securities:

☐ Blue-chip fund with almost no downside risk and a secure 9 percent return

☐ Growth stock fund with a 6 percent return and, with appreciation, a total of 10 percent

☐ Convertible corporate bonds in solid companies with a solid 8 percent return.

At this point, virtually no screening device can make the decision for you. The ball is 100 percent in your court.

If you want financial independence, you've got it when it comes to investing. *You are 100 percent responsible.* You make the decision. My advice: Apply a 24-hour gut-feel rule. If you're not a professional day-trader, and you're not convinced, sleep on it. If it still feels right tomorrow, get into action. This is not procrastination; it just makes good common sense. I also believe it taps into the average investor's psychology, letting the message from the left-brain, rational side sink in and mesh with the gut, to determine if the deal's right or not on the basis of both brain and instinct.

Bottom line: Most of the time the security will still be available tomorrow and still as good a deal as it was today, if it was a good deal originally. Moreover, I believe this same technique actually applies to *all* your investment opportunities, even the ones you immediately love and are convinced you should invest in now, before they get away. Wait until the next day; if you feel just as good, go with your decision.

Remember: Building a portfolio of stocks, bonds, and funds is as much an emotional decision as it is a set of mathematical calculations. Balance

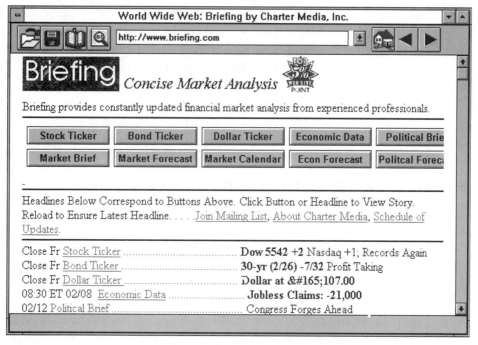

Figure 4.10   Briefing master menu: Concise Market Analysis.

the facts with your gut feelings and you are more likely to fill your port-folio with winners.

Step Five: Executing Your Trades with an Electronic Broker

Eventually it's time to pull the trigger. Fortunately, secure active trading already exists on the Internet. If the security issue bothers you, you can get in the electronic groove today. Begin your cyberspace trading with virtu-ally any broker through a separate dial-up telephone connection.

Until recently, Net technology did not fully support secure commercial transactions. Brokers feared that hackers could penetrate their computers via the Internet and raid all the accounts of the firm and its clients. How-ever, as the necessary encryption technology entered the market in 1996, *every NET*investor* can expect to be secure in trading stocks, bonds, and mutual funds directly on the Internet. And that's when the cyberspace excitement will really build to a fever.

Even with an electronic broker, you will still have to go through the process of establishing an account and credit, depositing funds in the account, and the other stuff necessary to satisfy the broker and the securi-ties watchdogs in the government. Surprisingly traditional, isn't it?

But as soon as the new secured transaction programs hit the market, we'll have a dazzling new global Wall Street cyberspace. Soon, you may even be able to do direct trading at any time of the day, with any exchange, anywhere on the globe. Your entire investment portfolio and online bank-ing deposits will be sitting on a single microchip *out there* in cyberspace, controlled by you from your hard drive. Now that will force everyone to think about financial independence. Jump in—start getting used to it now.

Step Six: Managing Your Investment Portfolio in Cyberspace

Managing your portfolio on a day-to-day basis is the key to successful investing. In fact, everything you do as an investor is portfolio manage-ment. As Telescan President David Brown says in *Cyber-Investing,* portfolio management "begins with the purchase of your first stock and continues as long as you own a stock."

Keep up with changing market conditions. Monitor financial news in the daily press and periodicals. Study analytical techniques and train on new or existing software programs. Periodically update your financial plan, asset allocations, and selection criteria. Explore the Internet for investor resources.

Review all stocks and funds in your portfolio on a regular basis. Decide whether and when to dispose of a security. And continually search for new opportunities in order to build a winning portfolio. These are the fundamentals of portfolio management.

You have to stay on your toes, regardless of the number of securities or the size of the portfolio. Markets, securities, and portfolios are dynamic and volatile.

In his book, *How to Be Your Own Stockbroker,* Charles Schwab recommends spending as much as an hour or two a day at first, just learning about how to invest wisely. If you're serious about building a successful portfolio, take Schwab's advice to heart. It's your money—act responsibly.

There actually are a few *free* portfolio management services on the Internet. Briefing.com has an Internet service that allows you to input your portfolio and other favorite stocks and track their performance based on current market conditions. The Websites of discount brokers such as Lombard and Aufhauser offer some modified portfolio management capabilities, in real time, of your portfolio account with them. And more are coming, usually for a modest fee.

CYBERSPACE INVESTMENT CLUBS: THE TOP FIVE USENET GROUPS

You will also find some solid peer support from other cyberspace investors *out there* sharing information on the five key Internet discussion groups specifically focused on investing topics. Check them out:

misc.invest	general discussion on investing
misc.invest.stocks	major and secondary exchanges
misc.invest.funds	mutual fund analysis and selection
misc.invest.futures	index options, futures, derivatives
misc.invest.technical	technical analysis for investors

Equally valuable are the specific discussion groups (also known as forums, conferences, bulletin boards, news groups, or chat rooms) at the major online services, America Online, CompuServe, and Prodigy. Start visiting these investment clubs regularly.

One of the more unique opportunities is *The Wall Street Journal*'s Personal Journal. For a reasonable fee comparable to the cost of the print version, Personal Journal gives you portfolio management capabilities, plus business and market news, digests of selected stories, and the ability to track some of your portfolio data. You'll also get some sports and weather information. This is definitely worth checking out, at least for the two-week free trial. Discover where Dow Jones is leading the Internet today. These guys are likely to dominate the financial cyberspace well into the twenty-first century.

Step Seven: Disposition of Securities—Criteria for Timing Sales

The sell side is definitely a trouble spot for most investors; emotions all too often take control and feelings override facts. Many investors get attached, even fall in love with their stocks. They may feel that it's un-American to sell a special symbol of our American blue-chip heritage (how could you possibly *betray* aunt Betty Crocker?)—as though it were something you should do in the privacy of your bedroom.

No wonder so many investors are not especially good at picking the right time to dump a stock, bond, or fund—and are *therefore weak in manag-*

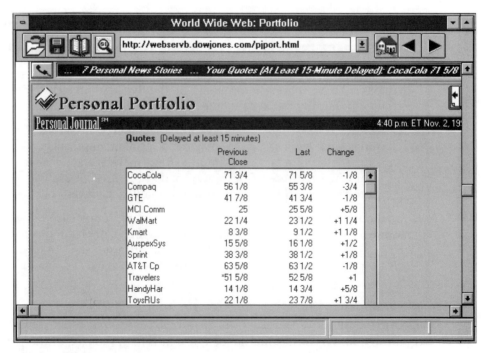

Figure 4.11   Monitoring your portfolio with Personal Journal.

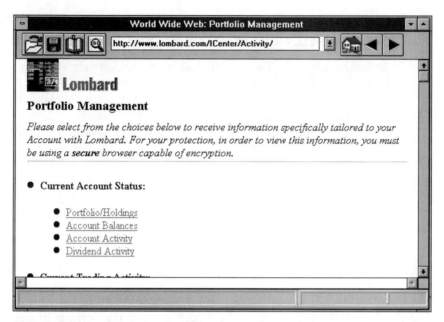

Figure 4.12 Lombard's Portfolio Management on the Web.

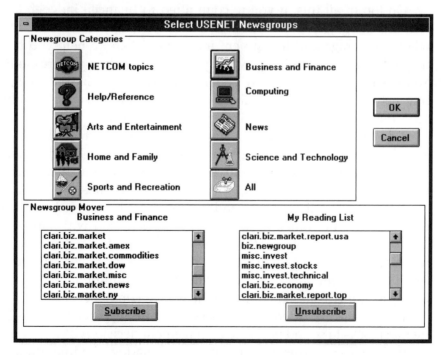

Figure 4.13 Usenet discussion groups on Netcom's Browser.

WHEN TO SELL FROM YOUR PORTFOLIO: FOUR KEY CRITERIA

1. **Industry laggard:**   The security has begun underperforming, lagging behind sector or industry leaders, for several quarters.
2. **Some fatal flaw:**   A change in management, negative market trends, or some other major change that impacts performance.
3. **Asset allocation shifts:**   Growth through appreciation may shift the balance in your portfolio. This and other externals may suggest revising your investment strategies and selling off some of your investments in order to improve overall performance of the portfolio.
4. **Lifestyle changes:**   Your personal situation is substantially altered (the obvious example being the loss of a spouse through death or divorce), demanding a new asset allocation.

SOURCE: "Hold 'em or Fold 'em," Gordon Williams, *Financial World* (October 1995).

---

ing their portfolios. They err in holding a loser or a bad fit too long, or jumping the gun and exiting too early, which can have a serious impact on the value and performance of the portfolio.

On top of all this, if you're committed to financial independence, no one else can give you one ounce of advice on when to sell a security. The whole brokerage and investment industry is there to help you *buy* what they're *selling.* Determining when you need to sell is *your* responsibility. You're stuck. On this decision, you likewise won't get one bit of help on the Internet nor will you get much help from the more specialized online services designed for individual investors like yourself.

The situation's not hopeless, however. In fact, in October 1995, *Financial World* magazine spotted us with four simple criteria to help investors pick the best time to get out of an investment. These include external market changes, portfolio considerations, and personal reasons.

The price paid for financial independence is eternal vigilance. Unfortunately, there's not much on the Internet to help you with this particular decision. You'll need one of the offline programs discussed in the last chapter. Even then, in every case, you are responsible for monitoring your portfolio, establishing performance criteria, and dumping losers (without letting a "guilty conscience" get in the way of common sense).

Finally, tax considerations can be so daunting that they too become mental blocks to sound portfolio management decisions. While taxes are of prime importance, they should never overshadow the importance of the basic investment criteria.

USE THE INTERNET . . . PLUS AN ONLINE SYSTEM

By the year 2000, the Internet will be an essential part of every NET*investing system used by cyberspace investors throughout America. That's right, virtually every investor will be on the Net as a direct result of its rapid growth, along with that of online banking, commercial online services, and other advances in telecommunications and computer technology.

*However, it's unlikely that the Internet will become the primary NET*navigator for investors.* You'll need what we'll call the *InternetPLUS.* Simply put, it's the Internet *plus* one or more of the Top-25 NET*investing navigators reviewed here—typically an online or dial-up service designed for cyberspace investors. The Internet needs structure and organization—a controller, an integrator, a navigator—something to harness, leverage, and maximize its enormous power *before it can be used effectively.* What's needed is *an InternetPLUS.* With this powerful combination—*the Internet PLUS your NET*navigator*—the cyberspace investor gets the best of all possible worlds.

Figure 4.14   Wall Street Directory: power tools for NET*investors.

BOTTOM LINE: THE INTERNETPLUS . . .
A NET*NAVIGATOR FOR CYBERSPACE INVESTORS

Every one of the Top-25 NET*investing systems we're focusing on is also designed to add the missing navigational link for the investor's system. Each of these NET*investing systems is *a computer-based navigator that integrates financial resources,* placing at your fingertips everything you need in a single system that ideally covers the whole investing process and saves valuable time.

Each of these Top-25 NET*navigators has pluses for investors. Each system *adds* its special blend of resources that are *not on the Internet,* such as offline analytic software, CD-ROM databases, online dial-up resources, and IntraNets. Some of these NET*investing systems achieve their goals better than others. However, they're all dedicated to helping the individual investor make better investments.

And that's why the InternetPLUS—*the Internet plus one of the other Top-25 NET*navigators*—is essential to your future in financial cyberspace. Your success as a NET*investor depends on your selection of a NET*navigator, so study them closely, choose wisely, and make certain you find the one that works for your unique investing style.

PART II

The Investor's Top-25 Navigators Online and on the Internet

How You Can Discover and Rate the Best Cyberspace Systems for Individual Investing

Today's *individual* investors are using a wide variety of high-powered new NET*navigators to compete against professional money managers and institutional investors in the cyberspace world markets. However, they aren't paying the $1,000 to $2,000 monthly fees per workstation that the big institutional money managers are paying for Telerate, Instinet, and the Bloomberg. Moreover, it isn't even close to the $500 a month professional traders pay for DTN Wall Street, Signal, and some of the other more expensive quote and data services.

Today's individual investor is getting the best technology at bargain-basement prices. As financial technology advances, individual investors can now arm themselves with powerful NET*navigators that virtually equal the high-powered systems used by those big Wall Street institutions.

The goal of this book is simple: We will identify the Top-25 NET*navigators being used by individual investors to win a cyberspace game previously reserved for the big institutions—and at a very reasonable cost to the individual.

HOW TO COMPETE WITH WALL STREET'S TOP MONEY MANAGERS— FOR UNDER $100 A MONTH

In fact, today's new NET*investors can easily get away with spending something in the range of $10 to $100 a month. That's right, that's all it takes to compete with the big institutions and money managers—enough to beat them, beat the key market indexes, beat the Street.

CompuServe, Reuters Money Network, America Online, StreetSmart, Dow Jones News/Retrieval, Telescan, and many more systems are *all available for under a $100 a month* for some first-class NET*navigators, often for a basic fee in the range of $25 to $30 a month. We're going to look at each of these top NET*navigational systems with you, and help you evaluate the ones best suited to your unique investing style.

TRUST THE NUMBERS—PLUS YOUR GUT INSTINCTS

Rating the NET*navigating systems described in this section will require you to mix objective and subjective criteria. But in the final analysis, the system has to work for you on a gut level.

Dow Jones News/Retrieval, CompuServe, or StreetSmart may fit *you* to a tee, but probably not someone else in your family or office. Their style of investing may fit better with all they discover on America Online's Personal Finance section, combined with NETworth and *Mutual Funds* magazine Websites.

Let's face it—you have a lot of portfolio dollars on the line. Your initial choice of systems could be one of the most important investment decisions you have to make. Take it very seriously—*and take your time.*

COUNT ON USING MORE THAN ONE NET*NAVIGATOR

Equally important—and this is crucial to understand, given the current state of development, the specific objectives of each system, the emerging new products, and the rapidly changing technological environment in cyberspace—you'll quickly realize that you may need to use more than one of these NET*investing systems in order to get the financial firepower you need.

In other words, although you have a primary systems navigator, such as Reuters Money Network or Telescan, it is highly probable that you will also, from time to time, prefer one or more parallel or alternative systems, to double-check your decisions, to reinforce your judgment, to minimize your risks. For example, you may want to check the rating systems of both Mutual Funds Online and Morningstar in researching a particular mutual fund.

YOUR RATING SYSTEM—THE ONLY ONE THAT COUNTS

When we set about doing our research, our initial goal was to develop a rational method of ranking the various NET*navigators available to today's individual investor. However, it quickly became apparent that not only are the systems themselves quite distinctive, the technology changing so rapidly, and the needs of the investor in a constant state of flux, but what works for one investor—what fits physiologically and psychologically—may be quite inappropriate for another.

So, it became obvious that, in the final analysis, each individual investor must determine the best system for them. And as objective as we want this decision to be, it remains a very personal one—as personal as selecting which cereal to eat or what movies you enjoy. Nevertheless, the decision is neither random nor irrational; it is merely personal to *your* unique personality and investment style.

RATING INVESTORS' NET*NAVIGATORS: A TEN-POINT CHECKLIST

Key Elements	How You Rate Each	
1. Systems integration	25%	_____
2. Online/Net connections	5%	_____
3. Personal financial plan	5%	_____
4. Financial news databases	10%	_____
5. Searching databases: historic	5%	_____
6. Screening: analytic software	15%	_____
7. Selection: specific securities	10%	_____
8. Electronic brokerage	5%	_____
9. Portfolio management	15%	_____
10. Disposition of assets	5%	_____
Total NET*investing system		_____

So with that in mind, our goal here is to give you the facts so you can make an informed judgment and save time in the process. We will present enough facts about each of the key NET*navigators to help you make at least preliminary ratings as to which of the systems are worth actually testing.

We know all too well that selecting the right NET*navigator can be a time-consuming process—it sure was in testing each of the systems reviewed here. So we respect the process you are going through, whether you're picking your first NET*navigator, making a change, or upgrading.

BOTTOM LINE: FROM 1,000 RANDOM POWER TOOLS TO THE TOP-25 NET*NAVIGATORS

In our first book, *The Investor's Guide to the Net,* we identified over 1000 products and services for the cyberspace investor. That taught us a big lesson—and led to writing this companion book. We learned that the shear volume of cyberspace alternatives can be so daunting as to make an investor stick with familiar methods that do not require cyberspace technologies. So we decided to go from the shotgun approach in the earlier book to smart-bombing in this one.

We believe that merely by narrowing your choices from 1000 to the Top-25 and by presenting you with the key facts about each, you'll have enough information to make your own decisions, to carry the ball over the goal line for yourself. If we accomplish that much, we will have achieved our goal for this book.

Online and Internet Services for Cyberspace Investors

America Online:
Personal Finance Center

America Online does a remarkably solid job of delivering the primary financial services to today's NET∗investor. Moreover, once the NET∗investor logs online with AOL, the investor can quickly and easily zip around from one of these services to the other. For less than $10 a month base cost, you just might find everything you need on AOL.

You want stock quotes? Get all you want free with the basic package. Need to check on the top-performing mutual funds? Hop over to Morningstar. How's the market doing? Reuters and *Investor's Business Daily* keep you on top. It's all there on AOL.

Right now, America Online is a near-perfect one-stop/total-service package integrated into a single operating platform, a cyberspace superstore for many do-it-yourself investors. Plus, if you want to pull down special information from the Internet, AOL now provides its members with a simple gateway with direct access to the Internet through its new Web browser.

Let's take a close look at AOL, because, with all the current hype surrounding the Internet, it's easy to minimize the incredible values in the commercial online services.

CONTENT INTEGRATION: THE KEY TO SUCCESS

Why are over five million online investors already riding with this winner, AOL? Quite frankly, the NET∗investor just doesn't want to schlep all over the Internet searching for information of questionable value. Besides, it takes valuable time. True, Bill Gates and the other Internet gurus will tell

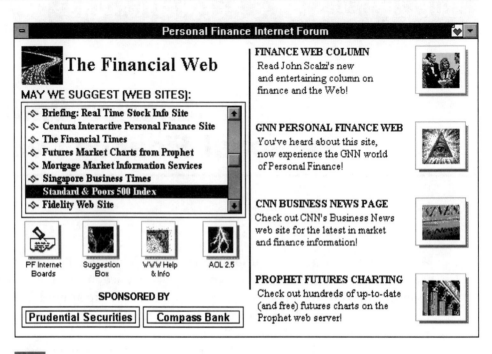

1.1 AOL's World Wide Web gateway for NET*investors.

LOST IN CYBERSPACE? AMERICA ONLINE IS YOUR SAFE HARBOR!

"Defying critics who expected customers to bypass AOL in favor of cheaper direct connections to the Internet, the company has instead become the dominant provider of Internet access. . . .

" 'The cognoscenti wonder why anybody would spend any time on America Online with all the free content on the World Wide Web,' said Peter Krasilovsky, senior analyst with Arlen Communication Inc., a media consulting firm in Bethesda, Md. 'But the truth is that when they're on America Online, they don't feel as lost in space as they do on the Internet. We've found some compelling evidence that people really do like America Online's services.' "

SOURCE: Jube Shiver, "Well-Connected: America Online's Deals Put It on Cloud Nine in Cyberspace," *Los Angeles Times* (March 12, 1996).

you that the Internet's the place to be, that it's a global shopping mall, uniting all people and eliminating distance and time.

Well, almost. That's the promise anyway. However, it's far from a reality today. And any services that actually do deliver on the promise will be the winners in Wall Street cyberspace. NET*investors are impatient; they want results and they want them now. Their time is valuable.

The fact is that AOL delivers quality service to the NET*investor today. It offers a solid package of services, all in one place. AOL is grounded in content integration, and that's the key advantage these one-stop/total-service online packages offer the NET*investor. Eventually, the Internet may deliver on the promise. But right now, any one of the online services is at least as good as, *if not better than, the Internet for cyberspace investors.*

America Online has been an aggressive marketeer for the past couple of years. It seems like almost everyone in America has received at least one free starter disk, and some of us have had to toss a few dozen away. Yet, under this glitzy marketing pizazz, AOL has, in fact, been adding a lot of valuable content providers. So let's explore these in detail.

AOL's Personal Finance has so much material about the markets, investing, stocks, funds, and corporate finance that it could be called the "investor's guide to the net"! Granted, it doesn't have the vast collection of resources to choose from that you'd get from CompuServe or Dow Jones News/Retrieval.

Yet AOL has some of the best resources for investors. Furthermore, the ones AOL offers are all packaged in one place, they're graphically appealing, and they are current, timely, and easy to access. So the average NET*investor has a solid platform from which to work.

By comparison, you might think of Dow Jones News/Retrieval and CompuServe as massive department stores—Macy's, for example, while AOL is more like one of those limited-menu restaurants that always has good food, fast and friendly service, and just the right ambiance. Or think of AOL as one gigantic cyberspace Price Club for cyberspace investors.

One thing you notice right away is the 6 key menu categories and a list of all the 40 to 50 specific services. The 6 main subdirectories are:

❏   Financial Newsstand

❏   Quotes and Portfolios

❏   Financial Forums

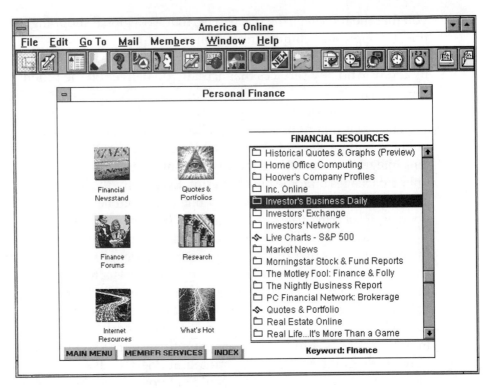

1.2 AOL's Personal Finance Services for NET*investing.

❏ Research

❏ Internet Resources

❏ What's Hot

From this vantage point, it's really quite easy to navigate around the AOL collection of NET*investing resources. The newsstand will quickly get you to the latest financial news and analysis.

For example, you get up around the time the market opens—let's say 5 A.M. You grab a cup of coffee, and you can sit down with the morning paper and catch up on what happened yesterday. After all, remember that print news reporters probably wrote all that stuff late yesterday afternoon or early evening before going out for dinner; the paper was likely printed before midnight, folded, bundled, thrown on trucks, and driven to your home, along with thousands of others.

AMERICA ONLINE'S SERVICES FOR THE NET*INVESTOR

Company and Market Research
- ❏ Hoover's Company Profiles
- ❏ First Call: earnings estimates
- ❏ Market Updates and Reports
- ❏ Morningstar Mutual Fund and Stock Reports
- ❏ Disclosure: EdgarPlus for Financial Statements (10Ks/Qs)
- ❏ Dow Watch: daily reports on the top 30 and more
- ❏ *Inc.* magazine's E-Zone, for entrepreneurs

Quotes: Stocks, Market Indexes and Mutual Funds
- ❏ Quotes: 15-minute delayed on specific stocks and the major indexes, plus NAV quotes for mutual funds
- ❏ Live Charts for the S&P 500 companies
- ❏ Portfolio Management: track your investments

The News: Newswires, Newspapers, and Magazines
- ❏ Reuters Newswires: reports on the markets; coverage of stocks, bonds, interest rates, commodities, gold, the economy
- ❏ *Investor's Business Daily* newspaper
- ❏ Nightly Business Report daily news summary
- ❏ *Worth* magazine
- ❏ *BusinessWeek* magazine
- ❏ *Chicago Tribune*'s business section
- ❏ *The New York Times*' business section

Mutual Fund Center
- ❏ Fidelity Investments' Online Investor Center
- ❏ The Vanguard Group of Investment Companies

Electronic Brokerage
- ❏ PC Financial Network, with a demo
- ❏ Quick & Reilly's reliable QuickWay
- ❏ U.S. Treasury Securities: buy direct
- ❏ Capital Markets Center: links to exchanges

Forums and Discussion Groups
- ❏ American Association of Individual Investors: solid support for 200,000 AAII members plus AOL's individual investors
- ❏ Motley Fools for Finance and Fun: a real online portfolio, stock tips, beginner courses, forums, library, surprisingly serious stuff
- ❏ Investors' Exchange and Investor's Network: meet and consult with corporate executives and access corporate directories
- ❏ Wall Street SOS Forum: technical analysis, timing, charting
- ❏ Decision Point Timing and Charts, for chartist and technicians

In other words, the print newspaper is old news by definition, compared to the online varieties now being uploaded and delivered around the world, around the clock.

Alternatively, before the print version arrives, you can flip on your computer, log in on AOL or some other service, click on the personal finance section, and head straight for the electronic newspapers section.

ONE-STOP FINANCIAL NEWSSTAND: PAPERLESS NEWSPAPERS

These *paperless*, electronic newspapers deserve your special attention. It would be easy to dismiss them as just an online fad, costing less than ten bucks a month, from which you can't expect any more than entertaining chatting and kid's stuff. Big mistake.

All individual investors are reminded that these same sources are also feeding your competition in the financial markets, the big institutional investors.

Maybe it's because I'm a former newspaperman, but I really do appreciate the valuable reporting of superteams such as the Reuters news service, *Investor's Business Daily,* and *BusinessWeek.* They never close and they are driven by writers and editors committed to providing the investor with solid news.

It's convenient to get them all delivered in one place, around the clock. In fact, AOL has so many news sources, I had the feeling of standing again in the main newsroom of the *Herald Examiner,* listening to the teletype, the phones, the typewriters, the chatter, the television—on the cutting edge of what's happening in the world.

So look closely at these alternative sources of electronic financial news that AOL delivers to you not only for less than the cost of *The Wall Street Journal* print version, but probably before the *Journal's* delivery person even gets out of bed! Moreover, your local newspaper may be rewriting or reprinting many of the Reuters stories, for example, so go to the source. Here are a few of the financial news sources AOL provides you:

❏ **Reuters Newswires:**   Here you get financial news reported by a top editorial team of 1,650 located in 120 news bureaus all over the globe. Reuters is the world's leading financial news organization with $3.5 billion in revenues. It must be doing something right, so while the coffee's brewing, warm up the computer and rediscover AOL.

　　Start your morning with AOL's Market News segments. You'll be getting the latest financial closings from Tokyo, Hong Kong, and London, along with the opening bell report on Wall Street. Reuters digs deep into the issues of currencies, economic indicators, precious metals—you name it; they report it. Frankly, it's surprising that Reuters doesn't get more credit on the AOL Market News marquee, since their reporting is so outstanding.

❏ *Investor's Business Daily:*   Here's another absolute jewel in the financial news reporting business—the choice of business decision makers. The *Daily* was founded by Bill O'Neil, author of the classic book, *How to Make Money in Stocks.* O'Neil's CANSLIM formula is the basis of his fortune—and maybe yours.

　　Investor's Business Daily's front page announces that its news is directed toward "important decision makers," and indeed it is. At 200,000, the *Daily's* circulation is about 10 percent of *The Wall Street Journal's,* yet much of the *Daily's* news and market data isn't found at Reuters, the *Journal,* or anywhere on a daily basis. *Investor's* is elite and unique.

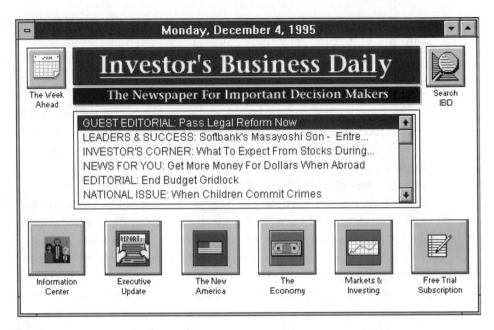

1.4 *Investor's Business Daily* "for important decision makers."

❑ *BusinessWeek* **Online:**   This source is backed by all the resources of its parent company, McGraw-Hill, also owner Standard & Poor's, another giant in financial market news.

❑ *San Jose Mercury's* **business page:**   A local paper of global importance, here is another fine source located right in Silicon Valley, the world's center of the information revolution. The *Mercury* was awarded honors for being one of the top electronic newspapers and is backed by all the resources of its parent, the Knight-Ridder organization, clearly the world's premiere resource for news about financial commodities and futures. At $2.5 billion, Knight-Ridder is one of the four giants of the financial news industry.

This is just the tip of the iceberg. There's much more top-flight news available, from *The New York Times, Worth* magazine, *Inc.* magazine, the *Nightly Business Report,* plus other great newspapers such as the *Chicago Tribune.*

We've deliberately taken the time to go over this in detail because you need to be aware that there is a surprising amount of depth available for

1.5 *The New York Times:* "All the news that's fit to print."

1.6 Market Reports: indexes, summaries, ratings, and analysis.

NET*investors at America Online's Personal Finance newsstand. It is definitely a bargain at less than $10 a month, even if that is the only service you use.

QUOTES FOR STOCKS AND MUTUAL FUND PORTFOLIOS

One of the great fascinations of the Internet's World Wide Web financial community are those teasers, especially "late-breaking headline news" and "five free quotes." They are advertising gimmicks that probably draw more high school and college kids than investors with real money to lay on the line.

At this stage of development, these Internet teasers are likely to draw a large crowd of curiosity seekers new to the Web, although that may soon wear off. Once you get the quote, so what? What do you do with it? If you have America Online (or one of the other services), you have unlimited quotes, plus the ability to automatically integrate the data directly into your portfolio. For example, here's what you can get from America Online regarding quotes for your portfolio:

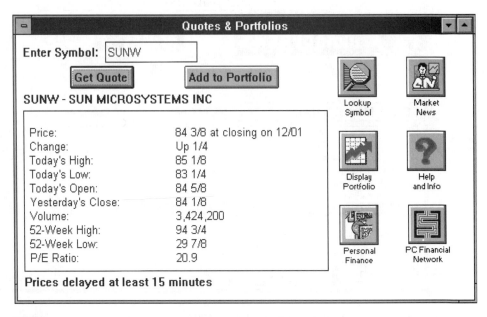

1.7 Build your portfolio: get quotes and other stock data.

❑ **Stock and fund quotes:** You get fast service looking up the ticker symbols, and drawing down quotes and other company data if you want it, without logging onto another Website.

❑ **Dow Watch:** This specifically focuses on the big blue chips—AT&T, Merck, GM, Exxon, IBM, GE—the drivers in the American economy, with big revenues and many shareholders. A few are probably in everyone's portfolio. And more than one astute financial advisor focuses long-term financial plans on these Dow Industrials. We pulled up J. P. Morgan as an example of all the financial statement fact you ever could want. Plus AOL has several analysts' commentaries available.

❑ **Hot stock news:** AOL has added a search provision that lets you uncover recent news about stocks you are researching.

❑ **Morningstar reports:** This is perhaps the most respected database, covering everything about America's mutual funds and, now, equity stocks. Morningstar not only gives you quotes, it also gives performance and other details. More important, with Morningstar you can select the top-performing funds from 27 categories, measured by returns from one month to five years.

❑ **Trends and technical charting:** For those NET*investors interested in going beyond the company fundamentals into technical analysis,

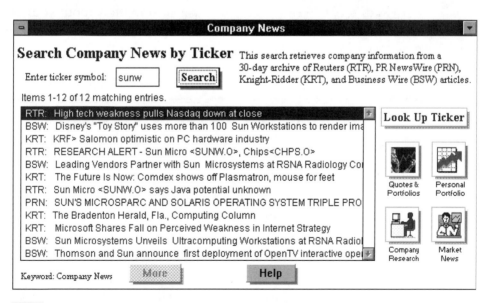

1.8 Expand on your quotes: search the latest company news.

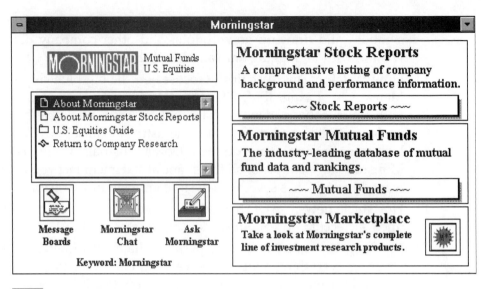

1.9 Morningstar stock and mutual funds quotes and research.

AOL's Decision Point service offers you assistance with Bollinger Bands and many other technical indicators.

In addition, you can also input basic information about your portfolio, automatically retrieve current quotes on your securities, and in this way keep track of your investments.

COMPANY RESEARCH AND ANALYSIS FOR NET*INVESTING

The wealth of high-quality information available to the NET*investor on America Online is really quite remarkable. When you click on the Research menu in the Personal Finance section, you'll immediately be able to access some of the best-known research databases for the fundamental analysis of stock companies and mutual funds, including:

❏ **Hoover's Company Profiles:** Business and financial facts.
❏ **First Call Earnings Estimates:** Past performance and future projections analyzed by the experts, from respected street resources.

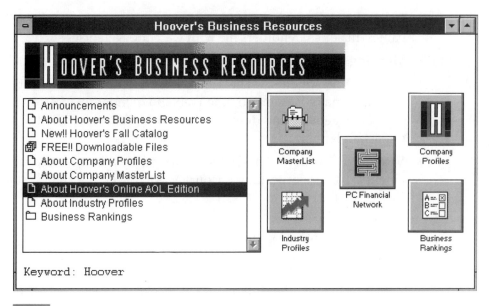

1.10 Hoover's business and industry resources.

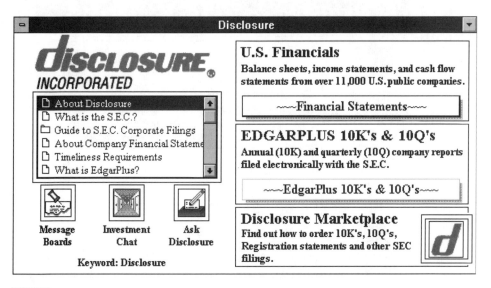

1.11 Disclosure Inc. for Edgar filings and financial documents.

☐ **Disclosure Incorporated:** Everything any one of the 6,500 public companies' major shareholders file with watchdog agencies such as the SEC.

☐ **Morningstar Research:** Detailed facts on all stocks and mutual funds.

☐ **Fidelity Investments:** The giant, with $365 billion in assets, which also has a major presence on the Web, independently of AOL. The AOL source is extensive and deserves your attention, especially the personal financial planner.

☐ **Vanguard Group:** Another mutual funds giant, competing with Fidelity. You are especially encouraged to check out the Mutual Fund Campus.

Armed with Morningstar for analysis, you might stay with just Fidelity and Vanguard.

America Online also offers the NET*investor an Investors' Exchange, with access to a few other interesting guides and directories, including:

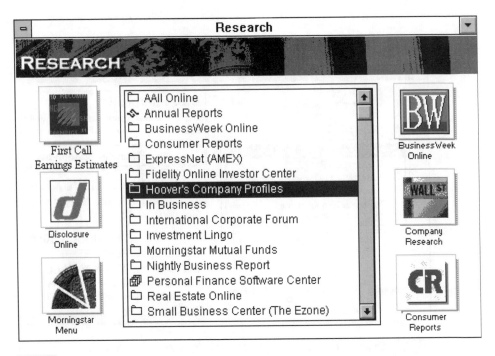

1.12 AOL's Research menu: the door to Corporate America.

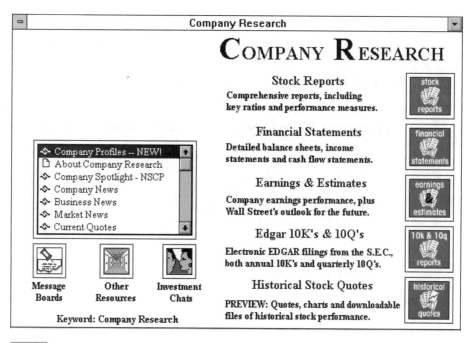

1.13 Company Research: financials, 10K's, earnings histories.

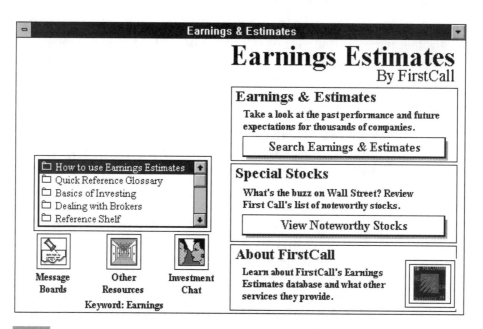

1.14 FirstCall Earnings: past performance and future projections.

❐ **Direct stock purchase programs:**   Go with the winning companies.

❐ **Dividend reinvestment programs (DRIPS):**   Keep investing in the winners.

❐ **Website addresses for public companies:**   More research information.

❐ **Exchange listings:**   Companies on the AMEX, NASDAQ, and NYSE.

❐ **Company-sponsored presentations and forums:**   You can "listen" online and ask questions of senior management; see upcoming schedule.

If all that exhausts you so much that you just can't remember the exact meaning of a DRIP, a call, or a swap, and you don't have a print dictionary near your workstation, then, AOL's Research section has an Investment Lingo file, which is an electronic dictionary for NET*investors. And for a down-to-earth break, check out the Motley Fools section, offering solid advice and a few investor-related jokes that might wake you up between all the hot stock tips.

TOPS IN CYBERSPACE INVESTMENT CLUBS

One of the great genius creations born with and embedded in the incredible Internet are the forums (also known as *bulletin boards, conferences,* or *discussion* and *chat groups*). This is global democracy and networking in its highest form, a true electronic meeting hall and shopping mall, where all are welcomed to learn and share.

From the beginning, AOL created its own forums for the discussion of common themes of interest. For many NET*investors, this is a perfect opportunity to get tips from peers, research leading-edge issues, discuss your favorite investments, compare notes about new software, and get leads for further reading on specialized subjects. It is a combination college seminar room, dormitory rap session, and graduate school library.

Obviously, all forums aren't dazzling expositions with brilliant new insights. Certainly anyone who has ever explored the Internet Usenet groups—the forerunners of the online forums—knows how limited forums can be. Often, they're no more than a mix of naive, melodramatic soap operas, hyped-up infomercials, and irritating classified ads.

However, the America Online forums—in fact, most online forums— tend to be naturally screened; that is, they are frequently monitored by

1.15 AOL's menu listing of Finance Forums.

a pro, which minimizes junk talk, and they are focused on a specific topic (such as Telescan users), thus requiring a prior level of expertise and interest. Some AOL forums that are of special interest to the NET*investor are:

☐ **American Association of Individual Investors:**   The premiere non-profit organization supporting the needs of individual investors and offering resources on software, stocks, funds, training, planning, brokerage, and more.

☐ **The Motley Fools:**   A must-see and one of the best sites in Wall Street cyberspace, with serious financial advice mixed with humor. Expect anybody this good to get worldwide exposure from a Website soon. They may not take themselves seriously, but *your* portfolio is deadly serious business to them.

☐ **Telescan Users' Group Forum:**   Focused support for serious investors using Telescan as well as other technical and charting systems for active trading.

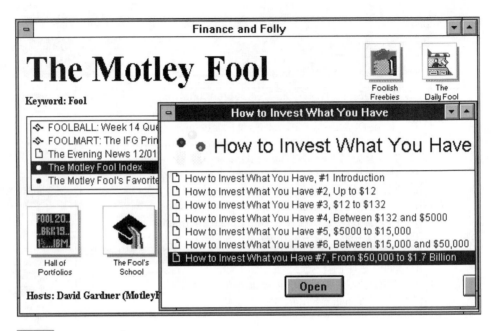

1.16 The Motley Fool teaches you how to invest.

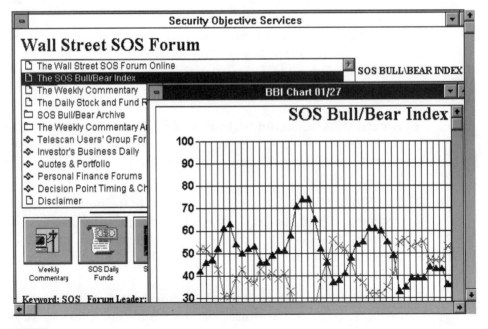

1.17 Wall Street SOS Forum and Bull/Bear Index.

❐ **Wall Street SOS Forum:** Another forum focused on technical analysis.

❐ **Decision Point Timing and Charts:** This forum features charts and graphs.

There are several other forums that fit a variety of financial and business interests, covering entrepreneurship, taxes, home ownership, real

---

KIPLINGER'S HIGH MARKS FOR MOTLEY FOOLS . . . AND FOR AOL!

"Investing can be fun! At least it seems that way when you log on to Motley Fool. . . . It's the brainchild of the Gardner brothers—Tom, 27, and Dave, 29—who serve up their advice with a lot of cheek and Renaissance-inspired whimsy. . . .

"The ten-stock Fool portfolio is decidedly high-octane, with above-average risk. The heaviest stake is in technology (holdings include America Online). . . .

"For stability, one-fourth of the portfolio is invested more or less according to a stock-picking recipe popularized in the book *Beating the Dow* (HarperCollins, 1991), by Michael Higgins, an Albany, N.Y., money manager. The Gardner brothers recommend it to beginning investors for its simplicity.

"Here's how it works.

1. **Identify the ten highest yielding stocks among the 30 companies that comprise the Dow Jones industrial average. . . .**
2. **From among those ten companies, invest in the five with the lowest-priced shares.**
3. **Hold for one year.**
4. **Repeat first three steps. . . .**

"The beating-the-Dow strategy produced an average annualized return of 20.6% from 1973 to the beginning of this year, versus the Dow's annualized return of 10.8%. In the strategy's worst year, 1990, the five stocks lost 15% versus the Dow's decline of 0.4%."

SOURCE: Gregory Spears, "Ready to Buy Your Own Stocks?" *Kiplinger's Personal Finance Magazine* (November 1995).

Kiplinger's is a great magazine for individual investors. You can also find *Kiplinger's* online at Prodigy. Also read *The Motley Fool Investment Guide*, by Dave and Tom Gardner (Simon & Schuster, 1996). These guys are nobody's fools; check them out.

estate investments, and a host of personal financial planning issues. In addition, most of the newspapers and magazines have their own forums with in-house experts, anchors, writers, and editors.

ELECTRONIC DISCOUNT BROKERAGE: DO-IT-YOURSELF TRADING

When the chips are down, when the next step is to put your money where your modem is, and when it's time to actually make that trade, AOL has more support for you. In fact, there are a number of ways to buy and sell shares, all right *out there* in cyberspace, accessible through your AOL NET*navigator:

❏ **PC Financial Network:** Probably the pioneer in online, electronic discount brokerage, this was started back in the early 1980s by the distinguished investment banking firm, Donaldson Lufkin Jenrette. It has the largest clientele in cyberspace, with over 225,000 satisfied customers and over 2 million executed trades totaling over $12 billion. In fact, PCFN often accounts for 10 percent of the daily trading volume on the New York Stock Exchange. Now that's cyberspace power.

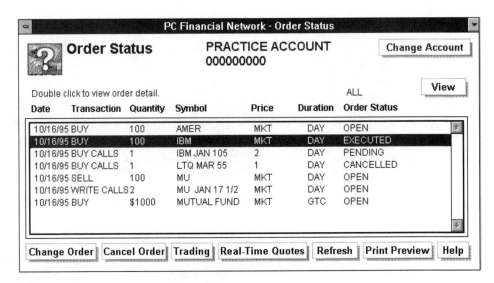

1.18   PCFN's Practice Account: an online trading demo.

❒ **Quick & Reilly:** This source offers QuickWay trading and is one of America's more aggressive electronic discount brokers. A stand-alone system (a high-quality, private-label Reuters Money Network product) is also available for total investment research and analysis before executing trades with Quick & Reilly.

❒ **Fidelity Online Xpress (FOX):** This is the Fidelity stock and mutual funds discount trading arm, which also provides access to FundsNetwork, your link to a cyberspace network of hundreds of top-performing non-Fidelity funds.

❒ **U.S. Treasury Securities:** Even the Federal government is now in the game of supporting cyberspace investors who want to avoid brokers and go direct. Find out how you can get U.S. Treasury bonds all by yourself.

You can also set up a hypothetical portfolio on AOL and trade it, as a learning tool and an opportunity to gain experience. Of course, it isn't the same as playing the game with real money on the line. In a similar vein, you can explore stock contests, games, and simulations, as offered by Fidelity Investments, for example.

AMERICA ONLINE: THE NEXT MAJOR INTERNET WEBSITE

As an example of the incredible array of possibilities offered by online services, America Online's offerings are very impressive. And with the intense hype now surrounding the Internet, it would be easy to lose sight of what these commercial online services *already* offer.

Moreover, now that AOL is offering its subscribers a gateway *out* to the Internet, it seems logical to assume that in a short period of time the gateway will also be reversed, allowing subscribers out there on the Internet to be able to get *from* the Internet *into* America Online—or any other commercial online service for that matter. This is especially true as AOL continues to enhance its content databases. Prodigy has already put it's Informed Investor service on the Web. It is probably only a matter of time before America Online and CompuServe follow the lead.

Simply put, it's logical and natural to assume that AOL will soon become an Internet Website that anyone, anywhere in the world can subscribe to. This is the obvious next step from a marketing standpoint, in order to tap into the massive audience growing on the World Wide Web.

BOTTOM LINE: ONE OF AMERICA'S
TOP NET*NAVIGATORS FOR INVESTORS

Two of the primary needs for every investor's NET*navigator—*content plus integration*—are well provided for by AOL. There's a lot all in one place. At AOL, the NET*investor will find a wealth of content necessary to handle all phases of the investing process, plus a central platform with which to pull it all together and make investment decisions.

For many investors, AOL has all that is needed, and it's hard to go wrong at $10 a month. Besides, AOL will let you try it free for a month. If you don't agree that it's worth that much just for the Reuters Newswires, *Investor's Business Daily,* and unlimited stock and fund quotes, then maybe you better stick to the free news you can pick up slowly surfing around the World Wide Web.

We want to conclude with a comment on the obvious. Our attention throughout this book is on tools for cyberspace investors. However, for ten bucks a month, the NET*investor gets access to a lot more than just the investment services outlined here—AOL has tons of information on sports, entertainment, travel, and weather, as well as E-mail available to the user.

From the NET*investor's viewpoint, however, that's extra—icing on the cake. It's true that if you use the service beyond the basic hourly allotment, you will get charged extra—but, heck, the phone company also charges you extra when you talk too long to your mother.

CompuServe: Global Network for Cyber-Investors

CompuServe must be considered the oldest commercial online service. Granted, Dow Jones, Reuters, and Knight-Ridder have been in cyberspace a lot longer with their digitized newswire deliveries, but CompuServe is the pioneer of the online business.

And like a good wine, CompuServe is improving with age. It first went online in 1969, in the old days of mainframes, providing electronic database services and computer time-sharing to business corporations. Then in 1979 it opened its doors to the consumer market.

The parent company, H&R Block, America's favorite neighborhood tax-services giant, bought CompuServe in 1980. H&R Block has awesome clout, with almost 10,000 offices worldwide preparing taxes for 17 million people. One in seven tax returns to the IRS is handled by Block, and they are known for their integrity.

Last year for the first time, CompuServe's earnings exceeded those of H&R Block's tax-preparation division, another example of the growth exploding online and on the Internet. This was enough that H&R Block took advantage of this year's hot market and brought CompuServe's stock public. The spinoff will be completed in early 1997.

HIGH-QUALITY NETWORK, CONTENT, AND SUBSCRIBERS

Today, H&R Block's CompuServe subsidiary has about five million subscribers in 150 countries worldwide, also providing online network services to about a thousand corporate customers. It successfully combines both commanding size and integrity, with a user-friendly network of electronic decision-making resources.

CompuServe's early entry into cyberspace and its reputation in the business community has earned it superpower status, both with content providers and consumers, thanks in large part to its focus on communications and networking technology, evidenced by its:

❑ **Extensive database of first-class content providers:** CompuServe has over 3,000 content providers supplying not only business and financial information but also a huge supply of resources for all sorts of consumers. In addition to financial and investing services, the opening menu will link you to top-flight databases with the latest news and the best data on everything from weather, sports, and movies to travel, education, and shopping. Plus it now provides a direct link to the

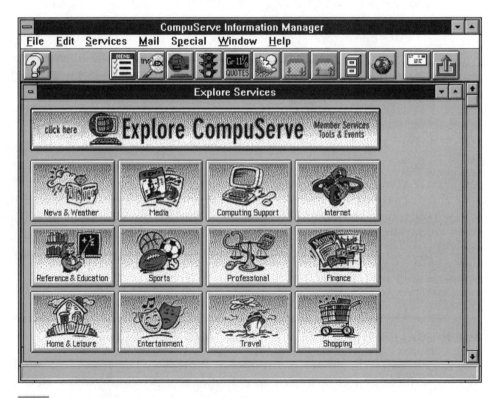

2.1 CompuServe's master menu of all services.

Internet. Fortunately, access to 90 percent of the total 3,000 content providers are included with the basic service fee.

❏ **Secure worldwide telecommunications network:** Early on, CompuServe realized that its reputation and success depended on developing a reliable communications network. As a result, today you can access CompuServe from local telephone numbers in every major U.S. city and worldwide in more than 150 countries. In fact, there are one million in Japan and another million European subscribers linked to this communications net. CompuServe has also been a leader in providing companies with secure, private IntraNets that link internal operations and departments with customers throughout the world, and it continues to develop this networking technology.

❏ **Expanding subscriber base of successful individuals:** CompuServe's average subscriber is an upscale, successful individual, including professionals and executives with average annual household incomes of $90,000. The demographics also indicate that CompuServe users are predominantly male (83 percent), college educated (71 percent), and average 41 years old. There is also a surprisingly large majority (54 percent) who have home-based businesses. Five million voices like this say that CompuServe must be delivering a first-class product—and the number of subscribers continues to grow.

CompuServe has been riding the crest of the Internet wave. Global subscriber growth exceeds 200,000 per month. Without a doubt, CompuServe will continue as one of the premiere online service companies well into the next century.

MASSIVE ONLINE DIGITAL RESEARCH LIBRARY

The key to CompuServe's popular and commercial appeal is the gigantic collection of content providers it has amassed in recent decades. In other words, CompuServe is clearly one of the master NET*navigators for the new cyberspace investor, having virtually everything you need for investing integrated in one single location, with many additional services.

In fact, the ability to integrate so many databases is what gives all three of the traditional online services—CompuServe, AOL, and Prodigy—such a powerful edge in the the online/on-the-Net race. Let's take a look at the resources CompuServe puts on your monitor.

❒ **Mutual funds:**   The *Money* magazine FundWatch is designed to help you screen and analyze over 5,000 mutual funds. Check out the Fund-Watch Top Performing Funds. Screen the total database based on pre-selected criteria, such as fund objectives, performance rankings, asset allocations, management companies, fees and expenses, and yield and risk. You can also get reports from two other winning databases, Morningstar and Value Line.

❒ **Current business and financial news:**   CompuServe has a news clipping and digest service, Executive News Service (ENS), designed to save you time by targeting and preselecting only the news you want from Dow Jones, Reuters, the Associated Press, and other national and world news services. In addition, you can access 50 national newspapers, including *USA Today, San Francisco Chronicle, St. Louis Post-Dispatch,* and *San Jose Mercury News.*

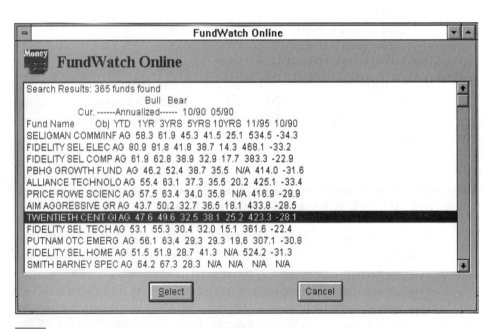

2.2 *Money* Magazine's FundWatch Online.

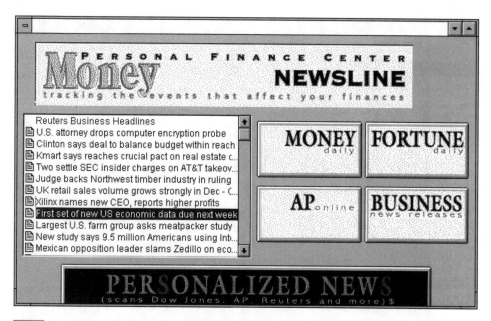

2.3 Newsline: AP, Reuters, Dow Jones, and more.

MUTUAL FUND HEAVEN: BORING BUT EFFICIENT

"You get into the basic investment services on CompuServe via a shell maintained by *Money* magazine, which also maintains a presence on Pathfinder, the Internet site for Time Warner (parent of *Fortune's* publisher). The baby-boomers and Generation Xers who have fueled the mutual fund explosion of the Nineties will find a lot to love here. The online version of *Money's* FundWatch provides excellent one-page summaries of any fund's performance, yield, risk, expenses, and holdings. The FundWatch screening program will also build a list of top-performing funds based on criteria you select, including type of fund (growth, income, international, etc.), yield, assets, risk, and fund manager. . . .

"Stock screening isn't pretty—CompuServe forces you into terminal emulation mode, so that your computer screen resembles a dinosaur circa 1980, with boring ASCII text and no graphics—but it's efficient."

SOURCE: Michael Himowitz, "Cyberspace: The Investor's New Edge," *Fortune* (December 25, 1995).

2.4 *Money*'s Personal Finance Center.

❏ **Financial and business magazines:**   In addition to all the national and international newspapers and the standout *Money* magazine, you also get *BusinessWeek, Fortune, Forbes, Inc.,* and *The Economist,* as well as other top names in first-class financial reporting.

❏ **Historical database:**   CompuServe's MicroQuote database is loaded with 12 years of history on more than 125,000 financial instruments: stocks, bonds, mutuals, options, and more. It is one of the best. Information on U.S., Canadian, and OTC exchanges, as well as foreign currencies, is available. This data and the charts are updated daily to the previous day's closing data. A good way to start the day is by looking at the previous day's activity by major markets, including most actives.

❏ **Financial quotes:**   The search engine helps you look up ticker symbols and check out quotes for your favorite stocks, funds, commodities, and indexes. Stock quotes are on a 15-minute delay. You can access the 600 market indexes, the DJIA, S&P 500, Nikkei, and whatever else suits

```
                              Current Quotes

    Ticker    Volume   High/Ask   Low/Bid     Last    Change Updated

    SUNW       85272     43.750     40.250    41.250   -3.500 03-Jan-96*
    MS          8323     83.500     81.500    83.500   +2.250 03-Jan-96*
    MSFT       39286     90.125     86.750    86.875   -2.875 03-Jan-96*
    IBM        31270     91.250     89.000    89.250   -1.625 03-Jan-96*
    NOVL       35655     15.625     15.125    15.250   -0.125 03-Jan-96*
    SP 500         0    623.250    619.560   621.320   +0.590 03-Jan-96
    HRB         3865     41.750     40.625    40.625   -0.500 03-Jan-96*

    All quotes are delayed.  CompuServe does not edit this
    data and is not responsible or liable for its content,
    completeness, or timeliness.
    * Most current news was at 23:50 EST for IBM.

    GO ENS ($)        Export        Detail         Help        Cancel
```

2.5 Selection of CompuServe's current quotes.

you, including a host of statistical input, volume, a/d lines, put/call ratios, and more. You can also get bond ratings from Moody's and S&P, commodity price quotes that go back more than ten years, plus option puts/calls on stocks and the major indices. And for research on international currencies, check out ADP's Global Report.

❑ **Company research:** Hoover's profiles are available and cover 1,100 of the largest companies; you can access the Disclosure company database as well. Other key databases are a mouse-click away, including Standard & Poor's, Disclosure, Value Line, Institutional Brokers Estimate System (I/B/E/S), and Zacks Earnings Estimates—everything you need for company research.

❑ **Fundamental analysis and screening:** With data from over 10,000 companies available to analyze, you can use any one of a number of excellent sets of selection criteria. Try *Investor's Business Daily* publisher Bill O'Neil's CANSLIM formula and other reputable methods for screening new opportunities for your portfolio. Screen securities on the basis of historical growth, financial ratios, book and market valuation, cash flow, sales, income, and other criteria.

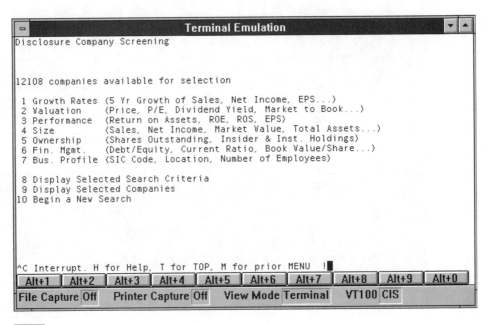

```
Terminal Emulation                                    ▼ ▲
Disclosure Company Screening


12108 companies available for selection

1 Growth Rates (5 Yr Growth of Sales, Net Income, EPS...)
2 Valuation    (Price, P/E, Dividend Yield, Market to Book...)
3 Performance  (Return on Assets, ROE, ROS, EPS)
4 Size         (Sales, Net Income, Market Value, Total Assets...)
5 Ownership    (Shares Outstanding, Insider & Inst. Holdings)
6 Fin. Mgmt.   (Debt/Equity, Current Ratio, Book Value/Share...)
7 Bus. Profile (SIC Code, Location, Number of Employees)

8 Display Selected Search Criteria
9 Display Selected Companies
10 Begin a New Search




^C Interrupt. H for Help, T for TOP, M for prior MENU  !█
```

| Alt+1 | Alt+2 | Alt+3 | Alt+4 | Alt+5 | Alt+6 | Alt+7 | Alt+8 | Alt+9 | Alt+0 |

| File Capture Off | Printer Capture Off | View Mode Terminal | VT100 CIS |

2.6 Disclosure's Criteria for Company Database Screening.

❐ **Global companies:** This includes information from databases such as Dun & Bradstreet and various foreign sources, including the *Financial Times* Analysis Reports Europe. Of special note is the fact that Compu-Serve has developed working connections with the key reputable databases in every major region, including Asia-Pacific, the United Kingdom, Europe, Latin America, the Arab world, the Middle East, and Russia.

❐ **Technical analysis:** If you're interested in betting on the short- and long-term trends, cycles, and turning points, you'll need additional software for timing turning points in the market and for particular stocks.

❐ **Expert opinions:** The database includes content from over 500 industry newsletters and 100 regional business publications, as well as reporting on more than 100 brokerage and investment research firms. It covers over 10,000 U.S. publicly held companies and 2,000 foreign companies—all the important ones.

❐ **Trading online:** Through CompuServe, you can set up an account with E*Trade, Quick & Reilly, and other brokers and make all your portfolio's trades online at a discount, without logging onto another service.

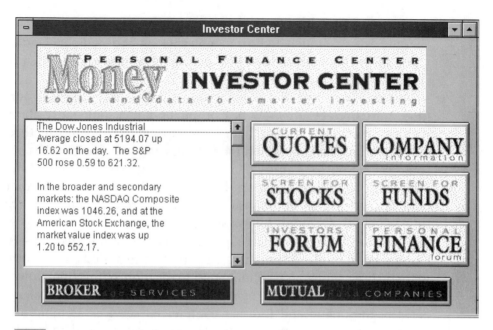

2.7　*Money* Investor Center: Tools and Data for Smarter Investing.

❐ **Investor education:** Investing is a lifelong process. Build your skills; educate yourself; test your ability to build and manage your portfolio. E*Trade will give you $100,000 in game money and a couple of games, without risking hard-earned funds.

❐ **Discussion forums:** CompuServe has a variety of solid discussion forums for serious investors, run by editors and experts at the major magazines, such as *Fortune, Forbes,* and *Money.* In addition, there are forums on taxes, small businesses, and new computer software.

❐ **Entrepreneurs and small business owners:** A large number of databases are available, offering services for home offices, telecommuting, and other entrepreneurial activities for small businesses. And this is just the start. You have ready access to all the other support services on CompuServe, such as entertainment, sports, travel, health, weather, and shopping, from more than 3,000 content providers.

CYBERSPACE COMMERCIALISM: CAUTION, METER RUNNING

There's so much information and they're so big that you can easily get lost in CompuServe. It's like walking around the Library of Congress, yet

CompuServe is well organized. As with other online services, you're charged extra for much of the data you click on or download. Don't get lost while the meter's running or you could be in for a shock when the next credit card bill arrives.

Is this a big deal? Not if you preplan, focus, and monitor your online time. Virtually every review of CompuServe has some story about users with astronomical bills, but that's to be expected for a company that's been on the leading edge of the online industry for two decades. Yes, there are some classic horror stories about CompuServe subscribers getting stuck with bills of a thousand dollars, but they still have hundreds of thousands of new subscribers every month. Also, you can reduce your risk if you take time to read the complex billing schedule.

This may be less likely to happen with other online systems—America Online, for example, where there are virtually no added charges other than for extra time. Still, you'd better expect to see more of this trend toward paying a la carte for every little byte of data you look at. It will accelerate in all areas of the online and Internet commercial services as more and more commercial services focus increasingly on the commercial bottom line.

It's your responsibility to watch how you select services and to use offline planning where possible. You can help yourself by using CompuServe's File

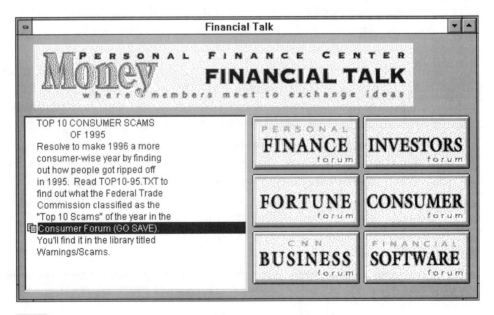

2.8 Financial Talk forums: business, finance, and investing.

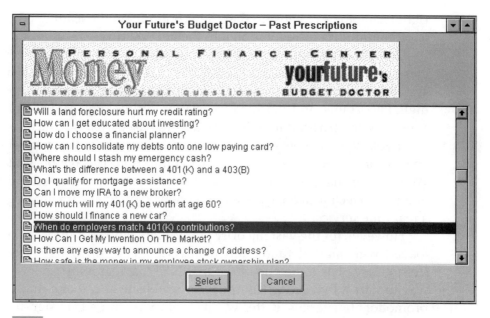

2.9   Budget Doctor: interactive financial advice for cyber-investors.

Finder CD to search files *offline first;* then you'll minimize online time by going directly to the required material. So don't let fears about hidden costs make you take something less than you really need for successful investing. Act responsibly, and you can coast by with a modest $20 to $40 monthly bill.

Let's face it, when you're working with such a huge collection of databases, you need a solid NET*navigator—and you, the pilot, must truly take control. Be thankful that you have access to such a wonderful research library, then make sure you use all of CompuServe's super navigational tools efficiently to monitor your online time and charges. If you just want to leisurely surf the Internet's World Wide Web, get a Netcom or similar local Internet access provider account that gives you *unlimited* time for about $20 plus the cost of a local call.

BOTTOM LINE: HIGH-TECH LEADERSHIP INTO THE TWENTY-FIRST CENTURY

CompuServe is definitely a five-star winner, a first-class NET*navigator for the serious investor. Moreover, CompuServe is investing heavily in all the right technologies to ensure that they continue on the leading edge of the telecommunications revolution into the next century.

CompuServe's own R&D has taken it into many advanced technologies, such as Internet interfaces with the acquisition of SPRY, cable delivery systems, multimedia publishing, CD-ROM, audio compression, personal digital assistants, and machine translation technology. And recently they teamed with Microsoft to build a Windows-based Web interface.

If you expect to spend a lot of time on the Internet's Web, you will probably want to add a separate Internet connection, to save on E-mail and Web-surfing charges. You'll also need some more sophisticated software if you're into technical analysis, and you may want to eventually upgrade to a real-time service.

However, for the vast majority of investors who are building portfolios loaded with mutual funds and relatively small portfolios of securities, CompuServe has to be one of the first NET*navigators to review. A good way to start is by visiting CompuServe's Website or call or e-mail for their promotional materials. Better yet, just jump in with a trial sign-up. You'll probably get five hours online for free to see if it satisfies your needs as an investor. It's time well spent, especially since you'll be working with whatever system you ultimately choose for a long time to come. It's all part of your cyberspace learning curve.

Prodigy: The Informed Investor Online and on the Web

Prodigy was the first of the online services to ramp up its subscribers with Internet access and a Web browser. In early 1996, it made another bold move by launching a new service for investors, on the Internet, independent of its online operations.

Why was Prodigy's action bold? The cyber-trend here was much bigger than Prodigy's decision. This strategic action signaled the first of many such moves by all the other online services as they began to create parallel but unique operations on the World Wide Web, *with services open to everyone with Internet access.* This heralds a transformation among the so-called online services.

In fact, the online services actually have no choice but to create open access to new subscribers on the Internet. The market is too big to ignore or leave to other, more aggressive, vendors. It would be like admitting members only to the doors of one anchor store in a regional shopping mall, while an anchor store at the other end has an open-door policy. Soon, competition for the mass-market consumer on the Internet will force all the "closed" online services to admit anyone on the Internet.

We are already seeing the rush of a whole new breed of Website-based services for investors—for example, Telescan, Schwab, Reuters, and *Mutual Funds* magazine. However, you have to give Prodigy credit; it's a pioneer in the true sense of the word. Among the traditional online services, Prodigy is the leader with its new investor service. But the rush is just beginning.

This trend is guaranteed to accelerate exponentially as online banking, secure credit card transactions, and the commercial banks grab a lock on the Net. Soon any subscriber *or nonsubscriber* with a Web browser will be able to access Prodigy, CompuServe, and AOL and charge it to some new universal InternetBank credit card. Eventually, the commercial banks could make this as easy as buying a day pass to the health club when traveling on business.

NEW PRODIGY: MORE THAN A FACE-LIFT . . . AN INFORMED INVESTOR

Prodigy's new image will surprise most subscribers and investors taking their first serious look at this service. In the past, press reviews would take frequent potshots at Prodigy's screen look, making flip remarks such as, Prodigy's "clunky interface will remind investors of the days when a Commodore 64 was the hot home computer."

Today, however, all that's changing, and it's time for a second look. The new Informed Investor Website is worth investigating, because Prodigy is rapidly converting to the more conventional and familiar Windows format, and, most likely, their "clunky" online screens will gradually be modified. Besides, as an investor aiming for a profitable bottom line and winning portfolio, what matters is the quality of the information. Your online service should be streamlined for results.

The comparison with other services is a bit unfair. After all, Dow Jones News/Retrieval and CompuServe both get away with some plain-vanilla, dull-gray graphics (arguing that their customers "just want the facts"). So

---

PRODIGY ONLINE: BEST ORGANIZED AND EASIEST TO USE

"Prodigy: just the basics. Prodigy has fewer resources than CompuServe and America Online. . . . Nevertheless, Prodigy is the best organized and the easiest of the online services to use. It may be all that most investors need.

"Prodigy's financial services are designed to be intuitive and complementary. One feature leads logically to another, and you don't have to search far to find what you're looking for. . . .

"The Verdict: Prodigy's intelligent design and ease of use make it a good choice for casual stock investors. But the mutual fund hunters and serious researchers will do better elsewhere."

SOURCE: Michael Himowitz, "Cyberspace: The Investor's New Edge," *Fortune* (December 25, 1995).

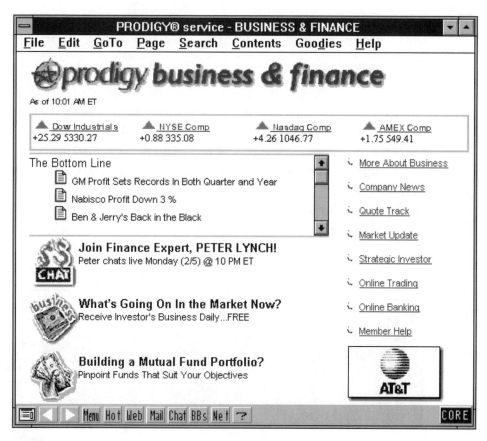

3.1 Prodigy's master menu for business and finance.

why pick on Prodigy for its unique play-school charm, rivaled only by
Quicken Deluxe's graphics (which certainly haven't hurt Quicken)?
Besides, this concern may soon be moot. Prodigy's screen format is slowly
being altered and is probably destined to become part of Web folklore. So
enjoy it while it lasts.

PRODIGY'S NET*NAVIGATOR . . . A SURPRISING WINNER

The NET*investors who are already into technical analysis and may be
using the super-sophisticated MetaStock and Telescan Platform may laugh
at the idea of Prodigy and America Online as competition for the Telescan,
Reuters, and Dow Jones NET*navigators. Let them laugh. Prodigy, along

with its siblings in the commercial online service industry, do serve the needs of many investors quite adequately. You may be surprised to know that:

❒ Dow Jones News/Retrieval is one of Prodigy's key stock quote resources. Prodigy reformats the data in a simpler, more logical way, actually structuring it to be more user-friendly to investors.

❒ *Individual Investor,* one of the top magazines in the field, has ranked Prodigy's Stock Hunter screening and selection program the best of its kind.

❒ *BusinessWeek* has concluded that AOL and Prodigy are "generally the easiest to get around in for PC newcomers."

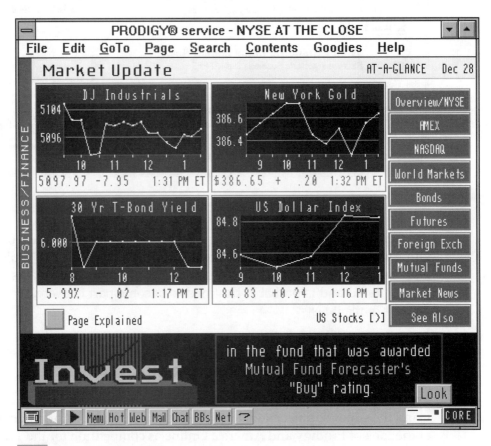

3.2 Market Update: DJIA, gold, T-bonds, and the dollar.

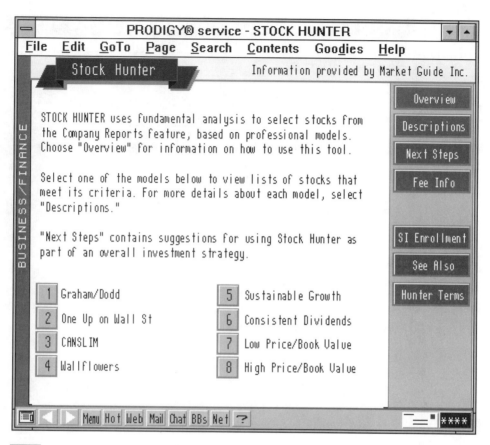

3.3 Prodigy's Stock Hunter: fundamental analysis screening.

The fact remains that Prodigy may be exactly what the new NET*investor should start with, and it may well be more than enough for more experienced investors who make few trades in and out of their portfolios.

Besides, even the NET*investor who has Reuters Money Network or Dow Jones News/Retrieval, for example, may want or need Prodigy for other services, such as entertainment, chat groups, or shopping. In other words, today's cyberspace investor is likely to have multiple systems including the following:

❑ **Primary investment navigator:** A super-powered but plain-vanilla system with all the data and analytics needed for trading and portfolio management—for example, Telescan, CompuServe, or Reuters Money Network.

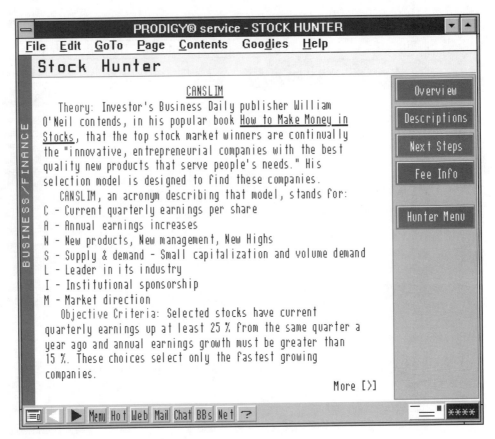

3.4 Stock Hunter: CANSLIM formula and stock screener.

❏ **General backup online service for family and investing needs:** Prodigy or America Online, for weather, travel, sports, entertainment, cooking, games, and all the other less-demanding elements that make life exciting.

❏ **Direct Internet access provider:**   If you start spending a lot of time on the Internet and its World Wide Web—say more than five hours a month—get something like WorldNet Netcom or EarthLink for essentially unlimited access for under $20 a month.

Be sure to monitor the charges, because they can add up quickly, along with an extra phone line, access calls, and so forth, as well as increasing charges for a cellular phone, cable system, and fax machine usage. Welcome to the Information Age. Information costs money and it is the basis of your future as a NET*investor headed for financial independence, but you'll have to spend it to make it.

PRODIGY: RATED NUMBER ONE FOR BANKING AND INVESTMENT

Prodigy's Investment Center is neatly and logically organized, which almost makes it seem like something's missing—especially by comparison with the gargantuan databases and more sophisticated navigation systems on CompuServe and Dow Jones News/Retrieval. Prodigy has the essentials for most investors, without the confusing, esoteric extras.

PRODIGY'S STOCK HUNTER: BEST STOCK-SCREENING TOOL

"Best Stock Screening Tool: Prodigy's Stock Hunter . . . The hands-down winner . . . runs screens, updated weekly, based on eight different selection methods . . .

"Best Portfolio Tracking and Online Trading: Prodigy . . . Its portfolio tracker is the only one of the big three commercial services that allows you to record commissions with the stock price . . . Prodigy also offers the easiest on-line trading through PC Financial Network."

SOURCE: Wayne Harris, "And the Winner Is . . . The Best of the Commercial On-line Services," *Individual Investor* (August 1995).

Here's what you get at Prodigy's Investment Center:

❒ **Strategic investor screening:** Use one of eight well-known investing systems, such as Graham/Dodd, Lynch, or O'Neil's CANSLIM to tailor your criteria, focus your screening, and select opportunities from the stock database. Here's an ideal research department for many cyberspace investors.

❒ **Tradeline performance histories:** Download price and volume charts on virtually every mutual fund, stock, and bond you'll ever want to research.

❒ **Company reports:** It provides all the fundamentals on more than 6,000 companies, as well as unbiased detailed financial information on all NYSE, NASD, and AMEX companies.

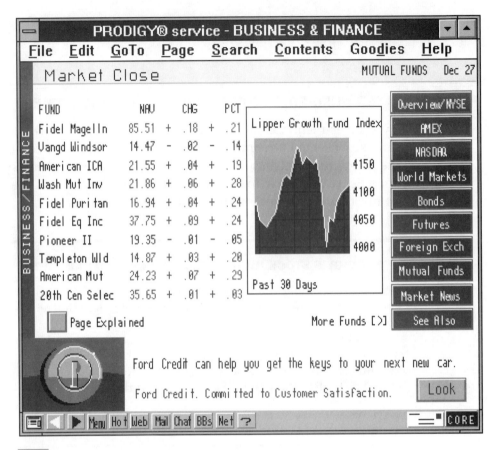

3.5 Mutual funds and other closing market statistics.

❏ **Wall Street Edge newsletters:** Daily stock tips are screened from more than 300 of the top financial advisory newsletters. Every day you'll get summaries of the latest (buying them direct could cost thousands of dollars annually). Coverage includes mutual funds, new issues, low-priced stocks, technologies, Dow theory, chartists, and growth stocks.

❏ **Quotetrack portfolio monitoring:** Use this service to update and monitor the current value of your investment portfolio, with alerts on news that might affect it.

❏ **Quote check:** This provides immediate retrieval of basic quote data for decision making.

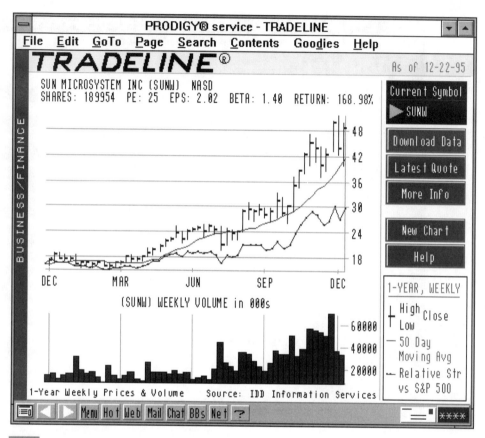

3.6 Tradeline: annual company price/volume charts.

❐ **Market and company news:** Get timely headlines and hot financial news directly from Dow Jones New/Retrieval, the same source used by market professionals. It includes information on markets, indexes, companies, and securities.

❐ **Money Talk and Investors Bulletin Board:** These are discussion forums where you can ask experts and peers about key issues on investing, software, specific companies, the economy, and so on.

❐ **Online banking:** You can hook directly into your account at one of the many participating banks, enabling you to view statements, transfer funds, and pay bills.

❐ *Kiplinger's* **magazine:** This is online access to one of the top ten financial periodicals published, with solid advice for individual investors.

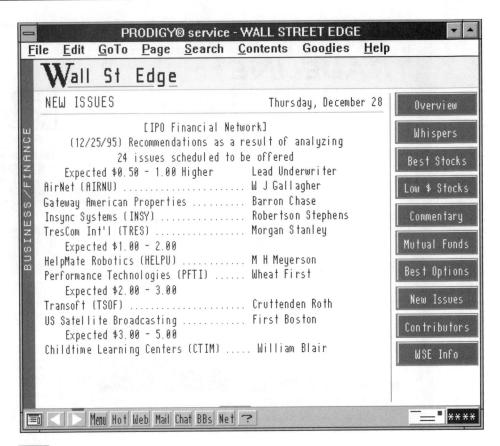

3.7 Wall Street Edge: financial advisory newsletters.

□ **PC Financial Network for trading:**   When you're ready, hot link to PC Financial Network, America's largest online discount broker, and close the deal. PCFN also has some investing contests to help you build skills.

Prodigy is like a limited-menu restaurant, a favorite hangout that doesn't confuse you with millions of unnecessary choices but offers just the right information for the kinds of essential decisions you must make as a new cyberspace investor.

Prodigy may well have everything you'll need. And, of course, you can always opt for a trial period to see if it fits your needs—as you can with virtually all the competing NET*navigators. If a super team like the *Individual Investor* says Prodigy is a winner, it is.

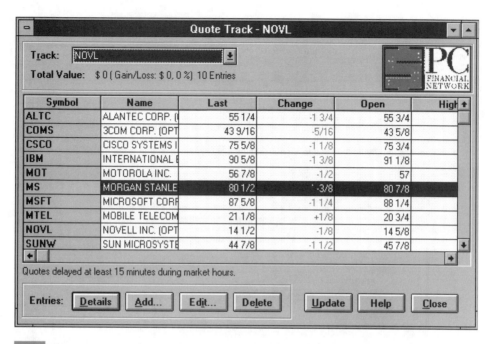

3.8 Prodigy Investment Center: new online format.

PRODIGY'S NEW WEBSITE: THE INFORMED INVESTOR

Prodigy's new offering on the Web—the Informed Investor—has a competitive base price of five dollars, with Prodigy's usual custom add-ons, such as company reports, Wall Street Edge, and historical stock prices. Prodigy is a respected online name and should give the competition a definite run for the money at this price, especially if it continues to stay competitive with the following excellent combination of services for NET*investors:

❏ **Market updates:** NYSE, AMEX, NASDAQ, mutual funds, world stocks, bonds, futures, and the currency markets.

❏ **Quotes:** Standard 15-minute delayed stock quotes and mutual funds.

❏ **News updates:** Dow Jones, AP, Business Wire, and the PR Newswire.

❏ *Investor's Business Daily:* One of the investor's best news sources.

❏ **Wall Street Edge:** Summaries of top financial advisory newsletters.

❏ **Tradeline:** Database for historic prices and volumes.

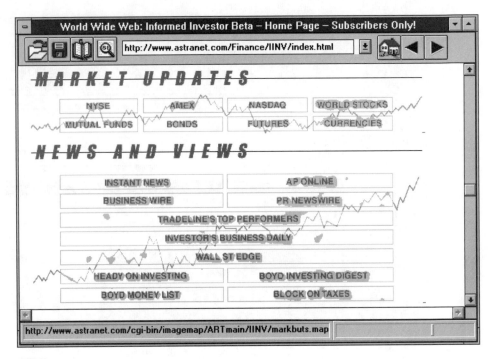

3.9   Informed Investor: Prodigy's new Internet Web service.

More will be added. The bottom line is that Prodigy is now making an important strategic move on the Internet that should improve its competitive position among the online services. This action should reinforce the accelerating trend to make more, better, and cheaper information readily available to the new independent investor.

Regardless of whether Prodigy succeeds in this bold move further into cyberspace, the overall competitive thrust of it is guaranteed to work to the benefit of the new cyberspace investor.

Reuters Money Network and WealthBuilder

Reuters Money Network is one of the more recent acquisitions of Reuters International, a British firm already operating 300,000 terminals for institutional investors in 150 countries. With revenues in the range of $3.5 billion, it is the largest information services company in the western world—larger and older than Dow Jones.

Like Dow Jones, Reuters has been using cyberspace delivery systems for the past several decades to help the large *institutional* investors make money by providing them with a number of products and services, including:

❒ **Information services:**   Real-time financial information is available on over 200 exchanges internationally using a network of 1,600 reporters and 13,500 employees. Reuters also owns the premiere market data service, Quotron, and the Teknekron Software Systems.

❒ **Transactions services:**   Reuters Instinet, Crossing Network, and Globex joint ventures with CME and CBOT are powerful private financial networks—IntraNets—linking brokers, institutions, and individuals throughout the world and operating much like a global securities exchange.

❒ **Media newswires:**   Financial, business, political, sports, weather, and general news are delivered everywhere, to newspapers, television and radio broadcasters, governments, businesses, and financial institutions. Reuters is tops in news for investors worldwide.

Reuters is everywhere in Wall Street cyberspace, although its British reserve lends it an air of understatement. Its low-key confidence befits a successful institution with a history dating back to 1851 that included worldwide coverage of Lincoln's assassination.

NEW MISSION . . . HELP INDIVIDUAL INVESTORS MAKE MONEY

NET*investors will now find Reuters news tucked in hundreds of cyberspace locations, as well as on most of the online and dial-up services. For example, it is online at AOL, Prodigy, and CompuServe, on the Internet at Yahoo and other Websites, and is also linked to many of the more powerful NET*investing systems, such as Telescan.

Reuters' transaction services were originally designed and marketed solely for the larger institutional investors, and these services are generally priced out of the market for the individual investor. However, there are some powerful indications that Reuters is now one of the principal architects of the trend toward cyberspace investing for the individual investor.

In fact, Reuters' massive information technologies and database delivery systems are already being repackaged to *target the individual investor as*

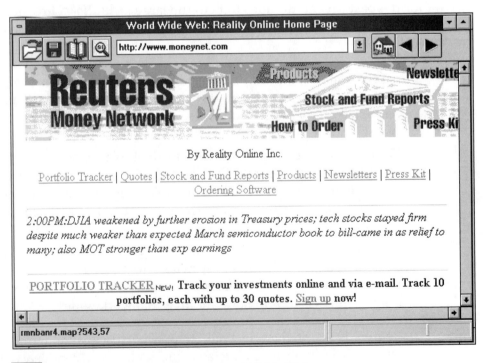

4.1 Reuters Money Network on the World Wide Web.

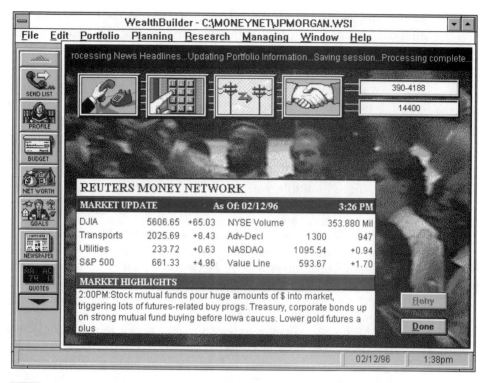

4.2 Reuters Money Network: Market Updates.

a prime customer. Most notable in this refocusing is Reuters' recent acquisition of the Reality Online Network, which, not surprisingly, was promptly renamed Reuters Money Network.

Reuters' commitment to the individual investor was further punctuated with their recent acquisition of Equis International, developer of MetaStock and other technical analysis software. Reuters is one of the superpowers of financial information that are, in effect, creating and organizing the new Wall Street cyberspace, which now includes both the *individual* and the *institutional* investor.

WEALTHBUILDER: A PLANNER FOR SUCCESS-MINDED INDIVIDUALS

The WealthBuilder personal financial planning software is part of the one-stop/total-service package offered by Reuters Money Network. Reuters' subscriber base includes "more than 150,000 success-minded people who are using WealthBuilder's powerful tools to meet investment goals and gain financial independence." This is accomplished by creating "a personalized financial profile taking into account your goals and tolerance for risk to produce an easy-to-follow, step-by-step investment strategy. Then, it helps you measure and update your progress."

We want to underscore Reuters' emphasis that "the key to any successful plan is the complete understanding of your own personal investment

---

REUTERS WINS EDITORS' CHOICE AWARD

"Keeping the multifarious needs of the average investor in mind, we award Editors' Choices to two programs that perform very different tasks. WealthBuilder . . . and Reuters Money Network. . . .

"The newly released windows version of WealthBuilder is very easy to use, extremely customizable, and includes all the extensive research capabilities of Reuters Money Network, which is also a fine package. Money Network gives you access to several on-line financial databases and generates a personalized financial newspaper that will put you well on your way to being a more savvy investor. . . .

"Although WealthBuilder doesn't have the technical-analysis prowess of MetaStock or Windows on WallStreet, it does have good filtering capabilities. And these can help investors make good choices over the medium or long term, which is what many people want. Then other programs that offer research or portfolio management just don't put it together as well as WealthBuilder does."

SOURCE: Editors' Choice Awards, *PC Magazine* (January 1995).

---

outlook." This emphasis focuses on one of the central features of most of these emerging NET*investing systems. Namely, the best systems strive to *integrate* a complete set of computer programs necessary for all seven tasks confronting every investor—from planning and analysis, to management and trading—creating a one-stop/total-package system that supports a logical, do-it-yourself approach to an investment portfolio, while honoring the investor's unique lifestyle and personality needs.

The WealthBuilder system of the Reuters Money Network accomplishes this task by including this sequence of eight processes:

1. **Your personal investment profile:** This uses two sets of questions to assess your risk tolerance and personal philosophy, complete with investment strategies.

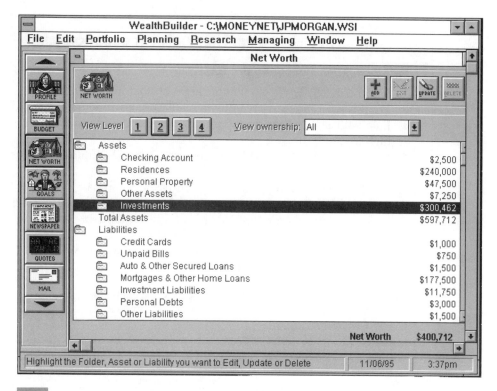

4.3 Your net worth summarized by WealthBuilder.

2. **Net worth financial statements:** This is a current, complete record of all your assets and liabilities.

3. **Financial goals and budget planning process:** This involves analysis of your goals and the income and expenses allocated to each, including goals tied to savings for your retirement.

4. **Portfolio management and net worth:** WealthBuilder guides you through the process of setting up portfolio accounts, inputting data about securities, and recording transactions to buy and sell securities.

5. **Customized retirement planning:** Based on your targeted goals, you can determine the amount of savings required, future investment, and income totals.

6. **Timeline forecasting your portfolio's growth:** A long-term graph gives you a visual snapshot summarizing your progress toward your goals, projected and actual.

118

REUTERS MONEY NETWORK AND WEALTHBUILDER

WEALTHBUILDER'S RISK ASSESSMENT QUESTIONNAIRE

Self-Evaluation Questionnaire Based on Your Tolerance for Risk

1. If you win a $500 bet, do you pocket it or go double or nothing?
2. What type of investor are you, on scale from beginner to advanced?
3. Rate your level of concern if making a $10,000 investment, from very high to minimum.
4. What are your preferred investments: CD, bonds, mutuals, stocks, or options?
5. Would you invest in options and futures: never, maybe, or yes?
6. Rate your level of concern if your investment lost 20 percent of its value.
7. What is your comfort level to take on a $5,000 debt for a potential $10,000 gain?
8. On which of these would you spend lottery winnings of $25,000: CDs, bonds, funds, stocks, or futures?

SOURCE: Adapted from Reuter's Money Network's WealthBuilder program.

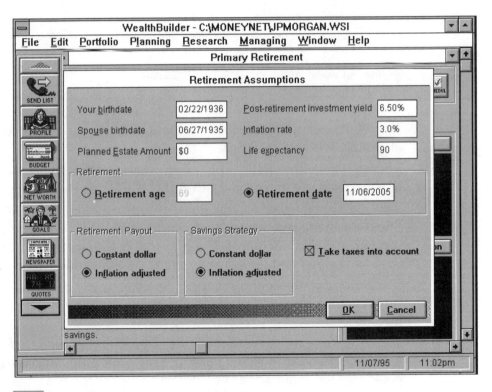

4.4 Revising assumptions to test what-if scenarios.

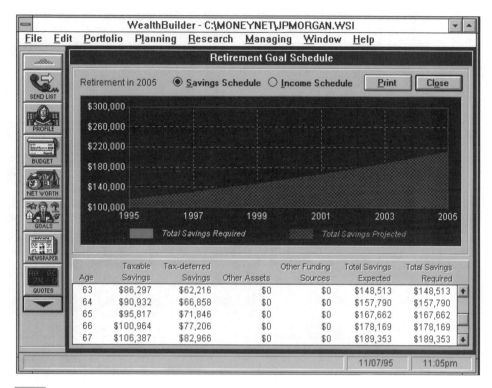

4.5 Your retirement goals, savings schedule, and shortfall.

7. **Flexible asset allocation and investment strategies:** WealthBuilder uses a sophisticated asset allocation system for both the current and suggested portfolios. It's flexible, so you can revise your assumptions and test other alternatives.

8. **Securities transactions and portfolio management:** The Wealth-Builder package includes Reuters Money Network with market news, quotes, research, analysis, and portfolio management.

If you're ready to pursue specific financial goals, WealthBuilder is a great tool. You can start setting aside funds for retirement or any other goal, such as planning for a new home or your children's college education. This personal financial planning system will give you a snapshot of your future financial picture leading up to that target, including future assets. And it will factor inflation into the growth of your portfolio.

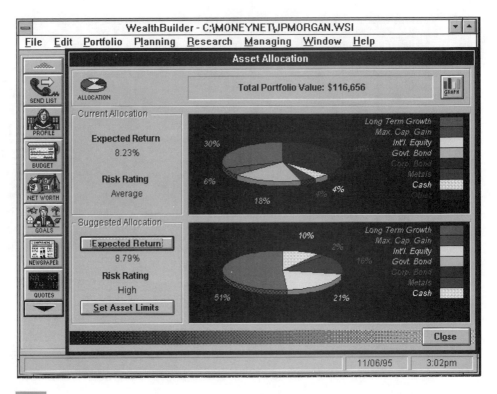

4.6 Current portfolio versus suggested asset allocations.

Equally important, the program is flexibly designed so you can easily input new facts and assumptions and test alternative futures. For example, you can easily and quickly make changes and test key factors such as:

❑ Saving another hundred dollars each month
❑ Taking more risks with other asset allocations
❑ What inflation does to your portfolio
❑ The impact of adding a specific new investment to your portfolio

Flexibility is one of the major features of the WealthBuilder financial planner. This program will crunch the numbers and generate new results for you instantly. Thus, you can test many more alternatives and assumptions, while improving your command of the investment process. Like so many of these new cyberspace investing systems, WealthBuilder is also a great self-teaching tool that encourages financial independence.

Furthermore, WealthBuilder's functions easily interface with the Reuters Money Network features: quotes, news, and investment research. In addition, with the Alerts Manager routine, you'll be notified immediately when selected criteria are triggered.

If you're a big Quicken fan, you can also get a Reuters Money Network designed specifically for the other major financial planning software packages. In marketing the Quicken version, however, Reuters' documents note, by way of comparison, that there are more options and greater flexibility with the Reuters WealthBuilder version.

However, Reuters' competitive advantage is now being challenged and may not last long. Recently, Quicken's parent, Intuit, also become much more aggressive in the Wall Street cyberspace investing arena, especially now that Intuit has added its Investor Insight online services to Quicken, thus taking aim squarely at the NET*investor market.

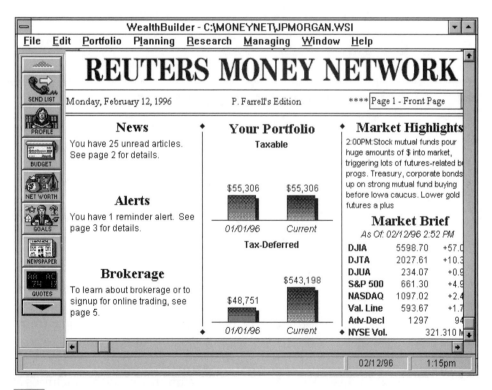

4.7 Money Network's newspaper format: front page.

INTERVIEW QUESTIONS: INVESTOR'S PERSONAL PHILOSOPHY

Self-Evaluation Questionnaire to Reveal Your Philosophy

1. Birth dates for you and your spouse?
2. Types of risks that concern you most: not enough return to reach goals or lost on a single investment?
3. Which best describes your risk tolerance (five choices from not losing any money to going for maximum return at high risk)?
4. Number of years until you retire?
5. Pretax income from the last three years with the next four estimated?
6. Monthly savings level?
7. Monthly retirement savings?
8. Money in tax-deferred investments (IRAs, etc.)?
9. Taxable portfolio with amounts needed in next 2 to 10+ years?
10. Experience with CDs, mutual funds, and money market accounts?
11. Experience with stocks, bonds, and futures (non- to significant)?
12. Newsletters of most interest to you: mutuals, equities, gold, bonds?
13. Interest in market timing and short-term trading?

SOURCE: Adapted from Reuters Money Network's WealthBuilder program.

THE NEW BRITISH INVASION INTO ONLINE AMERICA

The Reuters Money Network, an online investment service, is seamlessly integrated with its WealthBuilder personal financial planning software, and as such is one of the more powerful systems available to today's cyber-space investor. Reuters ads claim that it's "the fastest growing and least expensive online system available." It now has over 50,000 subscribers.

Here's what the new NET*investor can expect from the Reuters Money Network totally integrated system:

❐ **Personalized news:** This covers companies, markets, and economies, filtered and clipped according to your selection criteria, from Dow Jones News Retrieval, *Money* magazine, and Reuters Newswires, the largest global provider of news, including information from Reuters network of connections with 200,000 brokers, traders, and portfolio managers around the world.

❐ **S&P Comstock quotes:** On a 15-minute delay, this includes any stock traded on the NYSE, AMEX, and NASDAQ exchanges, with no extra per-quote or prime-time fees, and no connection charges.

TECHNICIANS GIVE REUTERS A BUY RECOMMENDATION

"It's amazing how cheaply you can get some really good research these days. . . . Nowadays, you can scan far more than [your broker] has time to scan and come up with not only good potential ideas but the background to evaluate the idea. . . . I'd put a buy recommendation on Reuters Money Network for stocks or bond investors."

SOURCE: John Sweeney, "Product Review of Reuters Money Network," *Technical Analysis of Stocks and Commodities* (February 1995).

❏ **Standard & Poor's Company Research:** This offers a database of 5,000 stocks and 6,000 bonds, plus you get the tools to screen and chart securities according to any criteria you select.

❏ **Morningstar Mutual Funds:** This offers a database of 7,000 mutual funds, with 40 data points on each fund, including returns, risk, and fees,

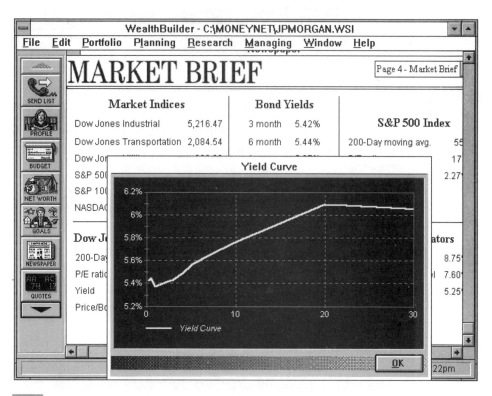

4.8 Market briefs and indexes: yield curve superimposed.

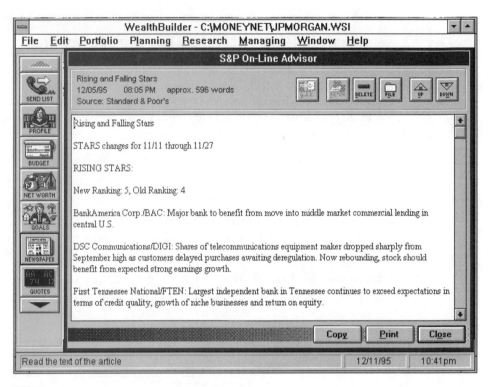

4.9 Standard & Poor's On-Line Advisor: rising and falling stars.

plus their five-star rating system so you can quickly search, identify, and analyze the high-performance funds by category (growth, income, small cap, etc.).

❐ **Bank rate monitor:** This feature tracks money market and CD information from thousands of institutions nationwide and includes the Veribanc safety ratings.

❐ **PC Financial Network:** America's biggest electronic discount brokers offer 24-hour-a-day online trading and real-time trade validation, plus discount commissions. PCFN is a subsidiary of the Wall Street investment bankers Donaldson, Luftkin & Jenrette and the Equitable Life Assurance Society.

❐ **Investment newsletters:** This includes *S&P Outlook, Donoghue's Moneyletter, Zacks Analyst Watch, Global Investing, Bond Fund Advisor, Oberweis Report,* and other financial advisory newsletters.

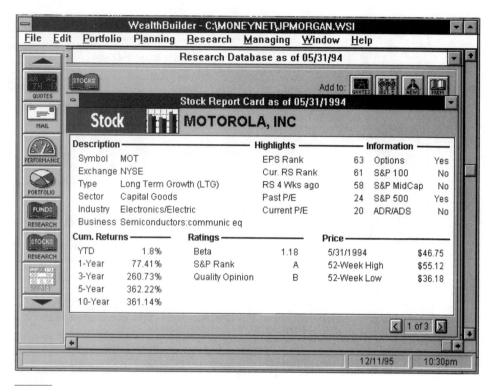

4.10 Company stock report and financial information.

☐ **Round-the-clock data availability:** This includes coverage of Wall Street and global market information, giving the cyberspace investor an edge on the market with a powerful arsenal of financial information, news, and hard data and the analytical tools to make timely, intelligent investment decisions.

The NET*investor gets all this cyberspace investing power for a modest setup fee of less than $50 and only $25 a month. Some of the services noted are extras, but the basic package is probably more than enough for most investors.

As if to embarrass the competition outright, Reuters also runs ads comparing the cost of its Money Network to several of the financial information services delivered to the professionals, in order to underscore its own competitive advantage to the serious investor who may not be a full-time trader. A comparison with CompuServe and Dow Jones News/Retrieval might be more apt, but the point is well taken.

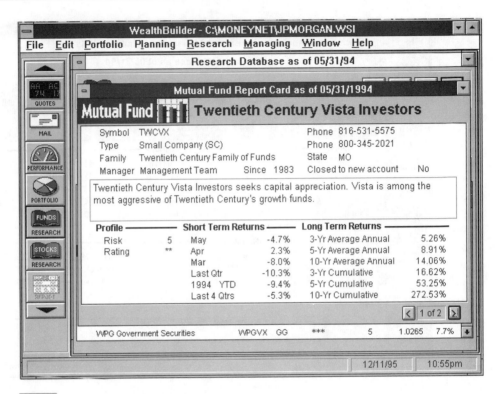

WealthBuilder - C:\MONEYNET\JPMORGAN.WSI

File Edit Portfolio Planning Research Managing Window Help

Research Database as of 05/31/94

Mutual Fund Report Card as of 05/31/1994

Mutual Fund **Twentieth Century Vista Investors**

Symbol TWCVX	Phone 816-531-5575
Type Small Company (SC)	Phone 800-345-2021
Family Twentieth Century Family of Funds	State MO
Manager Management Team Since 1983	Closed to new account No

Twentieth Century Vista Investors seeks capital appreciation. Vista is among the most aggressive of Twentieth Century's growth funds.

Profile		Short Term Returns		Long Term Returns	
Risk	5	May	-4.7%	3-Yr Average Annual	5.26%
Rating	**	Apr	2.3%	5-Yr Average Annual	8.91%
		Mar	-8.0%	10-Yr Average Annual	14.06%
		Last Qtr	-10.3%	3-Yr Cumulative	16.62%
		1994 YTD	-9.4%	5-Yr Cumulative	53.25%
		Last 4 Qtrs	-5.3%	10-Yr Cumulative	272.53%

< 1 of 2 >

WPG Government Securities	WPGVX	GG	***	5	1.0265	7.7%

12/11/95   10:55pm

4.11 Mutual Fund Report Card at Reuters Money Network.

HIGH QUALITY AT A REASONABLE COST

Reuters Money Network is able to keep costs down because it's programmed in such a way that you do most of the work offline. Updates are requested by a special dial-up system that logs into the Reuters database, grabs the requested new data, and logs off, without wasting any more time with you hooked online to Reuters than is absolutely necessary.

As a result, your online connect charges are kept to a minimum and Reuters can charge less because use of its databases is optimized. However, the downside is that if you need information that was not requested the last time you logged on, then you must go back online again. In that sense, it's not as interactive as when you stay logged on to a system. However, once you become familiar with the trade-off between online investment analyses and offline analytics, the discipline of defining and narrowing your data needs will be second nature.

BOTTOM LINE: NEW STRATEGY SHIFTS TO INDIVIDUAL INVESTORS

In Reuters International's 1994 annual report to its shareholders, Reuters emphasizes that, "We dedicate the bulk of your resources to serving banks, brokers and other organizations involved in the financial markets." At that point, the individual NET*investor was not yet a major factor in the corporate mission. However, that is rapidly changing.

With the acquisition of Reuters Money Network—comparatively small as it was for this giant with $3.5 billion in revenue—there is now a definite paradigm shift within the corporate mind of Reuters—at least a recognition of the emerging power of direct cyberspace investing by individuals. In fact, today, individuals can even tap into their elite Instinet service through various brokers.

REUTERS MONEY NETWORK: NEW NET*NAVIGATOR-OF-CHOICE FOR TODAY'S CYBERSPACE DISCOUNT BROKERS

"Brokerage Access . . . Many individual investors are getting an online connection to their brokers. . . . Our software lets you view your account statements and trade online at your convenience in the privacy of your home or office. . . . During early 1996, Reuters Money Network will give you access to even more of the largest and most trusted brokerage houses on Wall Street. Already, Reuters Money Network is shipping products available with Quick & Reilly, PCFN, and Charles Schwab. Several others will be available soon," including Accutrade.

SOURCE: Bob Pringle, "Helping You Make Better Decisions," *Reality Investor Newsletter* (Winter 1996).

Reuters has come a long way from the elite, expensive Instinet service for larger established institutional investors to the Reuters Money Network, WealthBuilder, and now Equis' MetaStock technical analysis services—all for the individual investor.

There are some extra charges for special reports, but, for the most part, the basic RMN package is quite inclusive and relatively inexpensive. It is a one-stop/total-service NET*investing system so that you are unlikely to get nickel-and-dimed for every piece of information requested.

Reuters Money Network is considered a highly regarded and competitive alternative when matched against the other NET*investing systems.

BusinessWeek says the Money Network "should pay for itself many times over"—definitely the kind of endorsement that invites cyberspace investors to seriously evaluate this Reuters NET*investing package first-hand. Reuters deserves a five-star rating and a test run.

Dow Jones News/Retrieval and The New Digital Dow

Like Reuters and Knight-Ridder, Dow Jones has been in Wall Street cyberspace for a long time—one of the original pioneers. The Dow Jones News/Retrieval (DJN/R) system was introduced in 1974, although various Dow Jones news services have been providing electronic information to businesses and institutional investors since the 1960s and earlier. Dow Jones/Telerate also began in the early 1970s, although Dow Jones did not acquire Telerate until 1987.

The DJN/R system was, of course, originally developed for the Wall Street institutional investors. In fact, *NET*investing as we know it—*electronic investment decision making by individual investors*—did not even exist way back then. Remember the context Dow Jones (and CompuServe) worked in when creating DJN/R:

❑ The *Apollo* mission had just landed on the moon.

❑ Wall Street institutions were using large mainframe computers and data on large tapes and punchcards.

❑ The personal computer did not even exist (and Bill Gates was still in high school).

❑ Individual investors competed "against" the institutional investor using only pencil, paper, and a lot of guesswork.

❑ The threat of Communism, the war in South East Asia, and The Bomb occupied our business, political, and personal consciousnesses.

In fact, while at Morgan Stanley just a couple of short decades ago, my only computer was a hand calculator and spreadsheets were typed on large-carriage IBM Selectric typewriters. Excel software hadn't been invented, and Microsoft didn't exist. In short, back then Dow Jones News/Retrieval was clearly on the cutting edge, an advance strike force defining Wall Street cyberspace.

DOW JONES . . . THE ULTIMATE WALL STREET INSTITUTION

In the past three decades Dow Jones has continued amassing gigantic databases with enormous content, responding to the diverse needs of Wall Street's demanding institutional investor. Dow Jones has one of the most complete databases for financial information, although it is delivered in a rather dull, boring (gray, pinstripe) graphic format that fails to convey its enormous scope and capabilities to today's individual investor—a factor which, along with its pricing schedule, may be a liability in marketing to today's NET*investors.

5.1 Dow Jones master directory to other Dow Jones Websites.

DOW JONES: BIBLE OF GRAY PINSTRIPE INVESTORS

"The name 'Dow Jones' is practically synonymous with corporate financial information. The Dow Jones Average is part of just about every TV or radio stock market report, and *The Wall Street Journal*, published by Dow Jones, Inc., is the bible of the gray, pin-stripe set. . . .

"Bottom line: If most of your online research needs are centered around corporate financial data, investments, or the international business scene, Dow Jones News/Retrieval should be high on your list of prospective acquisitions."

SOURCE: "Guide to Going Online," *PCNovice* (1995).

Aside from these concerns, the Dow Jones content base is all-inclusive so that (other than updates and new publications) it may *never* have to add a single existing business or financial resource. Moreover, with the new cyberspace technologies that enable links to virtually every database in the known world, individual investors should find this mega-system more generally available.

Until the early 1990s, Dow Jones was primarily focused on providing financial data services to institutional investors, including:

❑ **Dow Jones News/Retrieval:** Dow's premiere service for businesses and financial institutions. DJN/R delivers electronic and financial news gathered by a network of 1,000 professionals working in 50 bureaus globally, reporting news over the seven Dow Jones newswires, *The Wall Street Journal, Barron's,* Dow's *Smart Money* magazine and other news resources.

❑ **Dow Jones/Telerate:** An IntraNet or private network providing Dow's various newswire services as well as delivering the Telerate service, a quasi-stock exchange, operating in 85 countries internationally, with services by proprietary workstations. It was acquired by Dow Jones in 1987 and, as a group, currently generates nearly $1 billion in revenues—about ten times the revenues of DJN/R.

❑ **Dow Jones Newswires:** These newswires include Capital Market Report and Federal Filings, covering corporate legal filings with the SEC and other watchdogs; also accessible by individual investors through Private Edition.

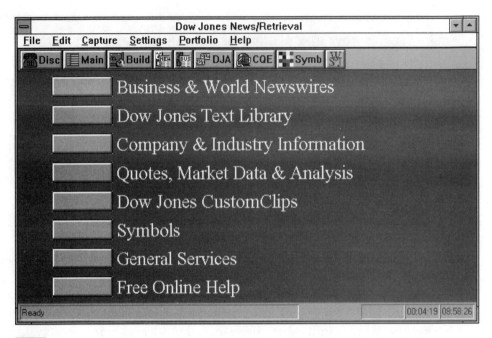

5.2 DJN/R opening menu: eight categories of services.

☐ **Electronic Publishing:** Everyone knows about Dow Jones' *print* publications, *The Wall Street Journal, Barron's,* and *Smart Money* magazine. Now Dow Jones is quickly moving into electronic publishing, especially the online *Personal Journal* and *Money & Investing Update* Web publication.

☐ **Dow Vision:** A corporate news service customized to fit specific business needs, including small businesses run by individual investors.

☐ **The Investor Network:** A time-sensitive video news service, including corporate interviews and financial news not normally covered in a timely manner. Similar specialized services are also provided by Bloomberg, Reuters, NBC, and CNN and can cost over a $1,000 per month.

With revenues in excess of $2 billion, Dow Jones remains one of the major power-players in Wall Street cyberspace. However, it is clear that the Dow Jones team is now focusing more and more on the *individual* investor market with many of their new services.

DOW JONES NEWS/RETRIEVAL: PRIVATE INVESTOR EDITION

*"Access the same financial information the pros use
for less than $1.00 a night."*

❏ **Daily quotes:**   Mutual funds, stocks, bonds, treasury issues, options, money markets, etc.
❏ **Historical quotes:**   For one year.
❏ **Index averages:**   Dow Jones from 1982.
❏ **Mutual funds: Daily quotes.**
❏ **Commodity futures and index quotes.**
❏ **Mutual funds:**   Performance reports on 1,500.
❏ **News periodicals:**   1,800 business, trade, and general publications in full text, including *The Wall Street Journal, Barron's,* and *Financial Times.*
❏ **Top news stories:**   Financial, business, and investing.
❏ **Clipping service:**   Scans and screens special interests.
❏ **Newswires:**   Dow Jones' seven, plus analysts' reports.
❏ **Insider trading:**   Reports on 80,000 individuals.
❏ **Wall Street Week:**   PBS transcripts.
❏ **Disclosure Inc:**   EdgarPlus database on SEC and other files.
❏ **Dun's Reports:**   7.6 million public and private companies, including 2.4 million international firms in 200 companies.
❏ **Media general research:**   180 industries and 6,200 companies.
❏ **Zacks Corporate Earnings Estimator:**   EPS for 3,500 companies.
❏ **S&P Online profiles:**   4,700 companies.
❏ **Innovest Technical Analysis reports:**   4,700 companies.
❏ **Investext:**   90,000 research reports on 14,000 global companies.
❏ **Other tools:**   For fundamental and technical analysis, investment portfolio management, and more.

DJN/R Private Investor Edition is available after trading hours.

THE NEW DIGITAL DOW: TARGETING THE INDIVIDUAL INVESTOR

Today's Dow Jones is aggressively pursuing the individual NET*investor with six separate electronic services, which, as it becomes more fully integrated into a single operating package, is potentially the single most powerful system available for the NET*investors. Dow's individual systems cover all the major decision areas necessary for effective investing. Dow Jones does have the most comprehensive network of databases for invest-

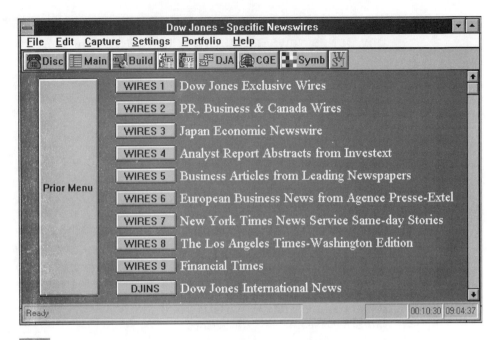

5.3 Ten major newswires on Dow Jones News/Retrieval.

ment decision making, and Dow Jones appears on the verge of integrating all six services into a single working system.

DOW JONES NEWS/RETRIEVAL: PRIVATE INVESTOR EDITION

The principal NET*navigator for Dow Jones' services for the individual investor is called Dow Jones News/Retrieval. The promotional material says that the DJN/R Private Investor Edition includes "the same informa-

---

DOW JONES' NAVIGATIONAL TOOLS FOR INDIVIDUAL INVESTORS

1. **Dow Jones News/Retrieval–Private Edition** (online/dial-up)
2. **Market Analyst** (offline software for technical analysis)
3. **Personal Journal** (the electronic *Wall Street Journal*)
4. **Money and Investing Update** (the *Journal's* Internet Website)
5. **Plan Ahead** (offline retirement planning software)
6. **Company and Market Data** (CD-ROM of prior year's stats)

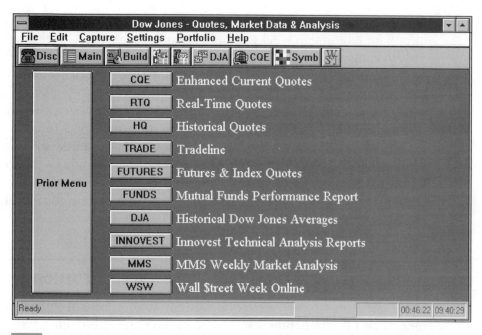

5.4 Dow Jones quotes, market data, and analysis.

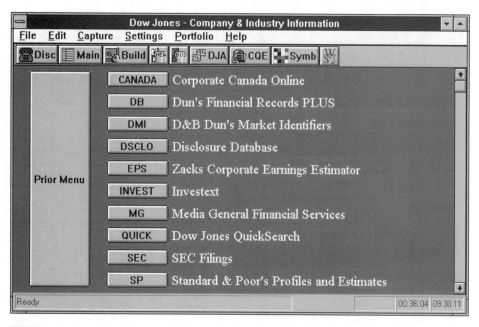

5.5 Company fundamentals and industry databases.

tion the pros use," and indeed it does. The base rate for the service is $30 a month for 8 hours on weekends and from 7 P.M. to 6 A.M. weekdays.

By comparison, the standard DJN/R edition used by professional traders during the trading day is billed on an a la carte pricing system that is both complicated and more expensive. However, to survive in today's highly competitive market for the individual NET*investor, the pricing of this service is likely to become more competitive in the near future.

Hopefully, it will also update its plain-vanilla graphics, with a snappy new image for *The Wall Street Journal* electronic versions—the Personal Journal and Money & Investing Update. The DJN/R database is so comprehensive it *needs* a more graphically alive presentation to communicate the enormous value of this package.

DOW JONES NEWS/RETRIEVAL: TECHNICAL ANALYST EDITION

The Dow Jones News/Retrieval system covers both technical analysis reports and fundamental research on market and companies. For individual investors who want more advanced technical analysis systems, Dow Jones offers another level of service for the NET*investor: the News/

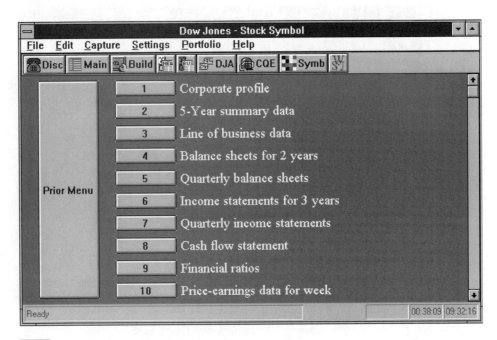

5.6 Ten key elements of corporate financial data.

MONEY MEETS MULTIMEDIA: THE NEW DIGITAL DOW JONES

Dow Jones' CEO, Kenneth Burenga, is the key strategist leading his company—and perhaps even the entire financial information industry—into the next century. Our "corporate mission is to supply business news and information whenever, wherever and however customers want to receive it. . . .

"*The Wall Street Journal* is a business information source that for its first 106 years just happened to be delivered ink on paper," but by the end of 1996 "you'll be able to get it in print, electronically in digital form and in video form via TV throughout the major financial centers of the world."

SOURCE: Paul Noglows, "Money Meets Multimedia: The Digital Dow Jones," *Interactive Week* (December 4, 1995).

Retrieval—Technical Analyst Edition, which is normally combined with the Private Investor Edition for $60 per month.

The Technical Analyst Edition includes the Tradeline securities system, 20 years of daily price and performance information on more than 200,000 securities. The data covers dividends, splits, distributions, and interest payments. It includes mutual funds and can be downloaded.

Recently, Dow Jones has retreated from highly competitive and specialized technical analysis products. This move is instructive from a strategic perspective, as a road map to help determine which way Wall Street cyberspace trends are going. We would expect to see them concentrate more on the mass market, the individual investor, someone who's not a professional day-trader, someone who may have a portfolio focused primarily on mutual funds with perhaps a dozen stocks.

The latest ads for Dow Jones News/Retrieval certainly emphasize this strategic focus, as they target the emerging NET*investor. Using the slogan, "for investors who do their best work at night," the ad is a bit misleading. The target audience is actually the professional and business executive who is, in fact, doing his or her best work during the day, at a day job, and checking the markets after-hours following a long day at the office.

NEW HIGH-TECH JOURNAL HOT-WIRED IN CYBERSPACE

Today Dow Jones is faced with intense competition from the commercial online services, such as AOL and Prodigy, with their colorful, glitzy graph-

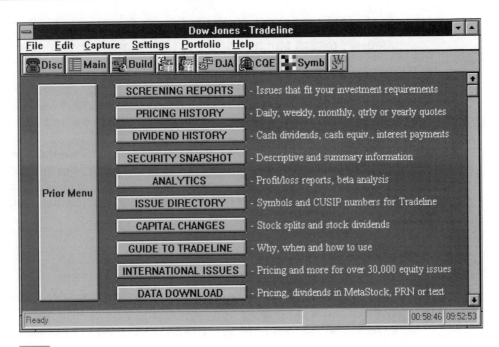

Tradeline screening: alternative investment criteria.

ics and other services designed to attract the television-bred audience used to being spoonfed facts in an entertaining format. Furthermore, new Web technologies such as Hot Java are opening up competition from many multimedia sources, forcing Dow Jones, as well as its fellow pioneers in Wall Street cyberspace, to go beyond the image of the basic News/Retrieval service that reflects the conservative corporate executive and institutional trader.

As a result, in mid-1995 the editors of *The Wall Street Journal* made a bold move, releasing two exciting new versions of the *Journal.* These new electronic publications—Money & Investing Update (at the Dow Jones Internet Website) and Personal Journal (online delivery, direct to your computer)—clearly show a break with the traditional bland image and incorporating the livelier style of quality graphics expected from today's hip online and Internet Websites.

Through these two electronic publications, the individual investor can access *The Wall Street Journal*'s enormous news-reporting database. Dow emphasizes that the Personal Journal, is "published for a circulation of one."

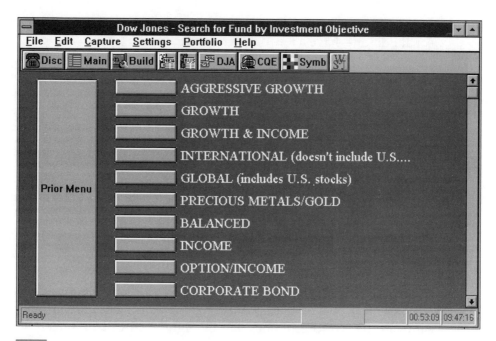

5.8 Mutual fund searches on ten investment objectives.

CYBERMANIA IGNITES *THE WALL STREET JOURNAL*

"Watch as America's most staid financial publication shows the world how to go digital . . . Dazzling design . . . The Update team obviously put a lot of thought into melding the vaunted content of the printed *Journal* with the technological advantages of electronic media. So far, they appear to have gotten almost everything right. . . . Each section—stock information, Heard on the Street, Credit Markets, Foreign Exchange, Commodities and Personal Finance—is immediately available with a click of a mouse. . . . Update has been able to include even more in-depth coverage than is available in the *Journal*'s print edition. . . . Get a more-than-once-a-day dose of the all-knowing *Journal*. . . . It's not just a free lunch. It's a free financial smorgasbord, with new features being added almost daily."

SOURCE: Wayne Harris, "Cybermania at *The Wall Street Journal*," *Individual Investor* (November 1995).

Some of these electronic versions—especially the more detailed online Personal Edition—have a few distinct advantages:

☐ **Front page:** Clipping and digest services available to help you focus on just the material you want.

☐ **Late-breaking stories:** Delivery anywhere, 24 hours a day, with updates at the click of a mouse.

☐ **Market coverage:** Quick summary of activity in the major global markets.

☐ **Personal portfolio:** Track your investments by monitoring quotes of specific stock and mutual fund assets.

☐ **Sports and weather:** Top team highlights and summaries, planning for global travel, and fashion tips (for men only).

Not only is this a visual break from tradition, it is a major break from the basic concepts of print publishing. Now you can get the best financial news in the world anytime, day or night. You can prescreen selections,

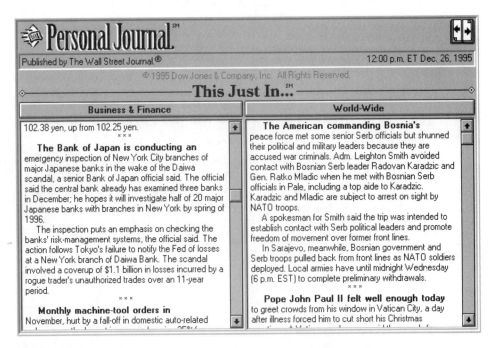

5.9 Personal Journal: news updates on the major markets.

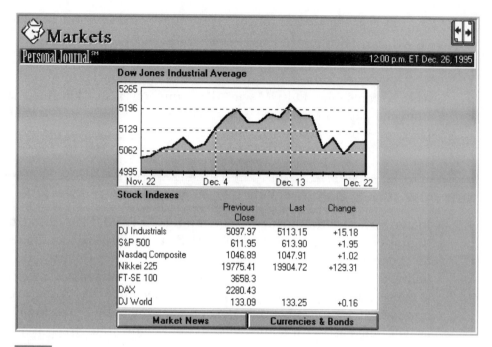

5.10 Personal Journal: tracking the major market indexes.

focusing only on material you need to review, and automatically retrieve information on your portfolio.

NEW HIGH-TECH DELIVERY SYSTEMS: HISTORICAL DATA ON CD-ROM

Today you can also get all the key information from last year's *Wall Street Journal* on a single CD-ROM. It's called "Review of Markets & Finance," at a cost of $75. It is a perfect database tool to help you analyze past performance of investments and select future opportunities. It includes:

❑ **Video and graphics** of *The Wall Street Journal*'s coverage of the markets from the previous year.

❑ **Articles and financial data** on each of the nine key investment areas.

❑ **Searchable news summaries** by company, industry, and dates.

❑ **Top news stories** of the year presented in video and articles.

❏ **Ten-year tracking** of consumer, economic, and investment data.

❏ **Glossary of financial and market terms** via hypertext links.

Dow Jones is the crème de la crème of the financial information business. A searchable CD-ROM with all the previous year's key financial news from the pages of *The Wall Street Journal* at this price is essential to the NET*investor's electronic library.

NEW DOW JONES MAKES FINANCIAL PLANNING EASY AND FUN

In one of the ads for the financial planning CD-ROM, Plan Ahead, the new digital Dow Jones tells us that "everybody looks forward to retirement. But few people look forward to planning for it." Then they smartly add spin by telling us that their Plan Ahead CD-ROM is easy and *fun to use*. Now *that* is a gutsy marketing approach. The new Dow Jones has taken a positive approach to a subject that for most humans (including investors) is about as welcomed as a visit to the dentist's office. Dow Jones treats it like a visit to the Magic Kingdom.

Plan Ahead is one of Dow Jones' leading-edge cyberspace products, providing high-tech information opportunities specifically for today's electronically powered individual NET*investor. Each chapter of Plan Ahead covers the basic questions facing every investor in the world and includes easy-to-use worksheets and built-in calculations so you can quickly test what-if scenarios, such as these:

❏ What are the best alternatives to plan for all my goals, retirement, home, children's education, estate planning?

❏ How big a nest egg will I have if I start saving now?

❏ What are the status of my investments and savings program?

❏ How can I best estimate my retirement expenses?

❏ How can I best analyze current and future spending needs and plan for any shortfalls?

❏ How can I choose from employer-based programs, 401(k), IRA, Keogh, and alternatives?

❏ What can I expect from social security benefits?

❏ What are the various investment strategies available, given my risk tolerance, and what are some appropriate asset allocations?

> **JOURNAL EDITORS TELL YOU "HOW TO RETIRE AS A MILLIONAIRE"**
>
> "You can do it—if you start early and 'plan ahead.' Planning is the key to a solid, secure retirement. And 'the best retirement planner on the market today' is Plan Ahead from the editors of *The Wall Street Journal*.
>
> "Easy-to-use, interactive worksheets include all your income, savings, assets and liabilities, and let you play 'what if' until you have a plan just right for you. And expert advice is just a click away. Informative videos featuring financial and retirement experts answer all your questions. . . . *Home PC* said, 'Plan Ahead sets goals that lead you to your pot of gold.' "
>
> SOURCE: "How to Retire As a Millionaire," Dow Jones advertisement (1995).

There's a narrator guiding you through the process and the graphics illustrate the concepts. Video interviews with experts are presented, and you can use a mouse to navigate from one section to another to truly make this planning relatively effortless. This CD-ROM is only $40, which is a real bargain.

Moreover, Plan Ahead is sufficiently flexible so that you can quickly make changes, not only to test your assumptions and alternatives, but also to review your progress and revise your plan to accommodate changing circumstances. Dow Jones' Plan Ahead lives up to its name.

BOTTOM LINE: NEW DIGITAL DOW TARGETS DO-IT-YOURSELF CYBERSPACE INVESTORS

The Dow Jones organization has been in Wall Street cyberspace for decades. Indeed, by virtue of their pioneering role on the cutting edge of financial information technology, Dow Jones has virtually *defined* the state of the art in electronic investing for the large corporate and institutional investor.

In the '90s, Dow Jones is recognizing the growing importance of *individual* investors and courting their business. Today's Dow Jones has a host of products specifically targeting the new cyberspace investor who is operating online and on the Net.

The electronic publications of *The Wall Street Journal* online and on the Web, CD-ROMs with financial planning systems and historic versions of *The Journal*, offline technical software, and new, competitive versions of News/ Retrieval are signs that Dow Jones, like the other major financial information vendors, recognizes the growing importance of the NET*investor.

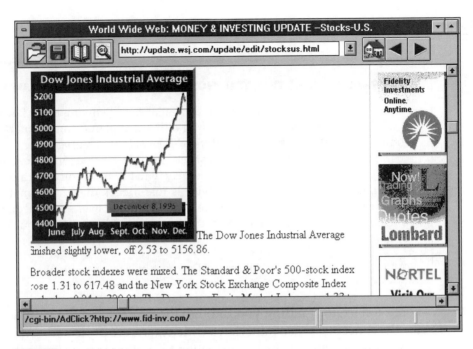

5.11 Update on the Web: latest financial news on U.S. stocks.

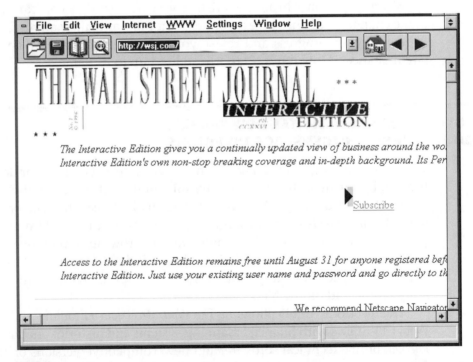

5.12 *The Wall Street Journal:* Interactive edition on the Web.

The new Dow Jones provides all the elements necessary for each of the seven steps in investment decision making. Its pricing system still seems geared to institutional clients, but that is changing, as are the graphics. The various elements of all these services could use more integration, but you can expect major changes there as well.

Dow Jones has been around too long and is too much of a competitor not to see and continue to take decisive advantage of market opportunities. In fact, just as it purchased Telerate to enhance its expansion in the institutional market, it is likely that Dow Jones will next acquire a Telescan—much as Reuters acquired the Reality Money Network—to speed its expansion in the individual investor market.

Bottom line: With Dow Jones' newest cyberspace power tools—the Barron's Online Website (www.barrons.com) and Investors Workstation, both created to "give subscribers even more powerful tools, hitherto used only by professionals"—it's clear that the new Digital Dow is accelerating its drive to solidify its position as a primary information resource for the independent, do-it-yourself *cyberspace investor.*

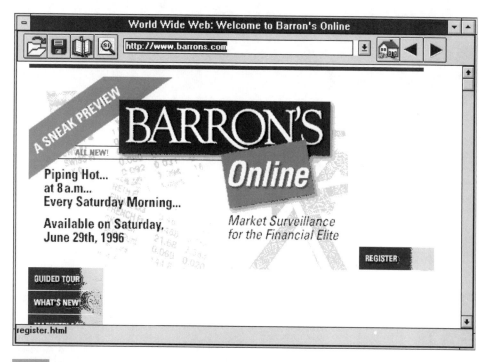

5.13 Barron's Online: company and fund research.

Telescan Investor's Platform, TIPnet, and Wall Street City

Cyberspace is full of rising stars. Suddenly shooting out of nowhere, they often rocket past the established giants at warp speed. It happened with upstart Microsoft and IBM in the 1980s. Similarly, the new information battleground of the '90s has had its success stories, most notably Netscape.

Telescan is definitely another one of them, a relatively new and growing public company built on delivering first-class financial information for NET*investing. And with over 100,000 customers, it must be doing something right.

NEW COMPETITION FOR OLD-TIMERS DOW AND REUTERS

Telescan is another excellent example of the new cyberspace investing systems being offered to today's NET*investor. In fact, Telescan's CEO David Brown wrote the book *Cyber-Investing,* which not only describes the Telescan investment system but also covers many important elements of the emerging field of electronic investing.

With over 100,000 investors and traders using the Telescan Investor's Platform, the company is a serious rival of both of the established giants, Reuters Money Network and Dow Jones News/Retrieval. It should surprise no one if someone like Dow Jones or Knight-Ridder were to acquire Telescan, as Reuters did with the Money Network—a logical strategic decision for a large firm to swiftly enter this new arena.

The playing field is leveling. The monopoly that institutional investors had in Wall Street cyberspace no longer exists. The ease and cost of entry to this arena are so low for new systems that a top-flight information services company with a first-class product like Telescan can quickly become a major rival of existing giants and carve out a sizable niche in the field.

In other words, Telescan could be a mini–Dow Jones News/Retrieval in the making. So let's look at the product itself.

TELESCAN: TECHNICAL ANALYSIS PLUS FUNDAMENTAL RESEARCH

The Telescan system for NET*investing actually includes a number of component parts to the package, and it has recently become one of the most advanced cyberspace systems available, being accessible on the Internet's World Wide Web.

Although the Telescan navigator's strong suit is technical analysis, it is equally powerful in fundamental analysis, too. There are two preliminary issues to consider:

6.1 Telescan Investor's Platform: master menu.

❑ **Charting, graphs, and mathematics:** If you have any reservations about an approach involving charting, pattern recognition, and in-depth mathematical analysis of stocks, this may not be the right system for you. (And if that's the case, you should consider the Reuters Money Network system, which forgoes the technical analysis tools and is based exclusively on fundamental analysis—with the exception of the add-on MetaStock technical analysis software.)

❑ **Technical plus fundamental analysis:** You should also be aware that a bonus of Telescan Investor's Platform is that it is not *exclusively* based on technical analysis. In other words, the Telescan system may be a more inclusive system, because it integrates fundamentals as well as technical analysis, as opposed to the competing Reuters Money Network, which is primarily based on fundamental analysis.

Perhaps even more important than the distinctions between funda-mental and technical analysis is the fact that *both* systems, Reuters and Telescan, have some very *similar* conceptual approaches:

❑ Both are solidly grounded in user-friendly **portfolio management** programs, rather than simply being focused on analyzing a stock in isolation.

❑ Both are solidly **integrated** packages of online connections and data-bases, complete with updates and offline analytics.

Both services deserve close attention by the serious investor looking for the best tools to navigate the world of cyberspace investing, keeping in mind that the Telescan Investor's Platform already fully integrates technical with fundamental analysis.

A SOLID FIVE-STEP SYSTEM FOR THE NET*INVESTOR

As you examine Telescan's material closely, you'll notice that it presents a simple five-step system of investing. These general steps are basic to virtu-ally any system of investment analysis and portfolio management and quite similar to the seven-step investment procedure we outlined earlier in this book. Our seven steps include more emphasis on up-front personal financial planning, which we believe is essential *before* starting with any investment analysis system. We also put more emphasis on the search and analysis steps in the process. However, Telescan's five-step process has the advantage of being simple, logical, clear, and user-friendly.

However, the mental steps that you, or any savvy NET*investor, goes through are essentially the same in both systems as you search for, analyze, select, and purchase securities. Eventually you develop your own method, a style of investing that fits your unique personality. And Telescan's *Quick Start Handbook* begins with a modest self-assessment of the value of their system:

> *You have purchased state-of-the-art research and analysis software that gives you the tools to make more profitable investments. You might be wondering how to use this tool in your daily strategy. Or, you may be trying to come up with an investment plan, but don't know where to start. You are not alone! [Here] is an easy 5-step plan that will take all the mystery out of the investment process, and provide you with a daily routine you can adapt to fit your goals and investing style.*

TELESCAN'S OFFLINE TOOLS FOR CYBERSPACE INVESTING

Proprietary Offline Analytics and Software Programs Necessary to Support Necessary Online and Internet Services for Cyber-investors

- ❏ **Portfolio Manager:** Accurately monitors and reports a portfolio's performance; tracks all purchases and sales with easy-to-use program tools.
- ❏ **QuoteLink:** Downloads current and historic price/volume data on about 80,000 issues and fundamentals into your analytic software.
- ❏ **Telescan Analyzer:** Fundamental and technical analysis based on its 20-year historical database; 80 indicators to pinpoint buy/sell opportunities; includes Quotelink interface.
- ❏ **ProSearch Module:** Screens stocks with your selection from 207 criteria to match high performance to your investment goals.
- ❏ **Mutual Fund Search:** Sorts through more than 2,000 funds using selection criteria designed to fit your unique investment criteria.
- ❏ **Options Search:** Instant search tool for more than 60,000 options and optionable stocks and spreads using an array of criteria.
- ❏ **ESearch:** Use Wall Street analysts' earnings estimates criteria; over 300 criteria to select and build your searches.

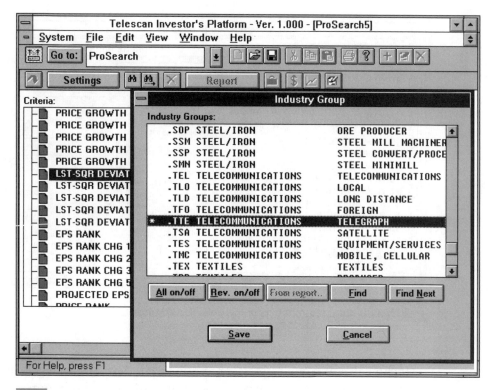

6.2 Telescan's superpowered ProSearch tool.

The five practical steps of the Telescan investment system are:

1. **Identifying potential new opportunities:** Telescan's 21 proven search strategies help you identify potential investment opportunities. Telescan's search tools begin with three different investing strategies based on momentum investing, insider trading, and value investing (undervalued stocks with increasing earnings and rising P/E ratios). Then they help you build other strategies to fit your special goals and investing style.

2. **Analyzing your prospects:** Evaluate each prospect using technical analysis and charting, then fundamental analysis. The system shows you how to access and retrieve basic company data, such as earnings estimates, market news, and research reports.

3. **Timing security purchases:** Here you maximize your portfolio's profit potential by timing your stock purchases with the best-known

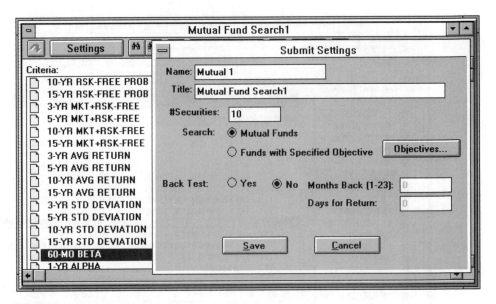

6.3 Mutual fund search: screening criteria and objectives.

technical buy signals. Telescan emphasizes that the system is actually "three-quarters fundamental" as an analytical methodology, "but our experience and our own testing of technical signals against historical markets have proven to our satisfaction that technical timing can add one to three percent annually to our returns." So it works, and in the world of investing, what works is what counts on the bottom line.

4. **Managing your investment portfolio:** Keep close watch on all your investment portfolios by managing asset diversification, monitoring performance, and staying current of trends and changing market conditions. Actually, this portfolio management process begins before the purchase of your first stock and continues indefinitely, as long as you have investments. And this process includes asset allocations, market analysis, diversification, and monitoring. From this *systems* perspective, the overall portfolio management process is NET*investing.

5. **Timing each security sale:** Improve your returns by using technical indicators to find the most advantageous time to sell. Telescan helps you assess the pros and cons of selling, how this affects its risk/reward ratio, and how all this impacts your return.

You'll find a more detailed description of this five-step *cyber-investing* process in David Brown's book by that name. Brown is Telescan's president, and his book is one of the best courses in online and NET*investing. Use it in conjunction with Telescan's online service and you'll have all you need to become a successful NET*investor.

Telescan's tech support system is also first class, quick to respond, and knowledgeable about the system, which can be better than having business school finance professors getting you up to speed.

TELESCAN WILL CHANGE THE WAY YOU VIEW INVESTING

"All the information Telescan has lumped together into its new Investor's Platform software package may seem daunting. If you can wade through it all, however, it could change the way you view investing . . . enough information for an army of Fidelity analysts. . . . The power and breadth of Investor's Platform, however, exact a price in terms of ease of use. The application does have a lot of drag-and-drop features that link various functions. In theory, this should make it easier to use, but it isn't intuitive, [however] if you want all that marvelous data, it may be well worth it."

SOURCE: Wayne Harris, "Handle With Care," *Individual Investor* (April 1996).

TOTALLY INTEGRATED SYSTEM ONLINE AND ON THE WEB

The Telescan system for electronic investing is a unique and complete package of services that includes offline analytics (computer software programs), as well as online and Internet Web connections (services for news updates and research). In fact, one of the main values of the Telescan package is that it integrates these features in one place.

In addition to the technical analysis software and search programs, with the "cyber-investing kit," as Telescan calls it, the astute investor can quickly and easily access and interface, on a subscription basis, with some of the more popular and valuable tools of fundamental analysis, including:

❏ Zacks Earnings Estimates
❏ Standard & Poor's MarketScope
❏ Morningstar mutual fund research

❑ MetaStock technical analysis software

❑ Charles Schwab's StreetSmart & online trading

❑ 20 online financial advisory newsletters

In short, Telescan is an excellent, *working* model of the emerging NET*investing systems. The best of these new NET*investing systems are one-stop/total-service packages, like Telescan. Each of their parts is neatly integrated into a working whole, and the key elements of the package are both the individual pieces and the systems integrator/navigator provided for you.

Telescan may cost more than America Online or Reuters Money Network, especially when you start adding a few of the other services—the price could approach $100 a month. However, if you expect to use minimum time online, you will also find starter packages in the $10 to $50 monthly range, with the option of adding time and cost as your needs expand.

For our purposes, it is important to accentuate a system like Telescan's because it is designed to work as an integrated, one-stop system, a self-contained online workstation for the new independent investor, and as such becomes a working model for competing NET*investing systems.

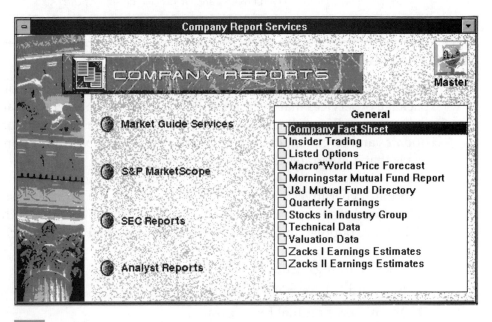

6.4 Company, SEC, market, and analysts' reports.

BARRON'S COMPARES TELESCAN TO THE COMPETITION

	Setup Cost	Monthly Fees
Real-Time Data Sources		
Bonneville	$532	$237–270
Data Broadcasting Corp.	$250–690	$170–600
DTN-Wall Street	$295	$38–60
Online Data Sources		
Dow Jones News/Retrieval	$0	$30–60
Telescan	$29–349	$15–99
Internet Data Sources		
InterQuote.Com	$0	$0–65
Quote.Com	$0	$0–135

SOURCE: Howard Gold, "The Electronic Investor—Data, Data Everywhere," *Barron's* (Aug. 28, 1995).

TIPNET: TELESCAN'S NEW NAVIGATOR FOR TODAY'S WEBSURFER

As if to underscore its intention of becoming the state of the art in cyber-space and the emphasis on the term *cyber-investing*, Telescan has "taken its show on the road"—the information superhighway, that is. Telescan now has a high-powered Website for investors—TIPnet—reflecting its commitment to using the new Internet technologies to their full advantage, and providing a top-flight service to the new global electronic investor.

Telescan is pushing the cyberspace envelope with this Internet Website. In fact, CEO Brown maintains, "TIPnet is the most content-rich and technologically advanced financial service on the World Wide Web." Content provided on the TIPnet Website includes:

❐ Securities quotes
❐ Downloadable stock graphs
❐ Company reports
❐ Stock and fund search tools
❐ Financial and business news
❐ Market summaries
❐ Advisory newsletters

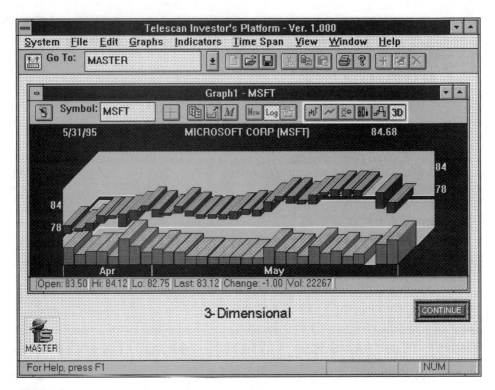

6.5 Telescan's three-dimensional price/volume charts.

❏ TIP talk discussion group

❏ E-mail

Most of the same content providers included in the online package are duplicated on the Web at TIPnet, including S&P MarketScope, Zacks Earnings Estimate, Morningstar, Reuters News, and various proprietary analytics and research modules. Registration is through special encrypted program modules.

BOTTOM LINE: TELESCAN IS A BIG-LEAGUE POWER HITTER

With the introduction of Telescan's Website, the big power hitters, those billion-dollar giants like Dow Jones, Reuters, Knight-Ridder, and Bloomberg, have a formidable competitor. Telescan's entry into cyberspace is reminiscent of the rapid rise of Netscape.

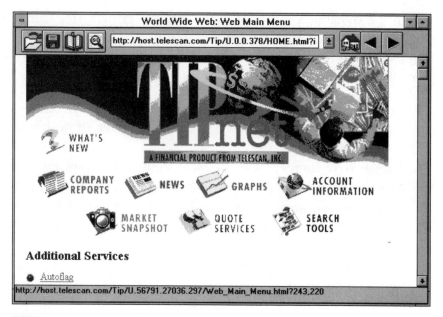

6.6 TIPnet's opening schedule of financial services.

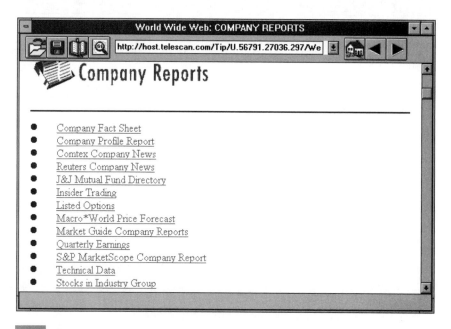

6.7 TIPnet/Telescan's company reports directory.

In the dynamic process of rapid Internet growth, Telescan's sudden high profile is likely to draw considerable interest from the Internet investing public. This increased base of satisfied customers could have the following results for Telescan:

❏ **Create a market niche:** Telescan could rapidly carve out a niche as a major financial information power at the upper stratosphere of Wall Street cyberspace.

❏ **Trigger new competitors:** Telescan could end up being regarded as another pioneer that paved the way for a flood of new competitors.

❏ **Encourage counterattack by existing competitors:** Telescan's sudden growth may trigger a major counterattack from the traditional financial services powerhouses.

❏ **Result in takeovers:** An acquisition by one of these big giants also seems highly likely.

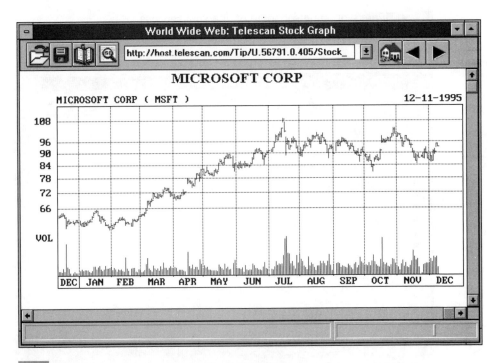

6.8 TIPnet charting downloaded from the Internet.

Mutual Fund Investing in Cyberspace

Fidelity Investments: Online Investor Center

Given its massive size, the fact that it has nearly a half *trillion* dollars under management, and its huge expenditures on electronic information systems, it should come as no surprise that Fidelity Investments is another of the leaders providing NET∗navigational services to the new cyberspace investor.

Today, Fidelity offers the NET∗investor five major vehicles to explore financial cyberspace—at least Fidelity's special corner of cyberspace:

❏ **Online dial-up:** Fidelity Online Investor Center on Prodigy and America Online

❏ **Internet Website:** Fidelity Online Investor Center on the Internet's World Wide Web

❏ **Offline analytics:** Thinkware, Fidelity's retirement planner software

❏ **Electronic brokerage:** Fidelity Online Xpress (FOX) discount brokerage service

❏ **Network of other mutual funds:** Fidelity FundsNetwork, to 2,200 American mutual funds

In addition, Fidelity is going online with some powerful new tools for electronic trading and real-time research. Like other new NET∗navigators, Fidelity is far from fully integrated, but it's aggressively working on products guaranteed to keep it in a leadership position. Moreover, the areas Fidelity is developing clearly indicate the *diversity in the entire industry's search for an ideal NET∗navigator* that will satisfy the high-tech needs of the new cyberspace investor.

The NET*investor should take special note of the Fidelity system as an example of how the new cyberspace investing terrain is evolving. Fidelity is using several technologies to serve the NET*investor: a commercial online service, an Internet Website, a network of other mutual funds, offline analytic software, and a dial-up transaction-based connection.

In the near future, you can expect more of these packages of alternatives from single vendors. Ideally, there will be better integration of the different *technologies,* plus better integration with *content* from other cyberspace information vendors. In this regard, Fidelity could learn an important lesson from services like Telescan and StreetSmart.

FIDELITY'S HUGE BUDGET FOR CYBERSPACE INFORMATION

Using the Information Systems (IS) perspective, you quickly get a sense of the enormous power of the Fidelity organization when you read about Fidelity Systems, the Information Systems team that manages all of the electronic processing for Fidelity's transactions. According to information in *Wall Street & Technology* and *Financial World,* Fidelity has a staff of 1,500 people and a total IS budget in excess of $350 million.

In other words, the Fidelity family spends more money processing electronic information than many mutual funds manage in total assets. Moreover, Fidelity accounts for 7 percent of the average daily trading on the NYSE. That's power. Nobody should ever doubt that Fidelity can throw around enormous weight in the financial markets.

In spite of these limitations, when all of Fidelity's services are evaluated as a single, evolving cyberspace package, the company still gets high marks for helping the online investor. It is a pioneer in cyberspace, and it promises more improvements for the near future.

FIDELITY'S INVESTOR CENTER AT AMERICA ONLINE

The online mutual funds have a surprisingly playful and disarming charm about them, if that's possible in the high-tech cyberspace financial world. You almost get the feeling of walking into your friendly local branch office and sitting down to discuss your future over a cup of coffee.

I feel at home when I enter either one of the America Online mutual fund centers, Fidelity Investments or the Vanguard Group. That homey feeling is a hallmark of the AOL services. If you're not a member, you may want to sign up—AOL's a pretty good deal, considering all the extras for the family as well as the excellent investor services.

Once in Fidelity's Online Investor Center at AOL, you'll find the following set of six menus that will give you access to all their online services:

❏ **Mutual fund library:**   This is an archive listing Fidelity's funds, and it will help you screen and uncover information about fund objectives, performance, management, and other fund data. The menu also has several separate subsections for various types of funds—money market, income, stock, and asset allocation funds. There is also a search function which lists their funds; however, it's not designed so you can automatically screen Fidelity's funds and select the top performers based on your designated selection criteria.

❏ **Brokerage and investment services:**   Fidelity offers a wide range of ways to invest through them. These include TouchTone Trader (phone), Fidelity Online Xpress (FOX online dial-up), BondDesk/Fixed Income Alerts, managed accounts for substantial assets, and FundsNetwork, a special service that helps you diversify outside the Fidelity family of

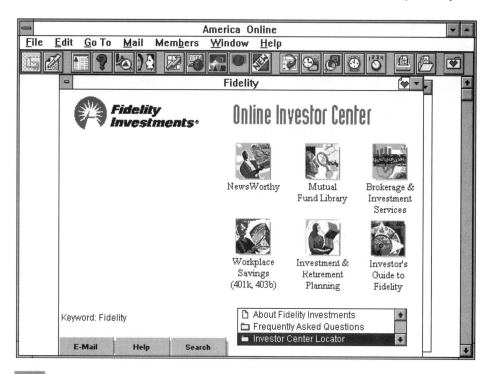

7.1 Fidelity's Online Investor Center at AOL.

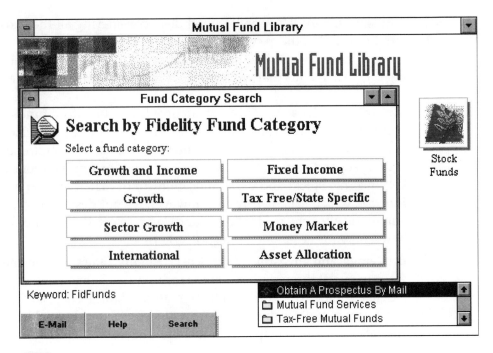

7.2 Searching mutual funds by category.

funds. FundsNetwork provides the NET*investor with access to more than 2,000 popular funds, such as Berger, Benham, Kaufmann, and Strong.

❏ **Investment and retirement planning:** A broad selection of education materials designed to improve your skills as an investor. Various modules focus on planning for retirement and other goals, such as the children's college education, taxes, asset allocation strategies, and the techniques of building a portfolio. Fidelity includes basic questionnaires and worksheets, similar to those on its Website, which will recommend one of five asset allocation strategies for you.

❏ **Workplace savings—401(k) and 403(b):** Fidelity also has a separate retirement planning module for nontaxable employer-based investments. Here you'll find educational materials on inflation, risk, future values, a quarterly market overview, and investment strategies, as well as the investor profile and planning worksheets.

❏ **Investor's guide to Fidelity:** Learn the mechanics of doing business with Fidelity—how to get quotes, methods of buying and selling fund shares, and types of accounts.

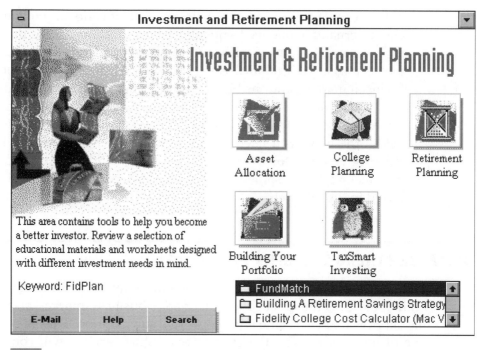

7.3 Investment and retirement planning with Fidelity.

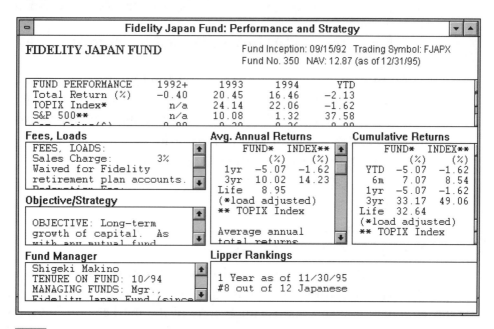

7.4 Specific fund data: performance and strategy.

❐ **News from Fidelity:** Here's their schedule of national seminars, articles, internal documents, frequently asked questions, and a dictionary for investors. In spite of the headline, "NewsWorthy," you will have to look elsewhere to find any real news. Fidelity offers nothing about the financial markets and the business world, probably because Fidelity is right there next to all the other great AOL news services such as Reuters, *BusinessWeek,* and *Investor's Business Daily,* which means you'll get all the news you need from the many other investor services on America Online. However well that strategy works at AOL, you can't help feeling there's something missing when the same system is transferred to the Internet.

DATABASE SYNERGY: FIDELITY PLUS AMERICA ONLINE

Perhaps the biggest advantage to mutual fund investors using the Fidelity online service is the great collection of *other* business, market, and investing services that also come with your AOL subscription. This, of course, is one of the reasons why the commercial online services will continue to attract investors, until we start seeing the next generation of comprehensive NET*investing systems located directly on the Web and open to use by any investor.

Other services available to investors subscribing to AOL include:

❐ **Morningstar Mutual Funds Reports and Quotes**

❐ **Reuters Newswires** with headline news and breaking stories on markets and the economy, stocks and bonds, commodities, currencies, and gold

❐ *BusinessWeek, Worth,* and *Inc.* magazines

❐ *Nightly Business Report* from NPR broadcasters

❐ **Business sections** of *The New York Times* and the *Chicago Tribune*

❐ *Investor's Business Daily* newspaper

❐ **Quotes,** including market indexes and securities

❐ **Hoover's Company Reports**

❐ **American Association of Individual Investors** discussion forum

❐ **Investor forums** from Telescan, Decision Point, Motley Fools, etc., where you can discuss all aspects of the markets and investing with other savvy investors

This integration of content resources adds a unique synergism to the Fidelity/America Online combination—one that also enhances the power of the Net itself as a master database for electronic investors. This combination substantially increases the value of Fidelity's specific services for NET*investors, and we believe these kinds of integration will continue to be a defining trend of the one-stop/total-service NET*investor systems developed in the next few years.

FIDELITY'S NEW WORLD WIDE WEB SERVICES

Talk about popularity: Fidelity's Website gets over 500,000 hits a month, with Websurfers stopping by from all over the world to see what the biggest of the big mutual funds is offering to the individual investor.

Imagine what a wonderful educational opportunity Websites like this can be in helping to introduce everyone from high school teens to seventy-

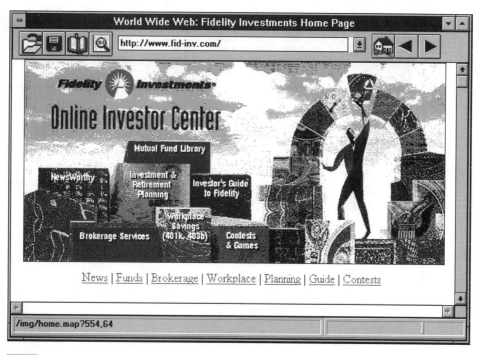

7.5 Fidelity Website: gateway to $365 billion in assets.

year-old retirees to the benefits of owning mutual funds, as well as introducing *them to the Internet as a way of life.*

With this cyberspace billboard out there for anyone throughout the nation and the planet, Fidelity is making mutual fund information generally available to anyone, anywhere. Soon these online offerings will not only be commonplace in our expectations, but the NET*investor will begin to wonder if there's anything wrong with a financial services company, fund, or money manager that's not online or on the Net.

Here's a quick rundown of the key elements of the Fidelity Website:

- ❑ **Mutual fund library:** Access to 50 of Fidelity's most popular funds, plus you can download and print the prospectuses.
- ❑ **Brokerage services:** Four ways to open an account, and all the details.
- ❑ **Workplace savings:** Get an overview of the market, learn the basics of investing, and start with the basic retirement planner.
- ❑ **Contests and games:** Develop your investing skills, make an educated guess on the Dow, and participate in a stock market simulation.

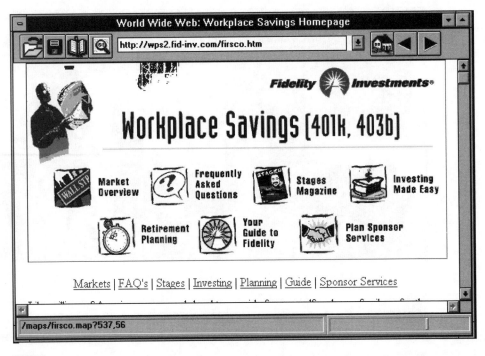

7.6 Workplace savings: market and retirement planning.

You can also get up-to-date information about Fidelity's ongoing seminars and events at its 80 centers around the United States.

Fidelity's Website is impressive. Although a somewhat scaled-down version of what's already on the AOL service, it's nevertheless a pioneering effort, considering the relative newness of World Wide Web. We're anticipating the next generation to hit Fidelity's corner of cyberspace soon.

FIDELITY ONLINE XPRESS: YOUR DIRECT LINE TO WALL STREET

This is one foxy broker taking advantage of the freedom to roam the chicken coop. The tag line on the FOX software package reads: "Your direct line to Wall Street." Today's cyberspace investor has a direct electronic link to the exchanges, bypassing Wall Street's establishment. And in emphasizing this, Fidelity reinforces the fact that the emerging new Cyberspace Wall Street is clearly not physically located in New York City.

FOX was a smart strategic move by the Fidelity mutual funds organization, which knows that many of its investors will invest directly in

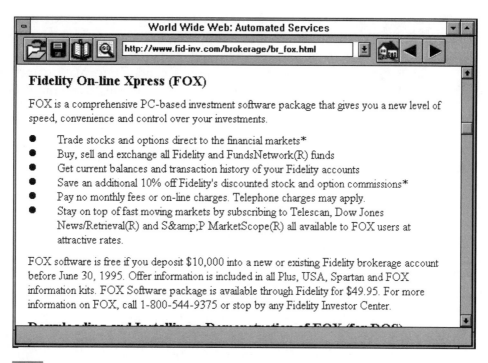

7.7 FOX: Fidelity On-line Xpress discount brokerage.

stocks. It also has a huge trading organization interfacing daily with the exchanges. Fidelity knows there's a major trend to discount brokerage. As a result, Fidelity wisely and strategically decided to create a separate brokerage team to serve its clients. And it's a two-way street: Its equity clients are also natural clients for the mutual funds.

Some of the key features of FOX are:

❏ Integration with other key market information resources, such as Telescan, S&P MarketScope, and Dow Jones News/Retrieval

❏ Real-time market quotes

❏ Direct trading of stocks and options

❏ Buying, selling, and exchanging Fidelity funds

❏ FundsNetwork which helps NET*investors trade and manage non-Fidelity funds

❏ Electronic monitoring of portfolio accounts

❏ Discounts on commissions and no fees

Like many of the online discount brokerage systems, Fidelity will give you the FOX software free if you open an account; otherwise, the cost is nominal. Moreover, the system is now converting to a superpowered Windows platform, integrating much more financial information and making Fidelity Investments an exciting competitor in this dynamic cyberspace investing arena.

THINKWARE: FIDELITY'S FINANCIAL PLANNING SOFTWARE

As you might expect, the Fidelity planning software focuses on mutual fund investments when it comes to asset allocations. And if stocks interest you more, once you develop your personal financial plan using the new cyberspace investment tools, you can also link with Fidelity Online Xpress (FOX) to trade stocks, bonds, and options.

Thinkware is appropriately named: It's a user-friendly program that encourages you to *think* and plan your future, then get into action and take control of it. This is first-class financial planning software that "makes it easy for you to experiment with your numbers." In fact, most of the new financial planning software has this primary *self-teaching* feature. Other Thinkware features include:

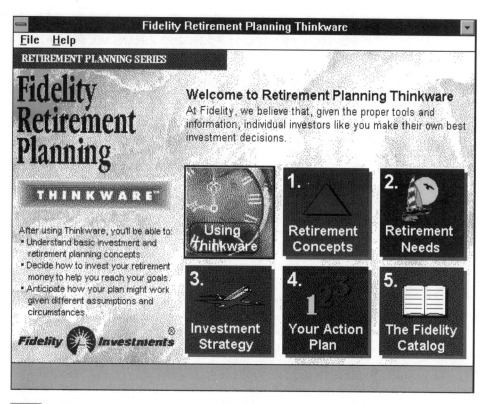

7.8 Thinkware: Fidelity's retirement planning menu.

❑ **Basic retirement profile information sheet:** The first step with Fidelity's financial planning software is the gathering of certain basic facts about you, both current and future expectations. (Note that each of these popular financial planning systems begins with a basic inventory of who you are in financial terms.)

❑ **Financial planning concepts:** Thinkware focuses you on the six key variables that impact your financial planning.

❑ **Calculation of retirement needs:** This software module performs the tedious calculations (numbers-crunching) necessary so you can test out what-if scenarios without restrictions. For instance, if you're currently planning to retire at 65 but you'd like to see how much more you'll need to save regularly to retire at 55, Thinkware can give you an on-the-spot estimate.

INVENTORY CHECKLIST FOR YOUR FINANCIAL PLANNING

Here is the basic financial information about you and your spouse that is input to Fidelity's financial planning software:

- ❏ Birth dates
- ❏ Number of years to retirement
- ❏ Current salaries
- ❏ Other income
- ❏ Desired annual retirement income
- ❏ Additional funds, if any, needed in retirement, to pay off mortgage or make major purchases
- ❏ Expected annual retirement income from:
    Social Security
    Employer pension plans
    Part-time work after retirement
    Amounts from asset sales, etc.
- ❏ Current investments in tax-deferred retirement savings with employers
- ❏ Current taxable investment accounts
- ❏ Annual savings you are currently adding
- ❏ Amounts your employer is contributing to your retirement account

You may want to compare this information with the basic data inputted into Schwab's FundMap planning software and note the similarities.

❏ **Investment strategies:**   Fidelity sums up this issue well: "With all the different investment vehicles available, how do you know what's right for you? The right strategy depends on your time-frame for needing the money, your experience with investing and comfort level with investment risk, and your financial circumstances."

❏ **Action plan:**   Here's the bottom line of this planning process, including a comparison of your expectations of income you'll need for retirement versus what you can expect based on current savings and today's nest egg. This information is then compared to the additional savings you'll need and alternative investment strategies necessary to help you achieve your goals of financial independence.

Because the Thinkware system is so simple, it also serves as a valuable educational tool that gets you *thinking* about the key issues—hence, its name. In fact, virtually all personal financial planning programs are identical in the kinds of data inputted. The differences in these programs are pri-

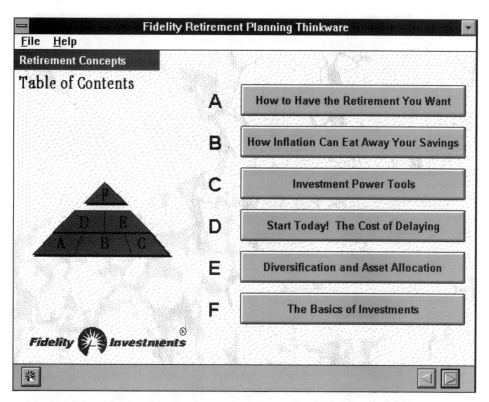

7.9 Basic concepts for the retirement planning process.

marily in the level of flexibility you have to examine alternative scenarios (more savings, higher-risk investments, etc.) and the kind of graphic and visual presentations of the results.

BOTTOM LINE: AN INNOVATIVE CYBERSPACE POWER PLAYER

An initial reaction to the Fidelity Website might be that it's a bit too self-centered, focused on just Fidelity, with little recognition of the existence of the financial markets or content from the outside world. For example, in the NewsWorthy section, there's no news from a major newswire like Reuters, nor is there something like a simple headliner displaying a real-time ticker of the major indices or that even suggests a connection with the dynamics of the financial markets. Fidelity's online and Net sites are static.

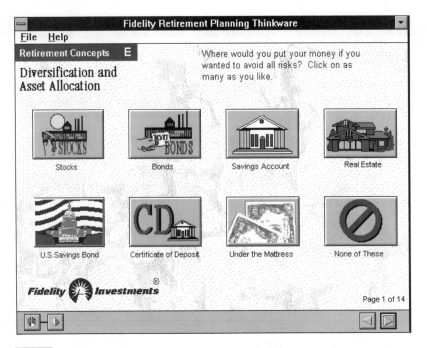

7.10 Portfolio diversification and asset allocations.

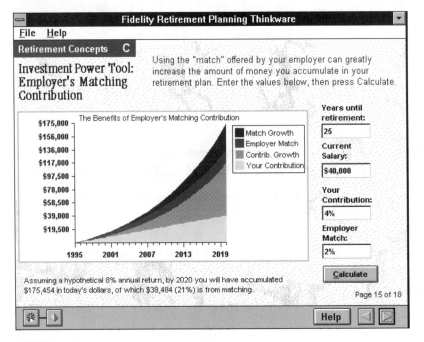

7.11 Power tool: employer's matching contribution.

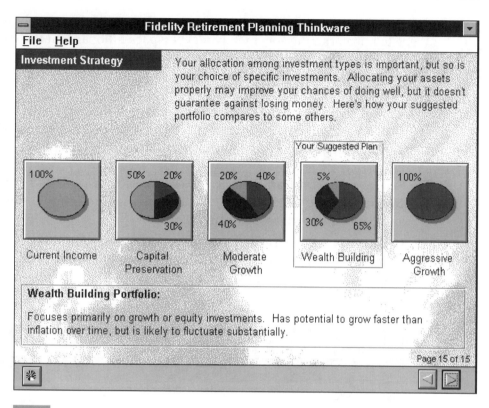

7.12 Fidelity investments Thinkware: five basic portfolio strategies.

However, it's important to appreciate that Fidelity's pioneering NET*investing system was originally with America Online—surrounded by high-powered news and other content providers. It may not translate as well as a stand-alone Website, but that is certain to change, as the next-generation Website is being developed by Fidelity. Regardless, Fidelity Investments is a first-class cyberspace competitor with one of the top-25 NET*investing systems.

NEXT GENERATION: TOTALLY INTEGRATED NAVIGATIONAL SYSTEMS

In Wall Street cyberspace, the next generation is never really more than a year away, and perhaps more realistically, not more than four months ahead. The technology is advancing so rapidly that, at any moment, the competition is likely to leapfrog the leading edge. Microsoft saw it happen with Netscape, and the same scenario will repeat itself on Wall Street as well.

One thing for sure is that any commercial entity that simply uses its Website for marketing—as merely a cyberspace billboard on the information superhighway—is liable not to get a second glance among the aggressive competition emerging as the Internet shifts from a *fragmented* highway to a *centralized* marketplace.

Moreover, Websurfers want to be entertained; the "billboard" concept is too static, and they want interaction. As a result, three major trends will create a paradigm shift for the mutual fund industry:

☐ **Secure financial transactions:** Web transactions will be secure and commonplace by the end of 1996, coupled with electronic signatures and paperless certificate transfers.

☐ **Integrated NET*investing systems:** The overwhelming trend is toward one-stop/total-service NET*investing systems that integrate historic databases, quotes, news content, analytics, and transactions.

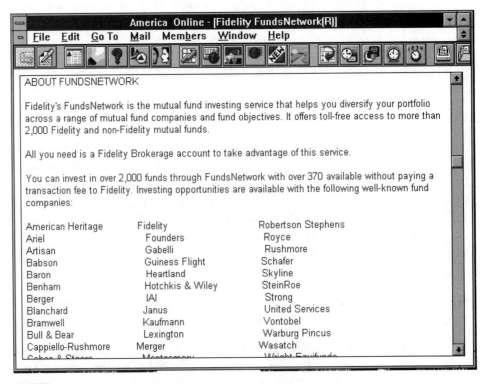

7.13 Fidelity FundsNetwork: access to 2,000 mutual funds.

❐ **One unified Super*FundsNetwork:**   Beyond OneSource and Funds-Network, there is definitely a supernetwork of mutual funds emerging, linking all fund networks and fund families, to avoid duplication and support the new cyberspace investor. In effect, it will be a securities exchange or marketplace in cyberspace.

As a result, it would be logical to predict that Fidelity Investments, as well as the other mutual funds, will develop Websites along the lines of this emerging Wall Street cyberspace model. In this scenario, it is highly probable that Fidelity Investments will integrate FOX and Thinkware with news and other analytics on its Website, as a totally integrated package of services.

And while there may still be a combination of Website, online, and offline products, the technology is clearly at a point where all the pieces can and must seamlessly operate as a single operating system that supports the NET*investor's primary goal of financial independence.

The Vanguard Group of Mutual Funds

The Vanguard Group of Investment Funds may not be quite as big as the Fidelity Group, but it is a tough competitor. Vanguard weighs in with close to $200 billion under management, about half the size of the mega-giant Fidelity machine. But the size can be deceptive—Vanguard has its share of winners, in spite of a more conservative approach.

The founder and CEO of Vanguard, John C. Bogle, laid out his philosophy in his book, *Bogle on Mutual Funds, New Perspectives for the Intelligent Investor.* He's been in the mutual fund industry for almost half a century and is one of its most respected leaders.

Vanguard is also one of the leaders on the emerging electronic Wall Street. For some time it has been exploring several major cyberspace vehicles to serve the NET∗investor. Vanguard's package of services includes:

❒ **Vanguard Online:**   Located at America Online.
❒ **World Wide Web:**   Vanguard's Website includes links from Morningstar, *Mutual Funds* online magazine, and others.
❒ **Offline financial planner:**   Software for retirement planning.
❒ **Vanguard FundAccess:**   Online fund trading and exchanges.

This is another supersystem for the NET∗investor. Vanguard is clearly one of the leaders in the business, but more significantly for the NET∗investor, Vanguard, along with Fidelity, are the pioneers of the *cyberspace mutual funds,* controlling about 20 percent of the total between them.

These two families of mutual funds—as well as key brokers such as Charles Schwab's OneSource, research organizations such as Morningstar,

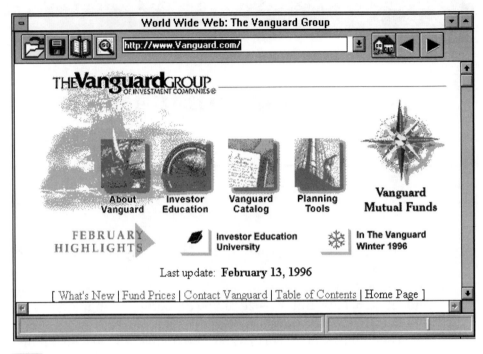

8.1 The Vanguard Group's Website master menu.

and magazines such as *Mutual Funds*—are setting the pace and forcing the other funds to compete in this arena for the new cyberspace-oriented individual investor.

VANGUARD'S WEBSITE: BEST RESOURCES FROM A FUND FAMILY

The Vanguard Group's Website offers many valuable informational tools for the Net*investor looking for opportunities to successfully invest savings. In fact, *Mutual Funds* magazine says, this Website "offers on-line fund investors the most comprehensive array of services and information on the fund sponsor scene today." Let's begin by checking out the various subsystems of the Website.

Vanguard's Website has a number of planning tools, giving the NET*investor another opportunity to do a little personal financial planning *before* just grabbing the first investment that catches the eye. The Vanguard planning tools include:

❏ **Investment Personality Profile:** This is a short multiple-choice test designed to uncover the amount of risk you are willing to accept. Once you answer all the required questions you get your answers in the form of a risk profile.

❏ **Retirement Savings Calculator:** Again through the magic of software on the Vanguard computer and your Internet connection, all you have to do is input the data. The remote computer does all the calculations and feeds back an answer from your specific, personal information, such as retirement planning goals, marital status, household income, current savings, personality risk profile, age and retirement date, and life expectancy.

Input your answers to their questions, and Vanguard's remote computers calculate the resulting amount of savings and any surplus or shortfall, with recommendations for making up any shortfall.

❏ **Portfolio Investment Mix:** Calculated from your age, risk tolerance, and future retirement goals, the Vanguard cyberspace magic continues with rapid calculation of the most likely asset allocation for your per-

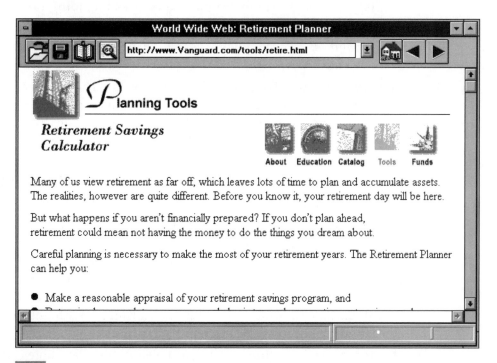

8.2 Planning Tools: Retirement Savings Calculator.

sonality. Like Fidelity's Website calculators, Vanguard's are also great for a first pass or a quick check up if you're an experienced investor.

Later you may want software such as WealthBuilder, Quicken, or some other more sophisticated offline software with budgeting and portfolio management capabilities. Each will provide not only more details, but also a retrievable file for future use and, more important, each of them is better *integrated* into an overall NET*investing system that provides a more comprehensive array of investment services.

❐ **Fund Information:** Although you're restricted to information about the Vanguard funds when you log onto their Website, once there you have the ability to check out more than 80 no-load funds in the Vanguard family. The information available at your cyber-fingertips includes:

> *List of fund categories:* Vanguard's funds cover all the primary categories and are designed to fit investor objectives and specific investment strategies. Based on your specific asset allocations, you can quickly access information about any class of funds to see if it fits your needs. There are nine categories including tax-exempts, fixed-incomes, growth, and international.

> *Search engines:* These quickly search all Vanguard's funds by name or category.

> *Daily fund prices:* They are updated every day. This menu prices and returns with the net asset values (NAVs) along with year-to-date returns and average annual returns for the last one, five, and ten years. Similar data is provided for Vanguard money market and bond funds.

> *Fund prospectuses:* Download or E-mail a request and get a print version through the U.S. mail, so you can do more detailed research.

Moreover, if you want more information and an independent rating of any one of Vanguard's funds, you can quickly log onto the Internet Websites of Morningstar and Mutual Funds Online and get a third-part evaluation. Both Morningstar and Mutual Funds Online are independent organizations that you can count on for an honest report. You'll get both the facts and a rating ("5-star" is Morningstar's highest) against other funds using solid, industry-accepted criteria.

❐ **Electronic Fund Trading:** Vanguard also outlines a whole collection of services for actually buying and selling funds, such as the Vanguard

FundAccess that sets up transfers from your fund accounts to your bank, and includes purchases and redemption services, deposits, and exchanges of funds.

HOW TO DIVERSIFY: WITHIN A FAMILY? . . . OR A NETWORK?

If there is one major limitation with Vanguard's Website, it is that you are "restricted" to information about one family of funds; however, the family is huge, with over 80 funds averaging $2.5 billion each. Therefore, it's highly probable that an investor could stick with this one family of funds and still diversify all resources into a mere half-dozen of Vanguard's top-performing funds.

And if even *that* seems too risky (because you've heard warnings to diversify all too often and you are reluctant to put all your funds with a single manager, no matter how well the individual funds may be performing), you do have one very important alternative. You can turn to Vanguard's FundAccess, which is similar to Fidelity's FundsNetwork and Schwab's OneSource, to make sure that some of your portfolio is diversified *outside any one family*. Vanguard, Fidelity, and Schwab are all structured to help cyberspace investors diversify beyond their immediate family of funds.

The reality is that today "the Net is your computer," and there still are substantial resources out there on the Internet, in cyberspace, available to any NET*investor, which means enormous flexibility and freedom.

VANGUARD FUNDS: PIONEERING WITH AMERICA ONLINE

One key reason Vanguard Online is so great is that it made a brilliant strategic decision early on to locate at America Online. On AOL, Vanguard customers are right next to so much other helpful information. Vanguard Online customers have the advantage of being handy to some of the best news, research, and other information anywhere in Wall Street cyberspace.

The AOL location automatically provided all that content to its subscribers. Presumably a Websurfer could go to other locations for similar information. Still, no matter how much performance, skill, and integrity you believe the Vanguard team has, it always makes sense to check out all your alternatives. Fortunately, an online location like AOL can supply some of that objectivity through competitive databases.

Think of AOL as a big regional shopping center, and Vanguard is one of the major anchor stores (like Sears or Macy's). Moreover, if you want to check out something on the Internet, AOL can quickly hot-link you through its browser.

The advantage is the accessibility of services such as top news from sources like Reuters, *BusinessWeek*, and *Investor's Business Daily*. The entire Morningstar mutual funds database and ratings systems is a fast click away, plus you can access Hoover's Company profiles, First Call earnings estimates and get quotes and more business services.

VANGUARD GROUP'S SIX RULES OF SUCCESSFUL INVESTING

1. Be **knowledgeable**—Learn, study, evaluate.
2. Be **consistent**—Develop a plan and stick to it, no matter what.
3. Be **balanced**—Hedge against future uncertainties.
4. Be **diversified**—Spread your portfolio's risks and returns.
5. Be **cost-conscious**—Be aware of commissions, fees, and expenses.
6. Be **skeptical**—Be your own person, an independent investor.

SOURCE: Adapted from Vanguard Online at America Online.

Sign up for America Online and check out Vanguard along with their other services. You get a bonus month free up front, so you can't lose—and if it doesn't work for your needs, drop it. But try it first; it just might answer your NET*investor needs.

Conversely, what Vanguard does provide at its America Online site adds to the overall value of the AOL services—and besides, their material is really quite nifty. You'll find the following new information at the Vanguard Online location:

❐ **Planning & Strategy:** This includes a basic course on mutual funds. Here you have an opportunity to develop investment goals and asset allocation strategies, including the investor's personality profile based on the risk profile and other personal financial needs. For example:

Growth portfolio: 80 percent stocks, 20 percent bonds.

Moderate growth: 60 percent stocks, 40 percent bonds.

Conservative growth: 40 percent stocks, 40 percent bonds, 20 percent cash.

Income portfolio: 20 percent stock, 60 percent bonds, 20 percent cash.

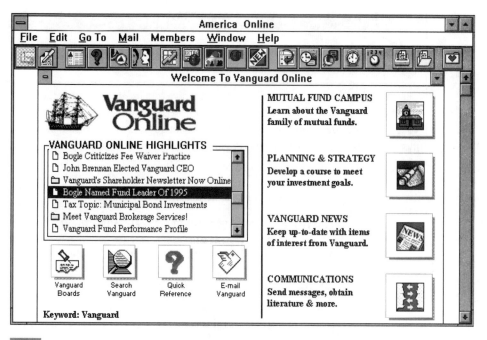

8.3 Vanguard Online: Master Menu at AOL.

In Vanguard's Portfolio Planner, the investor is forced to cut to the chase and pick one of these four basic asset allocation strategies quickly. This fits with something we've said several times: The key to a successful investment strategy is *action,* which boils down to the discipline of regular savings.

❐ **Mutual Fund Campus:** Vanguard has created something in the nature of a research library, where you can retrieve basic information about Vanguard funds, screen them according to performance criteria, and build a portfolio based on your asset allocation strategy. While the term "campus" is a bit misleading, this information closely resembles an educational center, as the name implies. At the same time, it is also a marketing vehicle for selling Vanguard's funds.

❐ **Fund Searches:** A NET*investor can check out the stats on Vanguard's 80 funds, screening the $200 billion by one of four screening criteria: fund category, objectives, type, and risk level.

❐ **Dictionary of Terms:** As you might expect, the Vanguard Campus has a dictionary with definitions of many of the key terms common not only to Vanguard but also to the mutual funds industry. In fact, this is another one of the great general advantages of all these online sites. For

Vanguard Funds Portfolio Planner

The Portfolio Planner presents four different ways to allocate your portfolio among different investments. Each of these allocations depends on a number of factors such as your age, your risk tolerance and your investment goals. For a detailed discussion of this, please refer to the Investment Planner in the Planning & Strategy area.

Choose An Asset Allocation:

GROWTH: 80% Stocks, 20% Bonds

MODERATE GROWTH: 60% Stock, 40% Bonds

CONSERVATIVE GROWTH: 40% Stocks, 40% Bonds, 20% Cash

INCOME: 20% Stocks, 60% Bonds, 20% Cash

8.4 The Vanguard Funds Portfolio Planner.

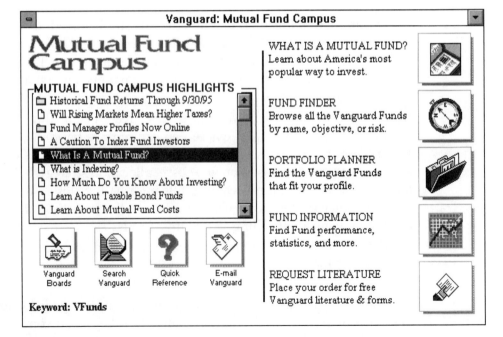

8.5 The Vanguard Mutual Fund Campus on AOL.

```
┌─────────────────────────────────────────────────────────────────┐
│  ▬            Fund Finder - Investment Objective              ▼   │
│                                                                   │
│   ⊕    Find Funds By              Defining    ┌─────────┐         │
│        Investment Objective       Investment  │ Terms   │         │
│                                   Objectives  └─────────┘         │
│                                                                   │
│   Select Funds By Investment Objective:                          │
│                                                                   │
│   ┌───────────────────────────┐  ┌───────────────────────────┐  │
│   │  Income & Pres. of Principal │  │         Balanced          │  │
│   └───────────────────────────┘  └───────────────────────────┘  │
│   ┌───────────────────────────┐  ┌───────────────────────────┐  │
│   │  Income & Low Principal Risk │  │     Growth & Income       │  │
│   └───────────────────────────┘  └───────────────────────────┘  │
│   ┌───────────────────────────┐  ┌───────────────────────────┐  │
│   │   Income & Moderate Risk   │  │          Growth           │  │
│   └───────────────────────────┘  └───────────────────────────┘  │
│   ┌───────────────────────────┐  ┌───────────────────────────┐  │
│   │     High Current Income    │  │      Aggressive Growth    │  │
│   └───────────────────────────┘  └───────────────────────────┘  │
│   ┌───────────────────────────┐  ┌───────────────────────────┐  │
│   │   Maximum Current Income   │  │    International Growth    │  │
│   └───────────────────────────┘  └───────────────────────────┘  │
└─────────────────────────────────────────────────────────────────┘
```

8.6 Finding funds by investment objectives.

example, even though Vanguard is pushing its own products, you also get an "electronic education" in the process. (So the use of term "campus" is really quite appropriate here.)

The Vanguard Online site at America Online is one of the pioneers of the mutual fund industry and for that reason it gets high marks. Vanguard plans to make substantial upgrades to its entire NET*investing system, so we can expect even better information support in the near future.

VANGUARD'S HIGH-POWERED FINANCIAL PLANNING SOFTWARE

Let's take a look at Vanguard's offline software, called Retirement Center. It's an excellent system, and has many elements in common with several other of the higher-quality personal financial planning software systems available today. You discover the usual modules you'd expect to see, and in this case, great graphs help make your financial decision making quite clear. The program includes:

❐ **Tutorial** covering basics of risk, return, savings, and more
❐ **Calculation of net worth** position

- ❏ **Overview of your savings** from various resources
- ❏ **Risk tolerance profile**
- ❏ **Asset allocations strategies**
- ❏ **Test of what-if scenarios** of available alternatives
- ❏ **Fund selections** for your portfolio

Vanguard's software is much more advanced than their "quick-and-dirty" personal financial planners found on either the Web or America Online, both of which are primarily intended as jump starts to get you thinking about investing. We would certainly recommend that any investor quickly upgrade from the Web and the online versions in order to plan his or her investment strategies in more detail.

In addition, the Vanguard financial planning software, and indeed any similar planning software, could be improved for the new NET*investor. The solution would require better integration of the software system with at least these four key elements:

- ❏ Independent mutual fund **research databases**
- ❏ **Personal budgeting** system
- ❏ **Portfolio management** system capable of handling stocks
- ❏ Open system with **nonfamily funds** (the emerging single global exchange)

THE VANGUARD METHOD OF LIFE-CYCLE ASSET ALLOCATIONS

"John Bogle, chairman of the Vanguard Group of mutual funds, says investors in their twenties and thirties should put virtually all their investment money in stocks. As you get older, you should gradually move some money into bonds, so that by the time you retire, you have about 50% in stocks and 50% in bonds, depending on your individual circumstances. In late retirement, say starting at 70 or 75, Bogle suggests an allocation of 35% stocks and 65% bonds."

SOURCE: Steven Goldberg, "Buying at the Top," *Kiplinger's Personal Finance Magazine* (July 1994).

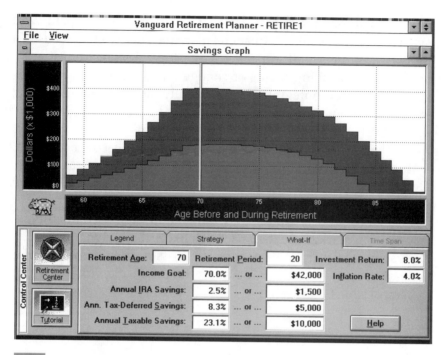

8.7 Vanguard Retirement Center: Savings Graph.

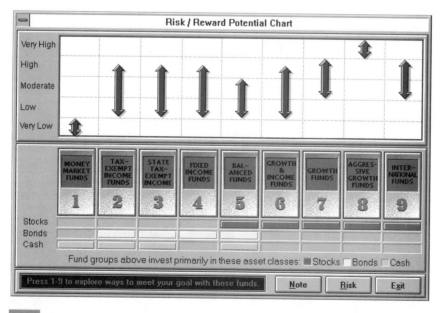

8.8 Risk/Reward Potentials Chart: various fund categories.

Frankly, without these features in today's highly competitive financial cyberspace, any system of financial planning services that focuses solely on its own products will appear out of step with the times and running against the prevailing winds of change that are rapidly bringing an open global network of integrated and mutually interdependent computers.

The NET*investor using the Vanguard Retirement Planner will definitely find many valuable features in it. In fact, we strongly recommend that you examine it closely, and you will discover many of the key features necessary to the better planning systems, such as WealthBuilder, Quicken, FundMap, and Telescan, all of which are well-integrated as NET*navigators.

Given today's fast-paced, dynamic, and highly competitive financial information market in cyberspace, it's likely that a dynamic leader such as the Vanguard Group will soon come out with an even more sophisticated, state-of-the-art planner, integrating financial planning broadly into a cyberspace NET*navigator.

NETworth's Website: The Internet Investor Network

NETworth is another of the early pioneers that paved the way on the World Wide Web back in 1994. Their stated mission: to provide the NET*investor "the most comprehensive mutual fund information online." Moreover, with the addition of equity stock and company fundamental data, NETworth wants to be all things to all investors, as "The Internet Resource for Individual Investors."

NETworth accomplishes its goal by offering a central Internet location for several reputable, established databases for financial information. The primary databases are Morningstar and Disclosure Incorporated, two of the most respected research organizations on Wall Street.

NEW POWER PLAYER ON THE WEB: NETWORTH, INTUIT, AND PARTNERS

Proof of NETworth's powerful position on the Internet was underscored in late 1995. Following the breakdown of its merger with Microsoft, Intuit (Quicken's parent company) became extremely aggressive as a major player on the Internet. As one of its first moves, it developed a consortium with over 20 major commercial banks to market its Quicken software for online banking.

Next, Intuit acquired Galt Technologies (NETworth's parent company), and this decision confirmed the strong leadership position NETworth has established on the Internet. More importantly, Quicken's bold move also reinforces both Intuit's growing position as a dominant force in cyberspace investing and illustrates a general trend toward rapid takeovers in the near future as a way of expansion on the emerging global Wall Street Web.

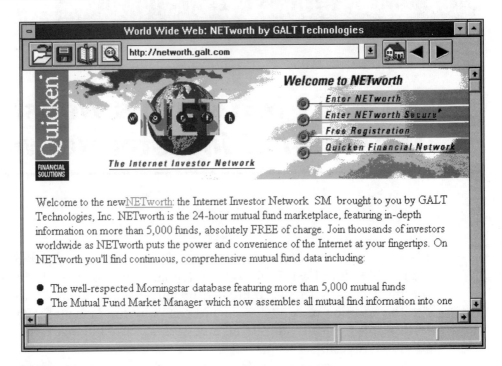

9.1 Welcome to NETworth: The Internet Investor Network.

Mutual Funds magazine was one of the original content providers at NETworth. In mid-1995, however, the magazine left the NETworth Website and has now developed its own rival Website. It is equally possible that NETworth's other primary resources, Morningstar and Disclosure, will jump ship and create competing Websites. More likely, each will expand its own Website *and* simultaneously continue serving NETworth customers.

Nevertheless, with the merger of NETworth and Quicken, NETworth will definitely continue as a major resource for the NET*investor, even if in a different form. Intuit's growing power with the commercial banks and the coming explosion in online banking virtually assures a bright future for NETworth, and probably guarantees the continued presence of both Morningstar and Disclosure.

In this dynamic environment, financial databases are likely to keep their options open and maintain existing network relationships even if they create their own Websites. Dow Jones and Reuters, for example, provide information to almost every other major online and Internet financial location, even though each has its own investor's NET*navigators—the Dow Jones News/Retrieval and Reuters Money Network, respectively.

NETWORTH'S INTERNET INVESTOR NETWORK: MASTER MENU

Mutual Fund Market Manager

❐ **Fund Search:**   Morningstar Research on 6,800 funds.
❐ **Performance data:**   Prospectuses and promotional.
❐ **Net asset value (NAV) quotes:**   From NASDAQ.
❐ **Meet the Experts:**   Weekly forum of fund managers.

NETworth Equities Center

❐ **Free stock quotes:**   From Standard & Poor's on 15-minute delay from the exchanges; also a great directory of links to key quote sources from brokerage firms and exchanges all over the World Wide Web.
❐ **Market Outlook:**   Analysis and forecasts by The Benham Group.
❐ **Fundamentals:**   Company information from Disclosure, Inc.

Internet Information Center

❐ **Investor Relations Resources:**   Links to company Websites.
❐ **The Insider:**   Links to other financial Websites.
❐ **The Forum:**   Internet links to mutual fund associations for no-load funds, 401(k)s and investor education.

Financial Planning Center

❐ Educational materials, worksheets, and tips provided by Quicken's Personal Financial Planner database.

Bottom line: NETworth offers a solid menu for the Internet investor.

POWERFUL NET*NAVIGATOR FOR BOTH STOCKS AND FUNDS

Although NETworth's initial mission focused on the mutual fund investor, it also has a large database of financial information on stocks and stock companies. As a result, cyberspace investors have an integrated navigator and do not have to jump to other Websites if they're looking for data on both equities and mutual funds. The databases for these two financial arenas are:

❐ Stock Database from Disclosure Inc.
❐ Mutual Fund Database from Morningstar Research

While it's possible that the Internet technology may soon develop so that the NET*investor's Web browser can integrate all the necessary infor-

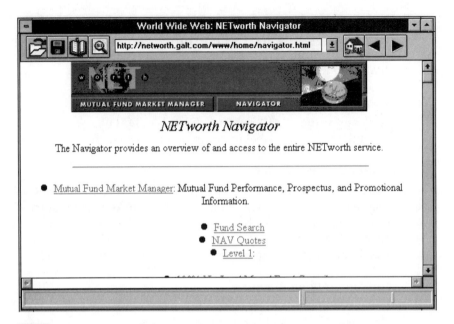

9.2   NETworth Navigator to stock and fund information.

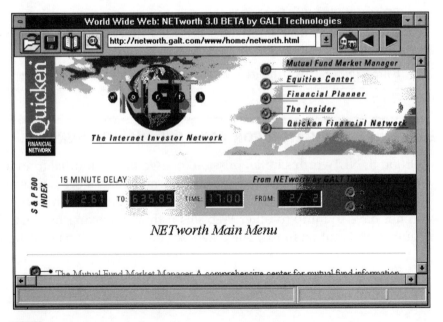

9.3   NETworth's Investor Scoreboard: the S&P Index.

mation—permitting easy linking to several free and for-pay services—the technology's not there yet. So given the current state of the art, NETworth provides a decided advantage over other Web resources that focus on just stocks or just mutual funds.

Let's take a close look at the collection of investor's resources NET-worth provides at its centralized, integrated NET*navigator.

MUTUAL FUND MARKET MANAGER: LINKS TO TOP PERFORMERS

NETworth's mutual fund information includes substantial promotional materials direct from the fund managers, as well as independent third-party databases. Obviously, such information tends to be biased and must be carefully scrutinized when you do your due diligence.

Nevertheless, the investor is given the opportunity for direct access to information on many of the best mutual funds. In most cases, you can download or order prospectuses. Keep in mind, however, that this information is basically self-serving promotional brochures and advertisements, including materials from about 60 prominent fund managers, with such respected and successful names as Kaufmann, Benham, Montgomery, Janus, Scudder, Dreyfus, Calvert, Twentieth Century, Lindner, Muhlenkamp, American Heritage, Value Line, and Oakmark.

MORNINGSTAR: PREMIER MUTUAL FUND RESEARCH DATABANK

Fortunately, NETworth balances the purely promotional materials supplied directly from the funds with some solid *independent* research. And even more fortunate is the fact that NETworth's primary source of independent mutual fund information is the highly respected Morningstar Mutual Fund database.

Morningstar's data can also be found at AOL, CompuServe, Reuters Money Network, and InvesTools. And their best strategy may be to keep it that way, marketing and selling their mutual fund database and research to any information vendor willing to pay for it. In many ways, Morningstar's dual role as an information retailer and wholesaler, like Reuters and Dow Jones, probably makes more sense than promoting and focusing on its own one-stop Website in competition with its own vendors.

Previously, Morningstar's print publications were promoted on the NETworth Website, although this is now being revised. However, the same

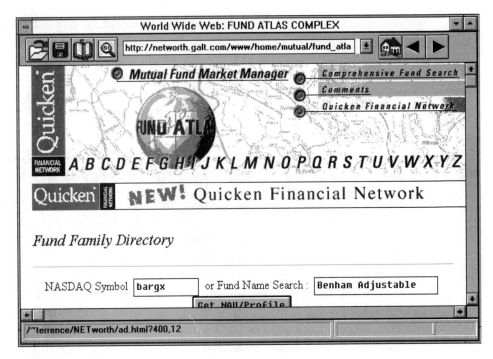

9.4 Morningstar database: NAV quotes, profiles, top-25 sector screens.

Morningstar database is the basic input for NETworth's mutual fund profiles and searches. The print versions of the Morningstar database include:

☐ **Morningstar Mutual Funds:** This includes rankings of 1,500 key funds, plus historical profiles, performance/risk analysis, returns for 17 industry benchmarks, NAVs, expenses, turnover, ratios, tax, income and capital gains, holdings, and other key data. Analysts' reports are also included. On a single page, Morningstar packs in 450 key statistics on each fund, updated biweekly. The data is also available on disk.

☐ **Morningstar's 5-Star Investor:** This is a 40-page monthly newsletter, including fund industry news; market trends; performance analyses of fund sectors; investment basics with portfolio planning, management, and makeover suggestions; individual fund profiles to illustrate trends; and risk measures on the Morningstar 500, a select group of 500 open- and closed-end funds.

☐ **Morningstar's U.S. Equities:** Morningstar is now developing a super-database on 6,000 stocks, covering virtually every stock on the

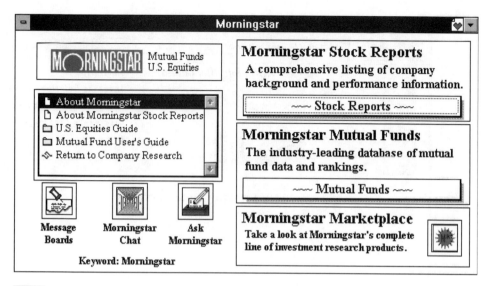

9.5 Morningstar stock and mutual fund reports at AOL.

NYSE, AMEX, and NASDAQ. This information is available on floppies, and includes 200 data points: prices, valuations, capitalization, income, cashflow and balance sheet information, and the key financial ratios.

Although you cannot yet directly access these three products on the NETworth Website, Morningstar's database underlying these periodicals is the basis of the mutual fund research data available at the site, including:

☐ **NETworth's Fund Search:** This is based on Morningstar's database of 6,800 mutual funds. Input the fund symbol (you can search for it first if necessary) and up come the stats and a graph of historical data and a profile.

☐ **NETworth's Fund Profile:** This provides statistics and graphs directly from NASDAQ through an electronic data feed through S&P Comsat.

☐ **Principia Mutual Fund Software:** Although not mentioned at the NETworth Website, Morningstar also offers the Principia offline analytic software, which covers 6,200 funds with 98 columns of data, updated monthly.

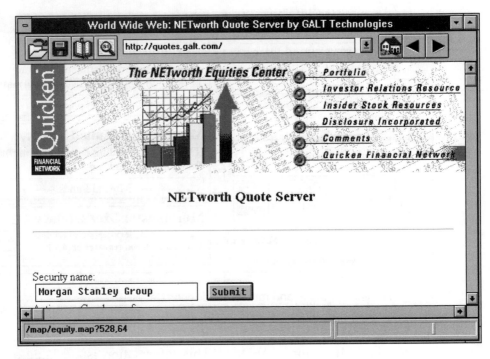

9.6 NETworth Equities Center and Quote Server.

This new cyberspace software is designed so you can create your own screening criteria, on a weighted basis, and retrieve the information that fits your personal rating system. In addition, you can create a portfolio and follow it as updated information is retrieved.

Bottom line: Morningstar is first class—one of America's primary databases for mutual funds—and it is comprehensive and reliable. Like *Consumer Reports,* Morningstar refuses ads, which limits its potential revenues on the Internet and minimizes its exposure to the NET*investor. However, Morningstar has deliberately taken a less prominent role at NETworth as well as at AOL and other locations.

NETworth's success is based to a large extent on Morningstar data. Arguably, Morningstar could have gone direct and created its own Website without NETworth. It chose not to. As it is, you do get a lot, although a cyberspace investor may be able to get more of Morningstar at America Online, for example—more information that is much easier to use and from a more visually appealing source.

To its credit, however, NETworth saw the enormous new opportunities inherent in the Internet and brought Morningstar to the global financial community. And today, fortunately, if you want the crème de la crème of mutual fund research and analysis, you can still get a good bit of it free on the Web, thanks to NETworth.

NETWORTH EQUITY CENTER: MARKET, STOCK, AND COMPANY DATA

One of the distinctive advantages of the NETworth Website is the fact that NETworth has extensive information on stocks as well as mutual funds. Its Website information includes:

❒ **Free stock quotes and company fundamentals:** Price, volume, trends, symbol searches, ticker information, charts, research and analysis are available directly from Standard & Poor's, one of the most respected names on Wall Street. NETworth also supplies one of the most comprehensive directories of links to other free quote sources from U.S. and international brokers and exchanges everywhere on the Web. This is a perfect platform if you can spend a few hours collecting a few hundred quotes.

❒ **NETworth's Market Outlook:** This is a weekly electronic newsletter from one of the more successful mutual fund managers, The Benham Group, with commentary on the preceding week and a forecast of likely trends in the coming week.

❒ **Investor Relations—company Website resources:** Here is one of the best point-and-click Web directories for investors interested in getting financial information directly from the source. In one location, investors can quickly and easily link to the official Websites of publicly held companies, supplementing other company research materials.

❒ **The Insider—market and personal finance Websites:** This is another excellent Internet directory with links to key Website resources on U.S. and foreign companies, public offerings, ADRs, financial and business news, government and private economic statistics, advisory newsletters, portfolio management, taxes, foreign exchange, international trade, credit, insurance, and more. This is an excellent Internet master list.

❒ **NETworth Forums:** Access is provided by some key mutual fund associations. Here, the investor has access to major membership

9.7 NETworth's Market Outlook by The Benham Group.

groups, including the 401(k) Association, and a rather extensive Investing Guide from the 100% No-Load Mutual Fund Association. A glossary of terms is also available.

❑ **Disclosure Incorporated Database:** Disclosure is one of the best resources for company information, extracted directly from public filings on record with the Securities and Exchange Commission (SEC). Now Disclosure also provides mutual fund data.

Clearly, NETworth makes available to the cyberspace investor a great body of information on company fundamentals and equity securities. Stock quotes and company information are not only unlimited, they are currently free, which certainly attracts many investors to this excellent Website.

NETworth also has one of the best Internet Web directories with links to the key investor resources on the Web. And while Quicken adds an exciting new dimension to NETworth's reputation, the primary databases continue to be Morningstar for mutual funds and Disclosure for stock data and company fundamentals.

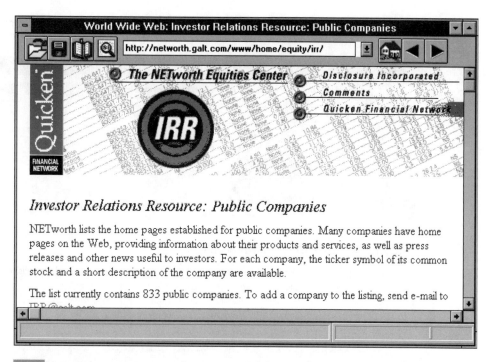

9.8 Investor Relations: links to public company Websites.

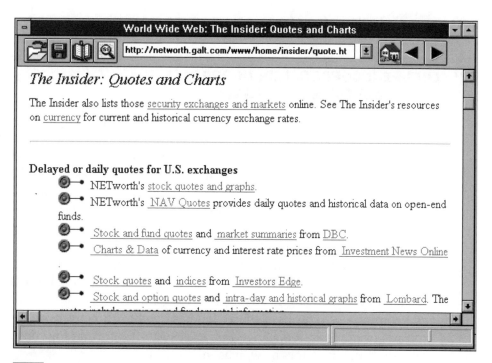

9.9 The Insider: links to other Web quote servers.

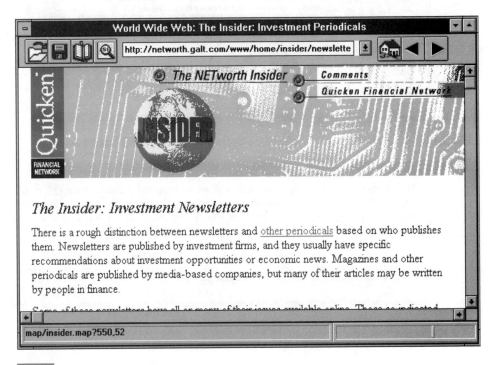

9.10 The Insider: investment newsletters and periodicals.

DISCLOSURE INCORPORATED: CORPORATE FINANCIAL DATA FROM SEC FILINGS

Disclosure is NETworth's main resource for stock and company data at the Website. Disclosure is now a subsidiary of Primark, an aggressive and relatively new conglomerate. A couple of years ago, Primark acquired Disclosure along with Datastream (real-time quote services) as part of Primark's strategy in entering a field previously dominated by Dow Jones, Reuters, Knight-Ridder, and Bloomberg. Morningstar also provides some financial information on equities, stocks, and company fundamentals, but Disclosure is the primary resource.

Disclosure Incorporated is an old-timer in financial cyberspace; it has been around for over 25 years—as long as the Internet itself. It understands what the NET*investor needs from its long experience of serving the financial community. The Disclosure database comes directly from the public records of the SEC, repackaged in an easy-to-use format for consumption by individual investors as well as institutions.

Public companies and their major shareholders file almost 400,000 documents annually. All this information is available to the public, but in its raw form from the SEC it can be unmanageable. That's where Disclosure comes in. Disclosure has been a reliable contractor for the SEC for over 25 years—a kind of data manager, packaging, marketing, and delivering financial documents filed with the SEC to anyone in the public. Their customers span the globe, including most major financial institutions, major money managers, research libraries, and law and accounting firms.

On Wall Street, Disclosure is synonymous with reliable public company information. Online you can tap directly into the extensive Disclosure database for a variety of services, many of which are included as part of your basic package from CompuServe, America Online, and The Microsoft Network. In fact, there are at least 40 different online services carrying some of the Disclosure offerings.

Fortunately, through NETworth as well as the various online services and Disclosure's new Website, the individual investor is now getting direct and timely access to more company financial information than ever before. Disclosure's services include:

❐ **SEC company filings:** The SEC Disclosure database has information on 11,000 U.S. companies whose securities are traded in this country. There are over 200 financial and full-text data entries for each company. Disclosure repackages the information, and cyberspace investors can retrieve summary company reports and screen investment opportunities.

❐ **EdgarPlus:** Disclosure's database of SEC documents offers many not included on the experimental Edgar Internet Project at New York University. In addition, EdgarPlus provides a formatting and search provision, making it easier to use than the basic government-sponsored Edgar database. Use this to look for electronically formatted 10-K and 10-Q reports, proxies, registration statements, and more, organized and indexed by Disclosure's proprietary system.

❐ **Basic database services:** Screen investment opportunities, conduct financial analyses, evaluate companies, compare market performances, and review portfolios with these services.

❐ **Stock Explorer:** Disclosure's new database covers a total of 4,000 companies, including the S&P 500, designed specifically for the individual investor with summary financial statements, p/e ratios, divi-

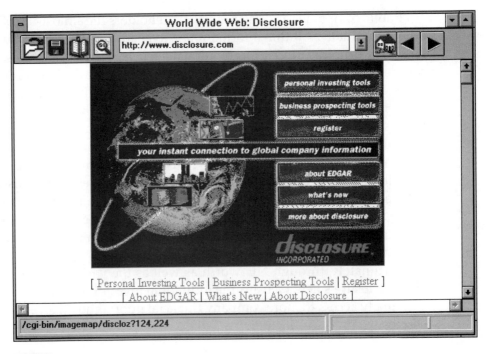

9.11   Disclosure's own Website: master menu.

dend yields, and historical and projected earnings estimates. Disclosure says it's "organized for hot investment prospecting."

☐ **WorldScope:**   Disclosure also provides similar corporate and financial information on another 12,000 foreign-based corporations, including a separate emerging markets database. This information is extracted from original documents and annual reports as well as other third-party resources.

☐ **New issues database:**   A comprehensive database of all new equity and debt issues filed since 1990 is available.

☐ **Canadian securities:**   Disclosure markets and distributes financial and management information on 8,000 Canadian private and government companies compiled by independent Canadian vendors.

☐ **Stock Tracker Portfolio Manager:**   Disclosure is a flexible software program that helps you manage your portfolio. Input your portfolio and other favorite stocks, configure the spreadsheet format so that you get all the information key to your needs, and Stock Tracker will automatically and instantly update the prices, alert you of major news items on stocks you're following, and provide you with essential company reports.

Disclosure has one of the most impressive databases available to the cyberspace investor. Disclosure has a long history as a reliable information link to corporations through its work with the SEC and other legal and financial resources on public companies. You will find them online, on the Net, and at many cyberspace locations.

BOTTOM LINE: NETWORTH IS PUSHING THE ENVELOPE IN CYBERSPACE

NETworth was one of the founders of the commercial Internet, taking risks and opening a path for many others to follow. It set the pace in this exciting new frontier. NETworth is also paving the way into the next generation

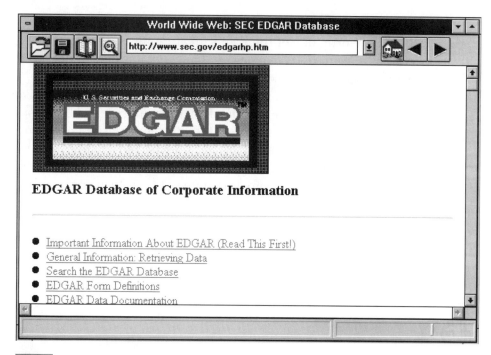

9.12 SEC/EDGAR filings: Disclosure's primary company database resource.

of Internet development and it is exciting to watch how it is developing. In the recent past we have observed:

❏ **Quicken/Intuit Merger:**   Intuit, the parent of the Quicken Financial Network, acquired NETworth, creating a new window to the electronic mutual fund investor. The acquisition should also provide Intuit with access to Galt's advanced Atlas transactions technology and, therefore, a secure channel between investors and their funds.

❏ **Disclosure and Morningstar:**   Last year, Disclosure merged with the Primark conglomerate, and it is developing its own Website. Morningstar could be a likely candidate for a cyberspace takeover and appears to be taking a much lower profile on the NETworth site, possibly tipping its hand to a move.

❏ *Mutual Funds* **magazine:**   Earlier, *Mutual Funds,* along with several major investment advisory newsletter publishers, left NETworth. *Mutual Funds* then created its own rival Website, serving Internet investors interested in mutual funds—and doing a great job at it.

This whole situation remains fluid, dynamic, and unpredictable. Today, NETworth, one of the Web's great pioneers, is not merely getting a face-lift as a result of its marriage to Quicken; it is also undergoing a rapid transformation into a major second-generation Internet resource.

Yet, no matter what direction this powerful global financial databank partnership of NETworth and Quicken, Morningstar and Disclosure takes, the larger context—the highly volatile Internet environment—will remain unpredictable and produce massive, unexpected changes in Wall Street cyberspace. Fortunately, in the end, the NET*investor will come out a winner, because these changes are guaranteed to create major new benefits for the *individual* investor.

Mutual Funds *Magazine Online:* *Website of the Future*

Mutual Funds magazine is another very powerful example of the enormous transformation impacting Wall Street as a result of the new cyberspace technologies—the Internet, private IntraNets, online dial-up services, offline analytic software, and all the other new electronic media.

Mutual Funds magazine's editor-in-chief, Norman Fosback, wrote his classic, *Stock Market Logic,* over 20 years ago, and it's still a best-seller today. The research organization he created, the Institute of Econometrics Research, now publishes eight financial advisory newsletters, and since 1994, it also publishes *Mutual Funds,* the only magazine exclusively focused on funds.

MUTUAL FUNDS ONLINE AND THE INSTITUTE FOR ECONOMETRIC RESEARCH

In addition, for over 20 years the Institute has developed and maintained one of the most complete independent databases on mutual funds, with over 500 data items on more than 7,000 funds, including 2,100 stock mutual funds, all of which are updated regularly for successful decision making by mutual fund investors. In fact, if the Institute doesn't have the information in its database, it probably doesn't exist. The major competitor in this field is the Morningstar Mutual Funds Research database (although other key fund databases do exist, such as Lipper and Value Line, they are not yet as readily available to investors in cyberspace.

Unlike so many of the early, one-person Websites on the Internet, this is a substantial, credible research institute making a serious, long-term

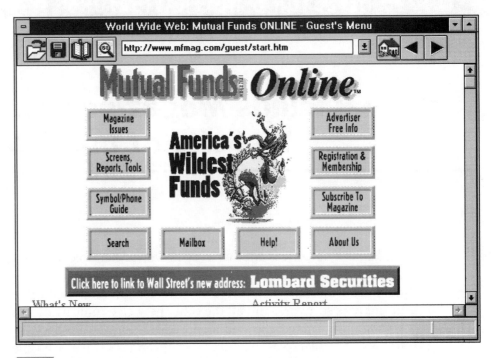

10.1 *Mutual Funds* Magazine Online: master directory.

investment in services for the new cyberspace investor. As a result, *Mutual Funds* magazine, a print periodical with a solid research database, has suddenly rocketed to the leading edge of the Wall Street cyberspace revolution. In fact, it may be a mini-Netscape of the electronic mutual fund publishers.

SOLID RESEARCH, PLUS NEWS AND ANALYSIS

In the initial stages of development of the Internet's Web, there were many Websites with information about mutual funds but few with the resources of *Mutual Funds* magazine and its publisher, the Institute of Econometric Research. The monthly publication, *Mutual Funds,* is the only magazine focusing exclusively on mutual funds as an investment vehicle.

Consequently, the conversion of *Mutual Funds* into an electronic publication that is available worldwide on the Internet is of major importance to the NET*investor. The database is potentially one of the most valuable resources available in financial cyberspace, especially since so many of today's investors are primarily fund investors, preferring diversification through funds rather than direct ownership of stocks and bonds.

MUTUAL FUNDS ONLINE: SUPER-DATABASE FOR RESEARCH

The Institute for Econometric Research is one of the most complete databases for the 7,000 mutual funds traded in America. Its magazine, *Mutual Funds*, has a circulation of 400,000 investors. More important, its Website is already getting hundreds of thousands of hits daily from cyberspace investors.

The editor Norman Fosback's book, *Stock Market Logic*, was originally published two decades ago. In addition to the magazine, the Institute has ten excellent publications on stocks and mutual funds:

❏ *Mutual Fund Forecaster:*   Profit projections and risk ratings.
❏ *Mutual Fund Buyer's Guide:*   Investment scoreboard.
❏ *Fund Watch:*   Chart service featuring high-performance funds.
❏ *Income Fund Outlook:*   Bond funds and money market funds.
❏ *Mutual Fund Weekly:*   Combination of the four fund advisories.
❏ *Market Logic:*   Full service on stock market and economy.
❏ *Investor's Digest:*   Market advice from hundreds of services.
❏ *The Insiders:*   Analysis and ratings of America's top investors.
❏ *New Issues:*   Guide to initial public offerings.
❏ *Stock Market Weekly:*   Combination of the four stock advisories.

These are mentioned here to emphasize that cyberspace investors using the *Mutual Funds* magazine Website are getting the benefit of the substantial backup research that also supports all their publications.

For more information, contact the Institute for Econometric Research at the *Mutual Funds* Online Website, at *http://www.mfmag.com*.

The Institute for Econometric Research has rapidly created a very powerful presence in financial cyberspace. In fact, it must be emphasized right from the start (and this is an important point for the cyberspace investor to understand) that the *Mutual Funds* Online Website is *not merely a graphic reproduction* of the magazine—it is far more. Think of it as *virtually* walking into one of the finest research libraries on the mutual fund industry. Here are some of the Institute's Website features that are available with the click of a mouse:

❏ **Mutual Funds magazine's latest issue:**   Here you can download a graphic showing the latest issue, including a screen with the table of contents. In addition, you can easily jump to key articles of interest while logged on the Web.

❏ **Search archives for prior issues:**   Another screen has the covers of the issues from the previous 12 months, with links to the contents of each issue.

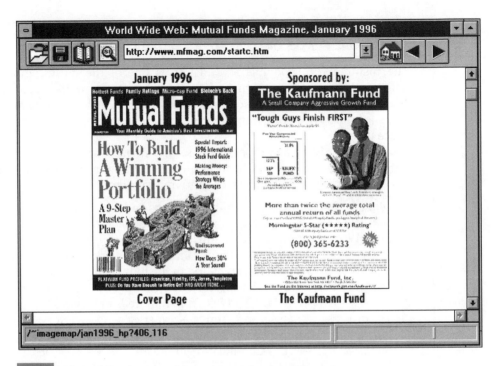

10.2 *Mutual Funds* magazine: cover and sponsor's page.

THREE KEY CRITERIA THE PROS USE TO PICK WINNERS

According to a *Mutual Funds* magazine survey of 100 leading experts on mutual funds, the three most reliable criteria used by professionals in advising their clients are:

1. **Past performance:** A consistent ten-year track record of returns.
2. **Consistent management style:** Fund managers have clear and focused investment strategies.
3. **Tenure of portfolio managers:** The team has longevity, including bear market experience.

SOURCE: "How the Pros Pick Winners," *Mutual Funds* (November 1995).

The magazine is extremely well written and insightful, with a regular selection of helpful, practical guidelines and commentaries on specific funds and industry trends. Fund investors should review this publication in addition to the Website.

❏ **Articles and fund research:** This Website has a special search feature that allows you to search and retrieve articles on specific funds; for example, 27 articles were accessed on topics related to the Fidelity Magellan fund.

❏ **Hotlist Alert:** You can create your own fund tracker by setting up a bookmark on your browser directly into the *Mutual Funds* Online Website and monitor it frequently for new information.

❏ **Database screening:** You have an opportunity to freely screen the *Mutual Funds* database using over a dozen criteria. Moreover, the site intends to add more search and selection tools using the complete fund database. The variables you can input for screening include fund type and objectives, size and risk-adjusted performance, load, fees, and expenses, total returns by year, and statistical measures.

If you are overwhelmed, you can omit some of the criteria (such as the statistical measure, beta, r-squared, and standard deviations); however, if you are serious about improving your investment skills, it's

10.3 *Mutual Funds:* research from previous year's articles.

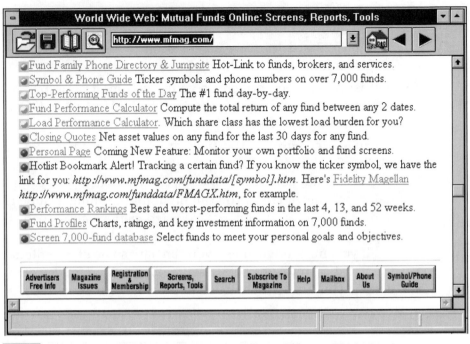

10.4 Directory of MFMAG's research tools for mutual fund investors.

worth learning every single analytical technique you can, including these screening measures. So experiment; see which work for you and why.

☐ **Total return calculator:**   If you want the bottom-line return of a particular fund for any specific period, input the symbol, the period you want included in the calculation, and it's calculated for you.

☐ **Mutual fund summaries:**   Using another search procedure you can retrieve all the essential information about your favorite mutual fund from one of the most complete databases available, including quotes, performance data, fees, expenses, and almost everything else you need for investment decisions.

☐ **Top-performing funds:**   There is an extensive screen with all the best (and also the worst) fund performers in the most recent period.

☐ **Website links:**   There is a directory of all funds, with links to individual Websites. Only a few of the larger funds (less than 100) had Websites in early 1996. Fortunately, telephone numbers are included so you

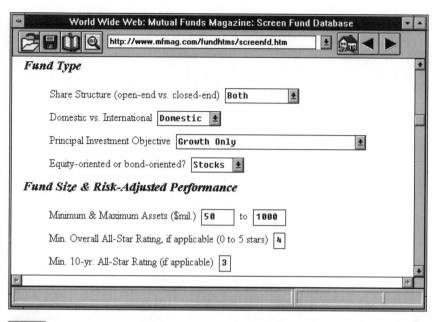

10.5 Search criteria: fund type, size, and performance.

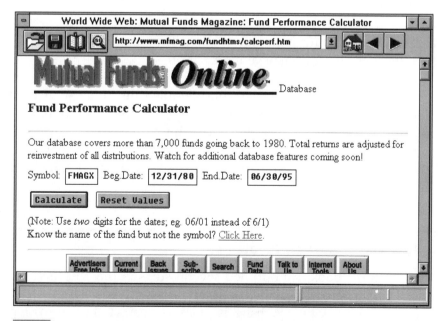

10.6 Online performance calculator for mutual funds.

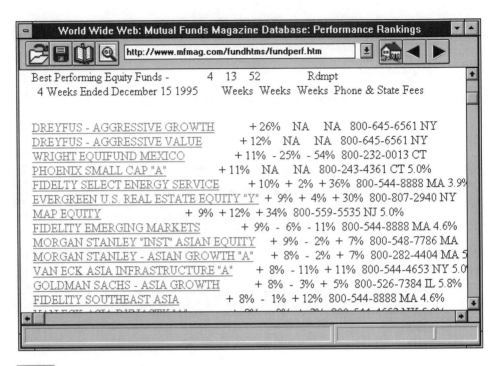

10.7   Ratings screens: best and worst fund performers.

can follow up for more information. They are cross-referenced to other key Websites for financial information.

Overall, this is a Website of considerable value to most NET*investors, especially since mutual funds are included in the majority of investment portfolios, particularly for the novice investor. Funds provide a perfect opportunity to satisfy the basic objectives of many portfolios, especially diversification of risk. No wonder an expert advisor like Bill Griffeth calls funds "the perfect investment."

A FOCUSED STRATEGIC MISSION

Earlier in the book, we outlined several steps in the NET*investing decision-making process, as a means of rating the top systems. When the *Mutual Funds* Online Website is stacked against the seven-step rating schedule and evaluated as an integrated NET*navigator you will see there are a few missing pieces (as there are with virtually every other system serving the cyberspace investor):

☐ **Stocks and company research:** There is no competitive information regarding stocks, bonds, and their companies, as indeed there are with other NET*investing systems—for example, CompuServe or America Online, which provide easy access to both fund and stock data from a single platform.

☐ **Executing trades:** As yet, you can't do any trading or exchanges as you can with Fidelity in-house exchanges, Fidelity's FundsNetwork, or Schwab's OneSource, where you can trade hundreds of funds from many managers.

☐ **Portfolio management:** With the exception of the Hotlist Alert, there are minimal portfolio management capabilities—certainly little comparable to what you'd find with Quicken, Telescan, or Reuters Money Network, for example.

In spite of these limitations and even though they are advertiser supported, as an integrated NET*navigator for the cyberspace investor, the *Mutual Funds* Website offers one of the best *independent* systems for NET*investors focusing primarily on mutual funds, a solid competitor for Lipper, Value Line, and Morningstar.

BOTTOM LINE: FIRST-CLASS FUND RESEARCH AND NEWS REPORTING

Mutual Funds magazine has apparently made a strategic decision to stay focused solely on mutual funds. In contrast, Morningstar (originally mutual funds only) and Disclosure (originally stocks only) are now expanding their databases to include both stocks and mutual funds. It remains to be seen which of these three organizations is strengthened by its strategies and which ultimately proves most successful.

In the final analysis, the Institute for Econometric Research certainly does have one of the most complete and reliable databases on mutual funds. Moreover, its data and recommendations can always be double-checked against other mutual funds databases, which is, of course, a generally recommended procedure.

Perhaps more important, *Mutual Funds* magazine has a super staff of analysts and editors who regularly turn out some of the finest analyses of funds, sectors, and trends in the industry, with a solid reputation for integrity. They are definitely committed to helping the cyberspace investor make informed, intelligent investment decisions.

As a result, *Mutual Funds* Online deserves a high rating among the NET*navigators for cyberspace investors. It goes far beyond just providing high-quality raw data into the depths of financial cyberspace to provide first-rate analysis and interpretation, and, in the process, it can help any mutual fund investor build a winning portfolio.

Discount Brokers
Online and on the Web

The New Cyber-Brokers: Discounts Plus Full Service

What a truly exciting time, filled with opportunities. The Wall Street cyberspace revolution is forcing the global investment community to restructure, creating massive uncertainties. Traditional institutions are being forced to respond to the challenge. Unexpected new opportunities are creating fortunes for the quick and aggressive. And the individual investor is transforming into a truly *independent* decision maker.

Newsweek, the *Los Angeles Times*, and many other publications called 1995 "the Year of the Internet," and the title fit perfectly. A strong entrepreneurial spirit dominated not only the financial press and television, but also the popular media. Every week saw yet another cover story in yet another magazine or newspaper—the cyberspace revolution is here.

THE WEB: EXPLODING NEW MARKET FOR TODAY'S CYBER-BROKERS

Into the center of this cyberspace electrical storm, several new financial superstores arrived *out there* on the new Web "shopping mall" that was attracting so much public attention. Some of the first of these Websites included PAWWS Financial Network, WealthWEB from Aufhauser & Company, and Lombard Internet Securities Trading. The financial and business press starting writing about them on a regular basis. This new generation of *cyber-brokers* became media darlings—certainly not at center stage like Netscape and Microsoft, but nevertheless hot news for hungry reporters and editors looking for sidebars to the main attractions.

Online trading really is not new. Other discount brokers, such as E*Trade, PC Financial Network, and Quick & Reilly, had been around for

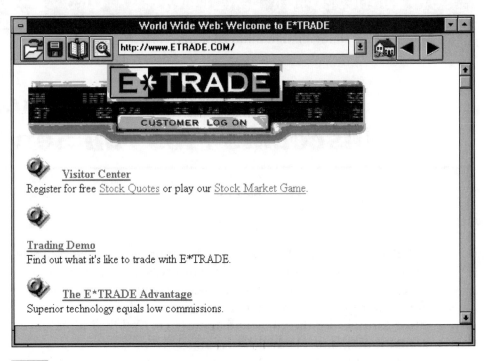

11.1 E*TRADE: Online brokerage since 1984.

several years in the online electronic brokerage business, offering basic trading-only services. They didn't have to offer anything more, because it was available elsewhere on CompuServe, Prodigy, and AOL. However, these new Web-based cyber-brokers began offering services in addition to mere trading: news, research, screening, management, and more.

WARNING: DEEP DISCOUNTS DO NOT ELIMINATE RISK FACTOR

"E*Trade slashed its commission price by 25%, cutting the cost from $19.95 to $14.95 for trades up to 5,000 shares of companies listed on the NYSE or AMEX . . . well below those charged by competitors like Quick & Reilly . . . which charges a minimum of $37.50, or e.Schwab . . . which charges $39 to trade up to 1,000 shares and adds 3 cents to each share after that. . . .

"Analysts warn, however, that just because it's cheap, trading through E*Trade doesn't make the stock market any simpler or less risky."

SOURCE: Adrienne Press, "E*Trade Cuts Online Trading Fees," *Money Daily Online* (February 17, 1996).

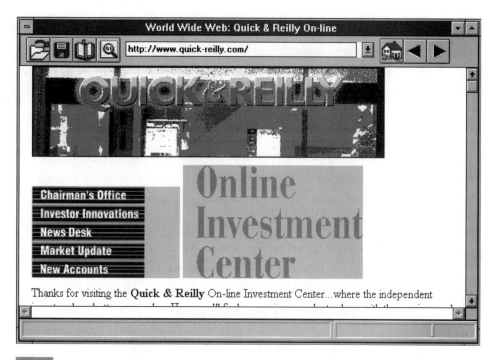

11.2   Quick & Reilly: Online Investment Center.

These cyber-brokers were, and are, the new breed of discount brokers. They are the leaders in electronic trading using this new Internet technology—a sign of things to come in the very near future. These new cyber-brokers are succeeding because they speak directly to the mind, heart, and wallet of the individual investor searching for the best possible tools available to help achieve the goal of financial independence.

1995 *was* unquestionably the Year of the Internet. *It was also the year of the online discount broker going full service.*

NEW CYBER-BROKERS: FROM TRADING-ONLY TO NET*NAVIGATORS

By the year 2001, virtually every investor will be online, through commercial services, online home banking, online commercial shopping, online brokerage, and online management of the investment portfolio. All 52 million shareholders will be literally *forced* online by financial institutions of one kind or another.

Similarly, *every* brokerage firm will be online (or out of business). This mass move online will dramatically change the nature of the brokerage

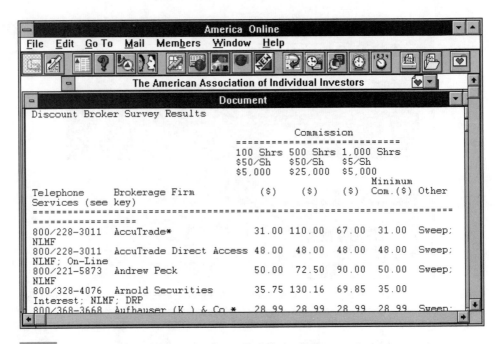

11.3 The AAII discount broker survey results: on AOL.

business as we know it, including discount brokerage in general, the nature of cyber-brokers, as well as the full-service retail brokerage houses, the Wall Street Establishment. In fact, there are at least three Internet trends that will impact this transformation of the brokerage industry in the near term:

Trend #1: Websites Become Essential Utilities—
No Special Marketing Advantage

As one astute financial executive at Vanguard astutely said, "the Web is the 800 number of the future." And the future is here today. The Internet and the information superhighway will become so crowded that there will be little distinction between cyber-brokers.

As a result, the *next generation* of cyber-brokers will either revert to basic trading-only online and on the Web, or they *all* will simply offer some private-label version of Reuters Money Network, for example, or any other NET*navigator selected by their customers. The distinctions will be minimal.

ARE YOU INDEPENDENT ENOUGH FOR DEEP DISCOUNTERS?

"Deep discount brokers aren't for everyone. They can best serve investors who do their own research to determine which stocks, bonds or mutual funds they want. To see if you fit that profile, take this quick quiz. If you agree with one or more of the following statements, a deep-discount broker may not be good for you.

1. I like to research my stock picks independently, but I rarely trade more than once or twice a year. *[Discounters may charge fees for inactive accounts.]*
2. I depend on brokerage research and want to obtain information I need on stocks. *[Discounters don't offer any research; but, of course, most online services offer electronic research and analysis.]*
3. I like to develop a one-to-one relationship with a broker. *[Discounters work on volume and usually won't even identify themselves by name.]*
4. I'm interested in trading stocks one day, but right now my portfolio consists mostly of no-load mutual funds. I'd like to consolidate my portfolio, make all my trades for free and get everything on one monthly, consolidated statement. *[Then you better forget discount brokers and stick with mutual funds.]*
5. If the market tumbles again, I'd like to try selling short—a first for me. *[If you need advice on short-selling . . . or any other investment technique or decision, you're better off paying the higher commission at a full-service broker until you're comfortable with what you're doing. Deep discounters do not build consumer education into their overhead costs, so you'll be going it alone.]*"

SOURCE: Tracey Longo, "The No-Frills World of Deep Discount Brokers," *Kiplinger's Personal Finance Magazine* (October 1995).

Trend #2: More Websites Will Charge for Fee-based Services— Fewer Freebies

An even bigger trend is restructuring the cyber-broker industry. Websites cost money to set up and maintain, and the owner's financial officers are likely to want a full accounting of its value-added or profit contribution. As a result, many Websites are now charging for data and services and offering less free information. We're already seeing a rapid trend among Websites severely limiting freebies.

Realistically, few cyber-brokers have the resources of a Fidelity or a Schwab. Fidelity manages over $400 billion; Schwab over $150 billion.

Moreover, the novelty of being a pioneer, with the media attention on your new Website, will fade when *every* discount broker offers cyber-brokerage and Websites are as common as pay phones in an airport.

Yes, you can still get some relatively innocuous free headlines from many sources on the Internet. You'll also find them in greater depth *live* on CNBC or CNNfn—and with analysis. And you can get a bunch of free quotes, which you'll have to retype into your personal computer.

But more and more, *you'll have to pay for* the information essential for investing in Wall Street cyberspace, even if it's just ten bucks a month for America Online. Otherwise, you'll be working with bites and bytes of information that are too little, too late, and too fragmented.

Trend #3: Websites Link into Single Global Marketplace—Less Isolation

Bill Gates emphasizes the centralizing marketplace quality of the Internet, in contrast to the fragmentation implied by the superhighway image of the past. This paradigm shift of perspective is crucial.

Some of the best examples of this consolidation trend are Schwab's OneSource and Fidelity's FundsNetwork, both of which are, in effect, private marketplaces or exchanges. And many more are coming on the market. With these, the investor has the opportunity to tap into hundreds of top mutual funds to buy, sell, switch, and exchange. This trend is likely to expand as more funds see the advantages.

Equity investors can also find access to private exchanges through Dow Jones/Telerate, Reuters Instinet, and Bloomberg. Global trading—commonplace for institutions—is also finding its way to the individual investor who can move money in and out of exchanges throughout the world. Soon the existing exchanges will see the need to develop new linkages and alliances in order to compete for the business of the new Web investor.

Another subtle aspect of this trend toward consolidation into a single cyberspace exchange is the growing awareness among corporations of the potential of the Web as an exchange. On the Web, such corporations are directly marketed to the new cyberspace investor who can buy securities without dealing with traditional brokers and the exchanges.

By the year 2000, the impact of these three trends will result in a new landscape for the brokerage industry. *All brokers will soon be cyber-brokers— including the big Wall Street firms.* They will have no choice because their customers are making the leap into cyberspace. Information and advice will be at a premium, on a fee basis. Cyberspace investors will need online

DISCOUNT BROKERS: ONLINE AND ON THE WORLD WIDE WEB

AccuTrade *(http://www.accutrade.com)*	800-598-2635
All American Brokers *(http://www.ebroker.com)*	800-553-9513
Aufhauser *(http://www.aufhauser.com)*	800-368-3668
Bull & Bear *(http://networth.galt.com)*	800-847-4200
E*Trade *(http://www.etrade.com)*	800-786-2575
Fidelity On-line Xpress *(http://www.fid-inv.com)*	800-544-5235
R. J. Forbes Group *(http://www.rjforbes.com)*	800-754-7687
Howe Barnes *(http://www.pawws.com)*	800-638-4250
Investex *(http://www.pawws.com)*	800-210-5496
Lind-Waldock *(http://www.ino.com)*	800-445-2000
Lombard *(http://www.lombard.com)*	800-566-2273
National Discount Brokers *(http://www.pawws.com)*	800-888-3999
PC Financial Network *(AOL/Prodigy/Reuters)*	800-825-5723
Quick & Reilly *(http://www.quick-reilly.com)*	800-634-6214
Charles R. Schwab & Co. *(http://www.schwab.com)*	800-372-4922
Muriel Siebert & Co. *(Siebert Online)*	800-535-9652
Jack White & Company *(http://www.pawws.com)*	800-753-1700

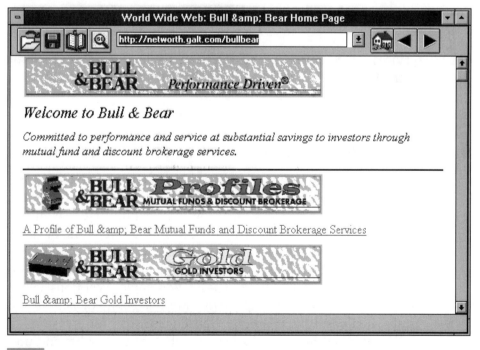

11.4 Bull & Bear: mutual funds and discount brokers.

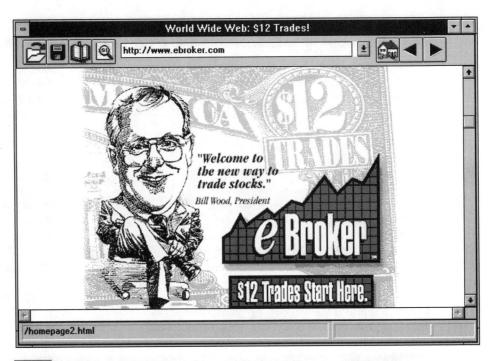

11.5   eBroker: deep-discount Web trades for do-it-yourself investors.

services as their primary NET*navigators. And fewer cyber-brokers will offer full-service online operations with *free* content, analytics, trading, and portfolio management.

THE ONLINE CHALLENGE: FULL-SERVICE OR TRADING-ONLY

In a relatively short time, most brokers will be cyber-brokers offering online trading, rather than mimicking America Online by offering news, quotes, and other services. Investors will get all that elsewhere, through online services such as Telescan, Reuters Money Network, or CompuServe, and a host of offline analytic software and databases that support the decision-making processes of the new independent cyberspace investor.

However, there are likely to be a few notable exceptions: cyber-brokers who were on the leading edge of the Internet technology curve and already established positions as unique Website resources for investors.

Highlighted here are the leaders who have gone beyond mere online trading services vehicles and have taken the initiative in attempting to develop some of the first full-service navigators online:

PCFN OFFERS "POWER FOR SELF-DIRECTED INVESTORS"

Since 1988, self-directed investors have turned to PC Financial Network, America's largest discount broker, to gain control over their investments. Now recognized as the leading provider of interactive brokerage services to the retail investor, PC Financial Network has executed more than 1 million online trades and currently holds over $1 billion in customer assets for online investors, offering:

Types of Investment Accounts	*Full Account Reporting*
Stocks	Alerts
Options	Order status
Mutual funds	Execution reports
Money market funds	Portfolio details
Bonds	History of accounts
Certificates of deposit	Account balances
Precious metals	

Types of Orders	*Decision Support*
Market orders	Stock symbols
Limit orders	Real-time quotes
Stop orders	Free investment research
Day order	Morning comment
Good till canceled	Credit and interest report
All-or-none orders	Economic and market indicators
Fill-or-kill orders	Individual stock reports
Margin or cash	Market wrap-up
Sell short	Week in review
Options information	

SOURCE: Adapted from PC Financial Network promotional brochures.

As the largest online discount broker, PCFN's alliances with commercial online services have obviously been quite rewarding. Now PCFN has its own version of Reuters Money Network to offer on the Net. Soon *all* discount brokers will be trading on the Internet, an infinitely bigger arena than AOL and Prodigy. That should create a virtual bonanza for the discount brokerage industry—and for the cyberspace investor.

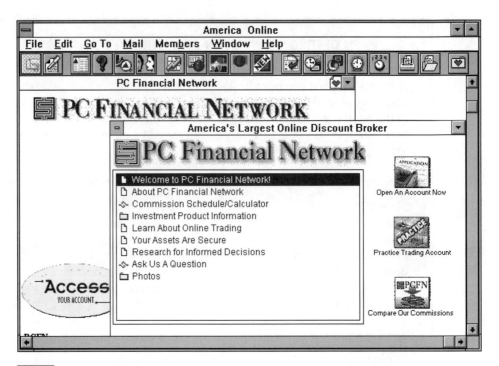

11.6　PCFN: discount subsidiary of Wall Street banker.

❏　Charles R. Schwab & Company, the ultimate pioneer in discount brokerage, cyber-brokerage, NET*navigators, and Wall Street cyberspace

❏　PAWWS Financial Network (Howe Barnes, Investex, National Discount Brokers, and Jack White & Co.)

❏　K. Aufhauser & Co.'s WealthWEB

❏　Lombard Internet Securities Trading

In addition, there are several other discount brokers that for some time have provided basic discount brokerage online. Now many of these are upgrading to online dial-up and Internet Website services beyond mere trading and are competing for both Schwab-type online clients as well as the full-service brokerage firms. This group of leading-edge brokers includes:

❏　AccuTrade

❏　E*Trade

❐ Lind-Waldock
❐ PC Financial Network
❐ Quick & Reilly
❐ Muriel Siebert & Co.

Schwab may have set the pace for the discount brokerage industry, first by offering discount rates, then offering electronic, online trading, and now full-service Internet and online brokerage. However, it's clear that these and other major discounters have no intention of watching the game from the sidelines. In fact, if anything the effect is the exact opposite. It's almost as if Schwab's success is nudging the others to become more aggressive—

CYBERSPACE TRADING: SEVEN ROADS LEAD TO ONE BROKER

AccuTrade, a discount brokerage firm in Omaha, Nebraska, was one of the early ones in the race, with an ad titled, "Cruise The Financial Services Super Highway," complete with a stylized road map of its services in discount brokerage, mutual funds, and insurance. Its strategy in delivery systems gives the investor *seven alternative ways* to work with AccuTrade:

1. Telephone: automated touchtone
2. DOS terminal emulation (some prefer the old way)
3. Windows-based platform
4. Personal data assistant (PDA or palmtop computer)
5. Fax machine (for hard-copy orders)
6. Internet: World Wide Website and E-mail
7. Telephone call to a broker

AccuTrade has a smart marketing strategy here. Let's face it: No one really knows which alternative will work best for individual cyberspace investors. More important, no one really knows which technologies will catch on or which new ones will come on the market in the near future. It's a chaotic crap shoot.

In the end, the customer—*the independent investor in cyberspace*—will control the shots, the marketplace dictates. And the successful discount brokers will follow AccuTrade's lead, accept the inherent uncertainty here, and acknowledge that, ultimately, the consumer has the power to vote on the direction Wall Street cyberspace will take. Actually, brokers have little say in the matter.

SOURCE: Interview with Pete Ricketts of AccuTrade (January 1996).

with deeper-than-Schwab discounts, with their own copycat OneSource fund networks, and now, with full-service online navigators for cyberspace investors.

BOTTOM LINE: THE NEW BREED IS A HYBRID

The fact that several discount brokers, including PCFN, Quick & Reilly, and other majors are now offering their clients a NET*navigator from Reuters strongly suggests that soon *every* discount broker could be offering much more than basic trading *just to stay competitive.*

This trend is quite fascinating, because it now appears that, in the process of taking full advantage of the new cyberspace technologies, *the discount brokers are all becoming full-service online brokers*—hybrids combining the best of both worlds. Next it'll be online banking. Meanwhile, the tradi-

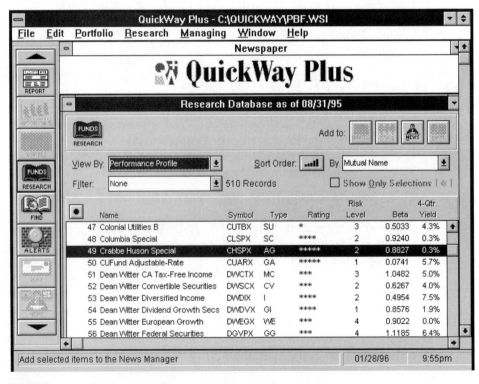

11.7 QuickWay Plus and Reuters Money Network.

tional full-service brokers may still be using telephones and counting on wealthy clients dependent on their advice.

With these trends and observations in mind, we will look more closely at the pacesetter Charles Schwab in the next chapter, before moving on to examine the NET*navigators offered by PAWWS Financial Network, K. Aufhauser & Company, and Lombard Internet Securities Trading.

Charles R. Schwab: StreetSmart Cyberspace Pioneer

Charles Schwab & Company has been a recognized pioneer in Wall Street cyberspace since the early 1980s—a leader offline, online, and on the Net. The company's cyberspace investing systems are what the financial techies call "killer apps"—state-of-the-art programs that work. In fact, it's safe to say that Schwab sets the standard with an ideal systems navigator for today's NET*investing.

Why ideal? It's quite simple. Schwab gives the new NET*investors what they want and need to make effective investment decisions that will

---

TWO VISIONARIES: CHARLES MERRILL AND CHARLES SCHWAB

"The financial markets have never lacked for visionaries, people like Charles E. Merrill, who started Merrill Lynch & Co. in 1914. Aided by an unapologetic flair for self-promotion, he built the nation's largest brokerage house by catering to the 'little guy.'

"The 1995 version of Merrill is Charles R. Schwab. With a blend of cutting-edge technology and old-fashioned sales and marketing, Schwab is once again radically altering how Americans of all incomes invest their money.

"He pioneered the discount brokerage following the deregulation of stock-trading commissions in 1975, and his San Francisco–based Charles Schwab Corp. remains the nation's largest discount brokerage. . . . Now he's struck gold again, this time with the exploding mutual fund business. . . ."

SOURCE: James Peltz, "Taking Stock of Schwab, Discounter Scores Again Pitching Mutual Funds," *Los Angeles Times* (August 18, 1995).

---

ultimately lead to financial independence—everything from planning to research, news updates to securities and analysis, mutual fund selection to trading and portfolio management. And more is coming.

In the revolutionary new world of cyberspace Wall Street, the pure label, *discount broker,* no longer quite fits the Schwab organization. Yes, it is a discounter, but it is also a *full-service online organization,* in competition with the best of the retail firms on the Street, most of which are still operating *offline.* Indeed, the major Wall Street houses are stuck in the cul-de-sacs and pit stops of cyberspace, while Schwab circles the track with a checkered flag. So, it's time to say that Charles Schwab is truly a high-tech, full-

---

CHARLES R. SCHWAB'S EIGHT PRINCIPLES OF INVESTING

"For thirty-five years now, I have been committed to personal investing. Behind this commitment has always been my desire to participate in the growth of America's greatest companies. And I have followed some basic principles I would like to share with you:

1. We all need a sound long-term retirement plan. Social Security and company pension plans alone are not enough.
2. As a rule of thumb, for every five years you put off investing, you may need to double your monthly investing amount to achieve the same retirement income.
3. Choose investments with a level of risk that makes you feel comfortable and that is appropriate for your long-term goals.
4. I believe in the wealth-generating power of stocks. Over time, stocks have outperformed all other investments and compensated for inflation.
5. Cash and bonds don't grow, they only pay interest. I include fixed-income investments and money market instruments in my portfolio only for diversification and liquidity.
6. Investing requires patience and the discipline to hold onto or add investments through down markets as well as up markets.
7. For more consistent and reliable outcomes, use asset allocation and mutual funds to create a broadly diverse portfolio—spreading risk over a variety of investments.
8. Investing doesn't stop when you retire. To make your money continue to work for you, don't shift all your money automatically into fixed-income and money market investments too early."

SOURCE: *"The Charles R. Schwab Approach to Investing" (http://www.schwab.com)*

service cyberspace Wall Street brokerage firm—which, by the way, also happens to offer discount fees.

As a result, Schwab is forcing the traditional Wall Street investment banks and retail brokers to compete on these new terms, *out there* in cyberspace, or lose the race for the new cyberspace investor's business—a race that will become intense as almost all investors (all 50 million) go online by 2000. Moreover, it is important to recognize this leadership, because you can expect that Schwab will continue to point the way as one of the leading suppliers of cutting-edge technology for independent cyberspace investing. Watch this company, invest in it, and use its technology.

MISSION: HELPING INVESTORS HELP THEMSELVES

Schwab's mission and corporate strategy are focused on helping the *individual* investor achieve a solid, winning future of economic freedom through financial independence. For quite some time, the Schwab team has

12.1 Schwab's mission: "Helping Investors Help Themselves"

been guided by a consistent philosophy that puts the power in the hands of the *individual* investor.

Charles Schwab's 1984 book, titled *How to Be Your Own Stockbroker*, is a classic and should be committed to memory by every new cyberspace investor. The opening chapter, "Why You Should Do It Yourself," clearly places you on solid ground for your cyberspace adventure, emphasizing our mutual conviction that "any investor can become truly independent" today.

Perhaps of most significance is Schwab's role in the history of Wall Street. He rocked Wall Street by leading the discount brokerage revolution back in the mid-1970s, and today he has replaced Charles Merrill as the champion of the "little guy." This is significant in a larger-millenium context, where technology rules.

The technological revolution that's creating the new information superhighway is having a major impact on the way the investment business is transacted on Wall Street. Today, Wall Street is no longer physically located in New York—Wall Street cyberspace is a global phenomenon, thanks to the new World Wide Web network.

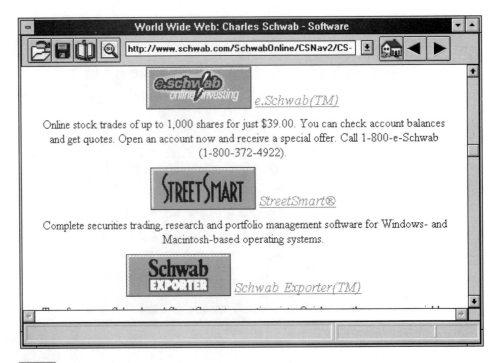

12.2 Charles R. Schwab: investor software center on the Web.

Charles Schwab's success and his role in investment history are products of this vision plus practical ability to *combine three diverse revolutions simultaneously into one single Wall Street cyberspace revolution:*

1. *Discount brokerage revolution*
2. *Information technology and Internet revolution*
3. *Revolution empowering the independent investor*

The phenomenal success of Netscape is a dramatic example of a revolution in progress. Similarly, in *MegaTrends,* John Naisbitt labeled the 1990s the "Age of the Individual." Charles Schwab is bringing Wall Street's information revolution onto Main Street and down to the level of practical realities for the individual investor, and in the process, he is turning Wall Street upside down.

STREETSMART: THE SAME INFORMATION AS THE PROFESSIONALS

Schwab's StreetSmart software is a perfect NET*investing system for the *independent* investor. *ComputerLife* magazine says, "This isn't toy research, but the same information professional investors pay hundreds to get." Charles Schwab is right; it "puts all the tools of a professional investment manager at your fingertips. . . . with StreetSmart you can invest like a pro."

Even the name is appropriate, incorporating both a strong marketing identity and a way to reinforce the cyberspace investor's goal of creating financial independence. Not only is StreetSmart a great NET*investing system, but its choice of electronic partners for investor services is impressive and once again emphasizes the direction of the Wall Street cyberspace revolution.

Schwab has made a strategic decision to integrate—*and jointly market*—the news, data, and analytic resources of some other key power players who have a hand in revolutionizing Wall Street. These include:

- ❏ Reuters Money Network
- ❏ Dow Jones News/Retrieval
- ❏ S&P MarketScope News
- ❏ Standard & Poor's Company Reports
- ❏ Zacks Company Earnings Estimates
- ❏ Morningstar Mutual Funds

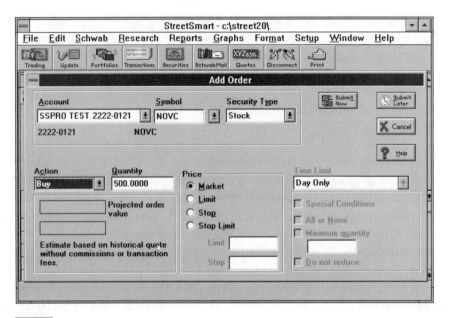

12.3 StreetSmart menu for placing orders.

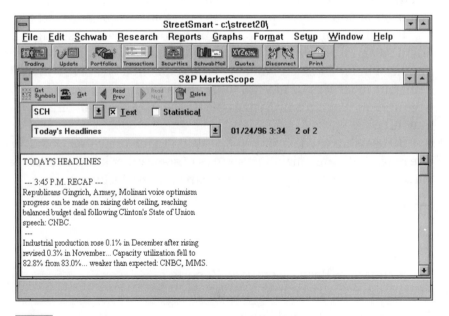

12.4 StreetSmart: headline news from S&P MarketScope.

Indeed, in the context of the emerging Wall Street cyberspace, it is significant to see how all of these leading information systems leaders are not only joined in cooperative marketing but are also designing their computer software programs to integrate their NET*investing systems with each other. This is a trend in this new cyberspace competition—indeed, *win-win* cooperation is actually more important to success than competition.

Install StreetSmart, open an account with Schwab, and you're on the way to becoming a street-smart, independent investor. And with StreetSmart you get a log of important features that'll make your investment decision making more effective:

❐ **Online trading:** For stocks, bonds, mutual funds, and options, plus confirmation of your orders. Buy and sell. Sell short. Switch/swap. Set limits and stop orders.

❐ **Transactions monitoring:** Order check status trades, cash balances, asset values, track assets, interest, and dividends.

❐ **Real-time quotes:** For your portfolio accounts; collect additional free quotes with each trade.

❐ **Market news and research:** Market news, company reports, earnings estimates, news clipping and digest service; StreetSmart also builds in hot news alerts on specified price/volume changes.

❐ **Screening securities:** Opportunities are based on your criteria for stocks, mutual funds, and other securities.

❐ **Performance graphs:** Create displays for investment returns, price histories, asset allocations, gains, and losses.

❐ **Mutual fund performance information:** Research, quotes, screening of 900 key mutual funds; from the Morningstar research database.

❐ **OneSource mutual funds:** Invest in hundreds of the top mutual funds outside the Schwab family of funds; no loads or transaction fees.

❐ **Portfolio management:** Customize reports and spreadsheets to fit your specifications and criteria. Simple point-and-click formatting. Updated snapshots of your portfolio's status.

❐ **Import/export data:** For taxes, planning, cash management, historical pricing, charting, and other compatible software.

❐ **Discounted commissions:** On trades and all third-party products.

❐ **E-mail communications:** The easy way to stay connected to your electronic broker.

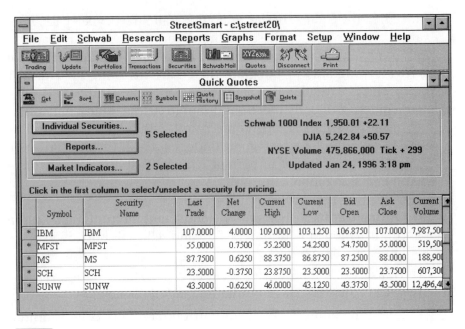

12.5   Quick Quotes: downloading selected stocks.

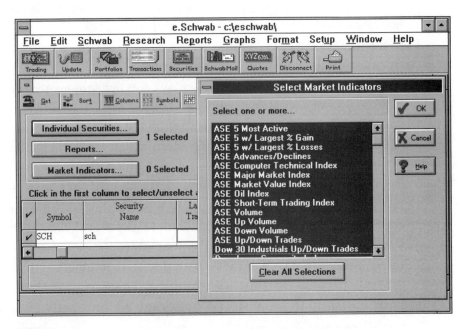

12.6   e.Schwab: market indicators for Quick Quotes.

12.7 SchwabFunds Family: $27 billion of no-load mutual funds.

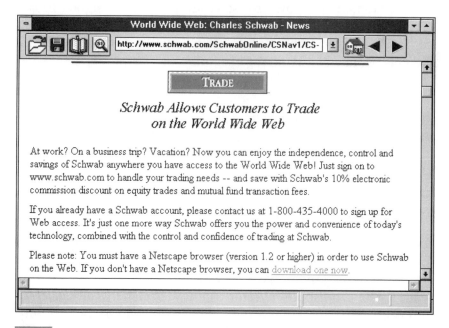

12.8 Schwab trades on the World Wide Web.

**SCHWAB'S ONLINE TRADING
100% INCREASE IN ONE YEAR!**

"Schwab doesn't mind using technology to cut its commissions. More that 200,000 of its 3.3 million customers now use its Windows-based Street-Smart software to enter their own trades online. Users of StreetSmart, which costs more than e.Schwab, can get limited trading advice from Schwab brokers.

"Schwab officials guess that roughly 15% of Schwab's orders from individual investors originate from PCs. Early last year, only 7% of its volume came from on-line investors.

"Trading on-line can bring significant cost savings. If an investor bought 1,000 shares of a $30 stock through a Schwab broker, the commission would total $166. The same transaction, using e.Schwab, would cost just $39."

SOURCE: Matt Krantz, "Order Entry on the Web: A Net Gain for Brokers," *Investor's Business Daily* (January 4, 1996).

StreetSmart is a powerful software package, designed to work effectively with a Charles Schwab online account. StreetSmart is also structured to work in conjunction with other investing systems—Telescan and Reuters Money Network, for example—or as an independent cyberspace investor's NET*navigator.

Online Access magazine gave StreetSmart its Hot Shot Award last year. StreetSmart is now the standard against which other products are measured in the discount brokerage industry and is obviously first choice for many new cyberspace investors.

e.SCHWAB FOR THE TRULY INDEPENDENT INVESTOR

Perhaps the clearest evidence of the trend toward creating totally independent investors is the new E-mail-only version of StreetSmart. This new variation of the innovative StreetSmart navigator is called e.Schwab, and with it, the cyberspace investor can now become totally *independent*. The ads call it "the future of trading, . . . the new, state-of-the-art computerized trading service." e.Schwab has all the intelligent StreetSmart basic features, plus these two key differences:

❏ **E-mail-only trading and communications:** These accounts limit investors to E-mail contacts only—no other advice, no telephone contacts with Schwab brokers, and no visits to Schwab branch offices are permitted.

❏ **Low flat-fee discount commissions:** These are available on all equity stock trades.

---

e.SCHWAB: THE ULTIMATE IN DO-IT-YOURSELF INVESTING

"Designed to meet the specialized needs of the online investor, e.Schwab state-of-the-art investment software for Windows gives you a higher level of control and convenience.

"Now, computer expertise has another reward—significantly lower commissions. . . . e.Schwab gives you everything you need to manage your own investments online—plus a low commission rate on your stock trades. It's fast. Efficient. e.Schwab rewards you for your computer expertise with added savings. . . . Put e.Schwab to work for you today. It's one of the advantages of today's technology. A better way to trade for the truly independent investor."

SOURCE: Charles R. Schwab, "e.Schwab Online Investing" (January 1996).

Schwab should attract a good share of cyberspace investors for this kind of deal *because it already fits the way they regularly do business today.* Branch office visits are rare anyway in this new age of technology. Moreover, as the online manager of the American Association of Individual Investors has said, many of the new breed of cyberspace investors prefer not to be bothered by brokers. On the other hand, in addition to creating an environment conducive to economic freedom for the new NET*investor, here is yet another powerful element of the inexorable trend (the Wall Street cyberspace revolution) that is forcing a paradigm shift in the way investing is handled throughout the world.

SCHWAB'S WEBSITE: NAVIGATION INTO THE NEXT GENERATION

One of the first things that strikes you when landing on the Schwab Website on the Internet is its mission statement: "Helping Investors Help Themselves." You know these brokers are on your side and want to help you *do it yourself.* Schwab's evolving Website is rapidly becoming much more than an advertising billboard (which best describes so many other sites) along the information superhighway's main trunkline, the World Wide Web. With the addition of trading on the Web, Schwab has gone way beyond dial-up online services and offline software into true cyberspace investing.

SCHWAB'S ONESOURCE: CYBERSPACE SHOPPING MALL FOR MUTUAL FUNDS AND PROTOTYPE OF A NEW GLOBAL EXCHANGE

"If you own funds with a medley of sponsors, you will get buried in paperwork. A cure for this problem: Schwab OneSource. . . .

"With a single phone call you can transfer assets from any OneSource fund to any other at no cost. Minimum investment: $1,000 per fund (higher at some funds). OneSource investors receive a consolidated statement, useful at tax time. Schwab also provides cost-basis accounting to ease tax calculations. . . .

"Schwab OneSource's weakness is that some very good fund groups do not participate. Among them: Fidelity, T. Rowe Price, Scudder, and Vanguard. Schwab will allow you to buy funds from these families for a minimum of $39 per trade through its Mutual Fund Marketplace program."

SOURCE: Mary Beth Grover, "Charles Schwab: the Matchmaker," *Forbes* (August 28, 1995).

Since the new secure-transaction technologies are expected to arrive on the cyber-scene soon, we're expecting another major new product from Schwab, possibly an interactive version of StreetSmart directly accessed on Schwab's Internet Website. Meanwhile, you can already link into a lot of information about the Schwab services on its Website, including:

❏ **OneSource:** Schwab's answer to Fidelity's FundNetwork, with electronic access to almost 1,000 mutual funds as well as the Schwab mutual funds; a spin-off of Schwab's Mutual Funds Marketplace started in 1984.

❏ **Software Center:** Find out all about how to get StreetSmart, e.Schwab, and the FundMap personal financial planning software.

❏ **Mutual Fund Tools:** Select List, Basics on Mutual Fund Investing, Basics on Mutual Funds, Morningstar Mutual Fund Reports, Mutual Fund Selector.

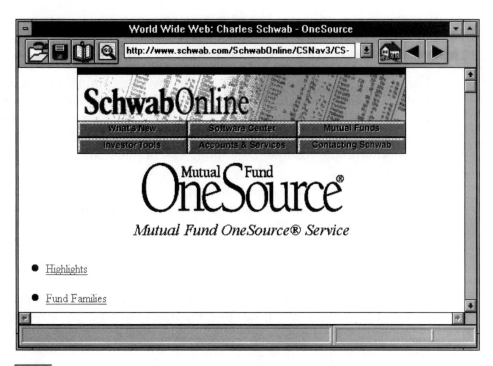

12.9 Mutual Fund OneSource: accessing top third-party funds.

❏ **Investment Advisory Services:** Professional advice on portfolio management.

❏ **Brokerage Accounts:** TeleBrokers, Schwab 500, and other electronic trading and management services.

❏ **Investment Library:** Order planning guides for retirement, brochures on investment basics, mutual funds, and prospectuses.

Schwab already delivers everything an investor needs through their online services, StreetSmart and e.Schwab. With these online services, all the content, news, analytics, planning, and other information essential to NET*investing are available to the cyberspace investor, on a dial-up basis if you are an account holder.

The next step in rounding out Schwab's arsenal of Internet weapons will be its Web-based, superpowered, interactive StreetSmart NET*navigator. And with that entry, Schwab's Website will finally fulfill its commitment to "helping investors help themselves," out there in cyberspace.

BOTTOM LINE: SCHWAB CONTINUES AS A PIONEER LEADING THE WALL STREET CYBERSPACE REVOLUTION

Charles Schwab is truly a visionary. He saw the coming impact of information technology and the power of Wall Street cyberspace to create a truly independent investor, as well as the enormous opportunities of a competitive fee structure for the brokerage world. And he's been transforming the competition, both discounters and the Wall Street establishment.

On top of that, he's an advertising genius. Names like "StreetSmart" and "OneSource" capture the essence of the particular product and red-flag the revolutionary trends on Wall Street, while tapping deep into the investor's emotional databank. After all, doesn't every investor want to become *street smart?* It's one step away from financial independence, isn't it?

Ultimately, the NET*investor's goal of financial independence is a battle fought one trade at a time. To do that, the investor still needs an electronic broker as a gateway to the exchanges. Just as you need a doctor to get a prescription and an attorney to appear in court, *even the totally independent* cyberspace investor trading from a cellular phone and a laptop in a Jeep on a Montana ranch still needs a broker—even if it's just a microswitch leased by an electronic discount broker at a telephone company.

Charles R. Schwab is on the cutting edge of this Wall Street cyberspace revolution. Since 1974 he's been *out there* shaking up old paradigms. Like Indiana Jones, he seems instinctively to know what's on the road ahead. Watch Schwab's strategic moves closely; they'll tell you what's next on the information superhighway—at least on the one being bulldozed through Wall Street from the West Coast.

PAWWS Financial Network

Security APL was founded in 1978 and is one of America's leading providers of portfolio analysis and accounting services for independent investment counselors and money managers. One of its roles as an IntraNet, an internal communications network for its corporate clients throughout the world, helping them with customers in their databases. Early on, Security APL saw the enormous opportunities of the World Wide Web.

PAWWS: ONE-STOP SHOPPING IN WALL STREET CYBERSPACE

"Once you've finished your research, check out the PAWWS Financial Network. The closest thing to one-stop shopping for financial services, PAWWS offers integrated portfolio accounting, research tools, and online trading. PAWWS is the Web storefront for a group of brokers and other providers that sell their services for a fee.

"For example, $8.95 a month gets you portfolio accounting that tracks dividends and interest received and updates the history of your transactions and holdings. Real-time quotes cost $50 a month. Access to research data on 2,680 companies is available from Ford Investor Services for between $10 and $20 a month. . . .

"In the end, deciding whether to log on to the World Wide Web or an online service comes down to your personality as an investor. If you like all your resources in one place, try America Online, CompuServe, or Prodigy. If you prefer to dig around and explore, check out the Web.

"*The good news is that no matter which way you go, you'll find cyberspace filled with useful information for investors. The bad news is that in the virtual world, just as in the one we're all used to, only you can make sense out of what you find.*"

SOURCE: Michael Himowitz, "Cyberspace: The Investor's New Edge," *Fortune* (December 25, 1995).

By early 1995 Security APL leaped ahead of the curve, out into cyberspace. Through its subsidiary, PAWWS Financial Network (Portfolio Accounting World Wide), Security APL became one of the first of the financial services companies to harness the power of this new Web technology. Since then its Website has become a media darling and an essential starting point for many curious investors and others surfing the Web. It generates millions of hits every month.

PORTFOLIO MANAGEMENT HITS WALL STREET CYBERSPACE

PAWWS became one of the early Websites for a couple of important reasons. It integrates in one Internet location several functions essential to investment decision making, including news, quotes, and portfolio management. In addition, it was the first to permit trading on the Internet.

Shortly after PAWWS opened its doors on the Web, Crain's *Chicago Business* noted that, "Stocks have been traded for several years through

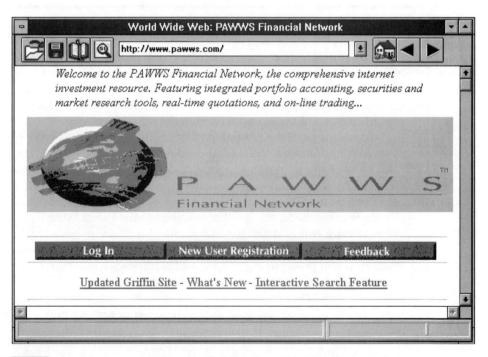

13.1 PAWWS Financial Network: Master Menu.

commercial services such as CompuServe and Prodigy. So, why haven't brokerages braved the Internet before?" For many in Wall Street cyberspace, the answer is obvious: "The Internet's loose structure is notoriously vulnerable to hackers, and trades can travel through a dozen unsecured computers between customer and broker."

Fortunately that didn't stop this pioneer. Security APL, PAWWS, and its brokerage partners took the risk, armed with the hottest new secured technology. They forged ahead in the brave new world of the Internet using Netscape's encryption software and led the way into the World Wide Web. The rest is part of the rapidly evolving history of the Internet.

"PAWWS BRINGS DO-IT-YOURSELF INVESTING TO THE INTERNET"

"Make your own personal investment decisions. Now you can handle every aspect of your investment planning by yourself, everything from research to entering trading orders.

"PAWWS' World Wide Web site now offers individuals the same tools professional money managers use to gather the information they need to make their investment decisions, to enter trades and to monitor the status of their investments—the first and only real time trading on the Internet55
."

SOURCE: "PAWWS Brings Do-It-Yourself Investing to the . . . Internet" (PAWWS

The PAWWS Financial Network's Website is developing into a rather substantial Internet "shopping mall" for the cyberspace investor. Here's what's now available at this one Website:

❑ **Quote Server:**   All the quotes you want for free on a 15-minute delay from the Security APL Quote Server. Plug in the ticker symbol and—bingo—you've got a full quote service for stocks and mutual funds.

❑ **Brokerage and Trading Partners:**   PAWWS has some excellent brokerage partners on this Website. These are respected names with solid backgrounds, providing the cyberspace investor with discount trading online and on the Internet, including:

—Howe Barnes Investments' Net Investor

—Jack White & Company's PATH On-Line

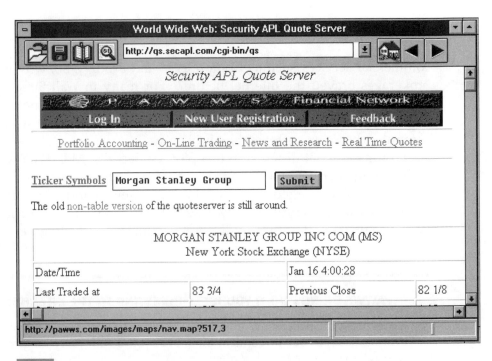

13.2 Security APL Quote Server in action.

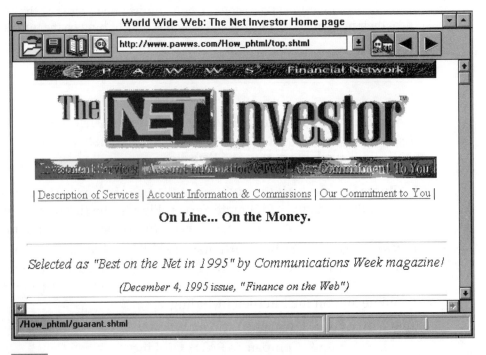

13.3 Howe Barnes Investments: NET Investor on the Web.

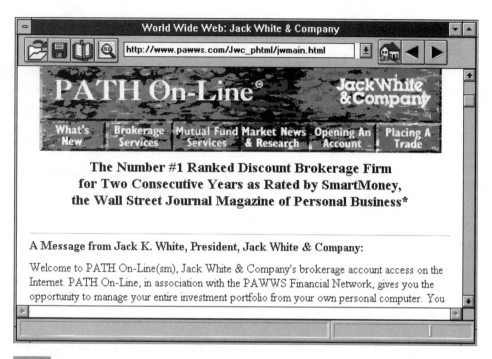

13.4 PATH On-Line: Internet access to Jack White & Co.

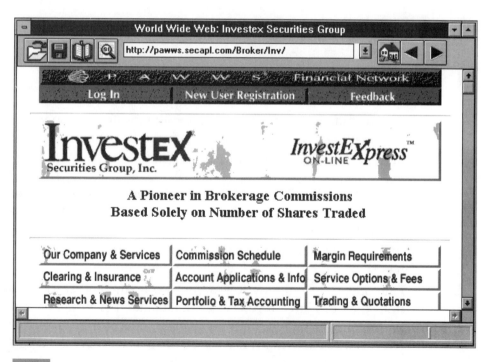

13.5 Investex Securities Group for online brokerage.

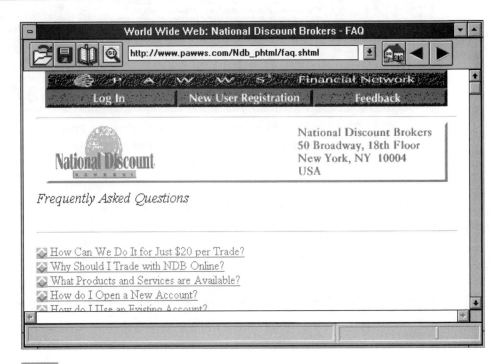

13.6 National Discount Brokers: basic trading FAQs.

—Investex Securities Group

—National Discount Brokers

Also included are some trading order demonstrations so you can actually experience how a cyberspace trade works with these cyber-brokers.

❑ **Market News and Analysis:** Direct from DTN Wall Street, this covers the securities markets, the same news available to DTN's cable and satellite subscribers. Markets covered include stocks, company earnings, derivatives, and government issues. Also available are S&P Stock Guide, Downing Technical Analysis reports, Fortucast Financial Timer, IPO Preview, and other respected financial advisory newsletters and reports. All solid financial research organizations.

❑ **Fundamental Company Research:** Company and stock information from the Ford Investor Services databanks. Ford offers a number of proprietary valuation analyses that are effective in projecting future returns. Its database covers 2,680 companies with over 90 data items on each company.

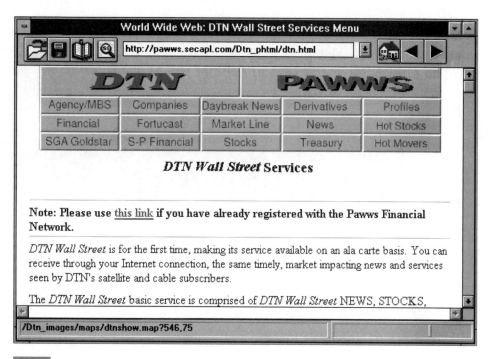

13.7 DTN Wall Street: news, analysis, and market reports.

❏ **Market Outlook:** Griffin Financial Services provides detailed commentaries on stocks, commodities, currencies, bonds, and interest rates.

❏ **Company and Stock Reports:** Griffin Financial also provides several series of reports on specific companies, earnings analysis, new issues, and trade alerts.

❏ **Portfolio Management and Accounting:** The basic portfolio management service that has made Security APL a success for many years is now on the Internet.

While many of these services are available only on a subscription basis, they're all right here in one location in cyberspace. Depending on your needs, it may be necessary to subscribe separately to the fee-based reports and services of Ford, DTN, and Security APL, each of which has its own pricing structure.

PAWWS and the Security APL organization must be doing something right. They're popular and they operate with integrity, offering a solid

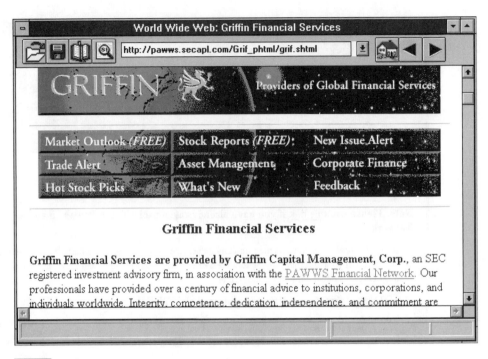

13.8   Griffin Capital Management for financial advice.

array of content for the cyberspace investor. Their Website attracts millions on the Internet every month, and, more important, they have well over 100,000 paying subscribers. Every new and seasoned investing veteran should check them out. PAWWS just might be the best NET*navigator for your needs in Wall Street cyberspace.

HIGH-TECH SOLUTIONS FOR PROS AND INDIVIDUAL INVESTORS

"Seems like just when you thought you've conquered your technology problems, the next thing you know all bets are off.

"At Security APL, we help keep portfolio management firms at the very top of the technology chart. No more bad investments, no more sluggish downtime and no worrying about real-time versus sometime-in-the-future. Only the finest, latest technology to keep you and your company as current as today's news."

SOURCE: Security APL 1995 advertisement.

Security APL's Website is another excellent example of the trend toward transferring sophisticated investment technologies into the mass market, *thus further leveling the playing field for individual investors.*

Tools previously reserved for the high-end professionals and institutional investors are now available to any cyberspace investor at a reasonable price. And this competition is guaranteed to bring in more top firms with more tools for the "little guy" in cyberspace investing—and to create further rounds of competitive price reductions on everything the cyber-investor needs: quotes, analytics, news, company and fund reports, and so on.

Security APL, PAWWS, Howe Barnes, and their partners deserve high honors for playing such a major part in creating this exciting moment in the history of Wall Street, rapidly transforming it into a global cyberspace marketplace in which power is being transferred to the new independent investor.

Aufhauser's WealthWEB

Aufhauser's WealthWEB is another of the early pioneers venturing into Wall Street cyberspace, ahead of the pack. You really have to admire these discount brokerage houses for seeing the enormous potential of the Internet, well in advance of the crowd, and taking action.

The American brokerage firm, K. Aufhauser & Company, began in 1981, and today, along with other well-known discount brokers, Accu-Trade, AmeriTrade, Ceres, and Amerivest, is a subsidiary of the TransTerra holding company. The firm Aufhauser has a strong tradition and history dating back to 1870 and the European Bankhaus H. Aufhauser.

Aufhauser prides itself on its reputation for reliability and service, which, along with one of the best discount structures available, has been an important factor in building a loyal customer base for the company. In fact,

---

THE SMART MONEY IS BETTING ON AUFHAUSER AND LOMBARD

"Unlike full-service firms, where you have one broker who watches over your account, discounters generally route your call to the first available person. . . . Who's manning the phones? To get a handle on that question, we queried the firms. . . .

"Two small firms share the prize in this category: K. Aufhauser and Lombard. They train even their brokers licensed by the National Association of Securities Dealers for one and a half and three months, respectively, before they are allowed to handle orders, and then insist brokers take one or two weeks of refresher courses each year. Finally, both firms send out customer evaluations to 100 percent of their customers."

SOURCE: Peggy Kalb, "Best & Worst of Discount Brokers: Broker Expertise," *Smart Money* (July 1995).

---

for one low flat fee annually, a frequent trader with an Aufhauser account has *unlimited* access to the exchanges. And that's hard to beat even for the deepest of deep discounters.

In one of its full-page advertisements in *Barron's* promoting its Website, Aufhauser emphasized the speed and low cost of trading with it, as well as the fact that WealthWEB was the most *informative* trading route, loaded with facts and reports for the individual investor. *Fortune, BusinessWeek,* and *The Wall Street Journal* have all reported quite favorably on WealthWEB and the value of Aufhauser's online services. Each one offered a solid endorsement.

WEALTHWEB: POWER TOOL FOR "SELF-DIRECTED INVESTORS"

The very name "WealthWEB" has a strong marketing punch for a Web location, grabbing you like the name "StreetSmart" does. This Website really is first class. Aufhauser was a true pioneer, like Schwab, early on developing its own Website based on the strong conviction that this was the wave of the future. And the gamble has paid off: The prediction turned into profits, for Aufhauser as well as its Internet customers.

ARE MERRILL LYNCH TRADES WORTH FOUR TIMES AUFHAUSER'S?

"Buying or selling 100 shares of Microsoft, for instance, can cost either as little as $24.99 in commissions at a deep-discount broker like K. Aufhauser & Co. or more than $100 at full-service brokers such as Merrill Lynch or PaineWebber. . . . The bottom line? If you don't want or use all the extras, there's no reason to pay for them."

SOURCE: Hui-yong Yu, "Schemers and Scalpers: A Look at Broker's Commissions and Fees," *Bloomberg* Magazine (November 1995).

Aufhauser emphasizes that, "Our WealthWEB service lets a customer access the same information their broker sees. They can price their portfolio, and based on the information they see, trade accordingly. All Aufhauser accounts are *self-directed—the customer will make all of their own investment decisions,* and communicate their wishes to us, via WealthWEB. The customer will also be able to access research materials for selected stocks via WealthWEB, to aid the decision making process."

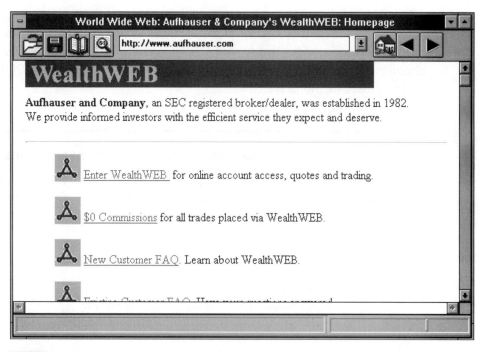

14.1 Aufhauser's WealthWEB for independent investors.

A WINNER WITH THE INDEPENDENT CYBERSPACE INVESTOR

As we see so often with the marketing thrust of these discount brokers, Aufhauser is clearly targeting *independent investors who are making their own decisions without relying on the advice of brokers.* In the new Wall Street cyberspace, we see many examples of this power shifting from the institutional investor to the individual investor. And nowhere is this more obvious than in the way the discount brokers have been marketing their online and Internet services in the past decade.

Like skilled Samurai warriors, the discount brokers are flowing with the tide of the battle, while using the strength of the enemy to their own competitive advantage. They know all too well that the power has also shifted from the broker to the individual investor, who relies on:

❐ Information available from remote electronic databases in cyberspace

❐ Individual decision-making tools as independent investors

As a result, a new breed of cyber-brokers like Aufhauser are giving the new breed of investors *exactly what they want: independent decision making in financial cyberspace.* So today, over 20 percent of Aufhauser's customers already use WealthWEB. It's easy to estimate that, by the year 2000, that will be closer to 100 percent.

"HOW THE RICH GET RICHER," IN AUFHAUSER'S CYBERSPACE

"Aufhauser WealthWEB. The *fastest*, most *informative*, and the *lowest* cost PC trading route available. Plus all the other resources Aufhauser has to offer . . . special WealthWEB features:

- *365 days a year*
- *Continuously updated quotes*
- *800 number or Internet access*
- *Buy, sell, replace orders*
- *Integrated with Touch-Tone telephone system*
- *Automatic confirmation immediately on execution*
- *Extensive securities database*
- *Search news by symbol or subject*
- *Equity research*
- *40 recommended issues*
- *Interest on short sales*
- *International bonds*
- *Account protected to $25 million*
- *Full cash management: free checks and MasterCard*

Never have so many, received so much, for so little."

SOURCE: "How the Rich Get Richer," K. Aufhauser & Company advertisement, *Barron's* (June 26, 1995).

WealthWEB is another fine example of the new breed of Internet navigators now available to the new cyberspace investor. Of course, you'll need an account at Aufhauser & Company to fully use the service. However, you need an account somewhere, and Aufhauser is certainly a solid, respected choice. After all, investing is serious business, as opposed to mere Websurfing, which can quickly become time-consuming, tedious, and unprofitable.

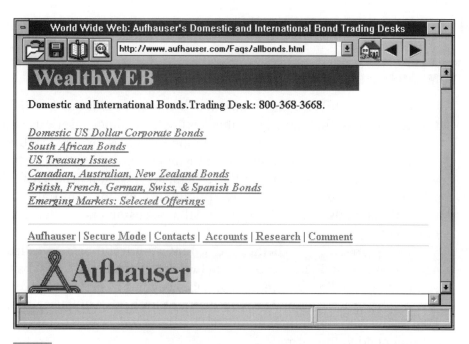

14.2 WealthWEB: Bond trading—domestic and international.

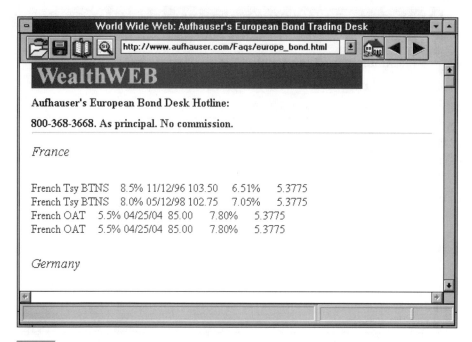

14.3 Aufhauser's European bond desk hotline.

BOTTOM LINE: WEALTHWEB IS A FIRST-CLASS NET*NAVIGATOR

Of course, WealthWEB also makes a substantial amount of free information available to the public, whether you're a customer, a serious investor exploring the Internet for new information resources, or just a Websurfing sightseer. And that is certainly one of the main reasons Aufhauser has created such a first-class tool for the cyberspace investor. The WealthWEB Website is indeed a wealth of free public information—and also a great marketing tool that's attracting potential new customers, as well as a curious press.

Soon *every broker*—whether a discounter by trade or a so-called full-service broker—will be a cyberspace broker, complete with a Website and some level of online information services beyond basic trading. Yet, even when cyberspace is crowded with discount brokers, Aufhauser's Wealth-WEB is likely to continue standing out in the crowd as a first-class resource for independent investors.

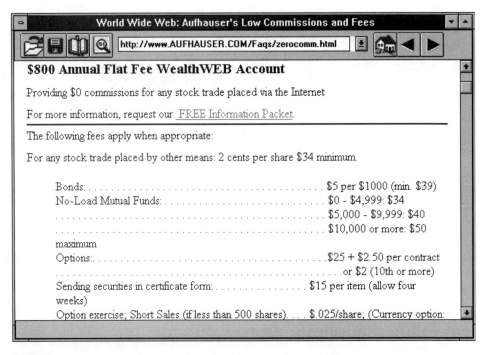

14.4 Aufhauser & Company: discount commissions and fees.

Bottom line: Backed by the Aufhauser brokerage and technical team, WealthWEB works as a top-flight navigator for the self-confident cyberspace investor. Stop by, check it out, and compare WealthWEB with the other NET*navigators that seem to fit your needs and style of investing. Discover which of these navigators works best for you—and get down to the core business of working toward your goal of financial independence.

Lombard Internet Securities Trading

Lombard Internet Securities Trading is a division of Thomas F. White & Company, a San Francisco brokerage firm. In 1995 *Smart Money* magazine awarded Lombard its top prize for discount brokers, along with Aufhauser. And that award was given before Lombard went public with its Internet Website and trading system. In 1996 Lombard received a similar award from *Barron's*.

The Lombard brokerage team went live with its new Internet system after spending a substantial budget and months fine-tuning the technology.

FORECAST: 75 PERCENT OF ALL TRADING WILL BE IN CYBERSPACE

"It took a dozen developers a year to produce, but moments after Lombard Institutional Brokerage's new Internet trading interface went live the firm was convinced it had a hit on its hands.

" 'We turned it on, and 10 seconds after that a trade went through,' recalled John MacIlwaine, director of technology. . . .

" 'We telephoned the guy and he said, "I'm totally comfortable with this. The interface is the best I've seen and I'm happy with it." '

"MacIlwaine said he watched with glee as new customers from around the world signed up for Internet trade order service. At the end of its one-week debut, Internet orders accounted for 8% of total volume. . . .

"Lombard executives believe that the Internet and other new media will eventually account for 75% of the firm's business."

SOURCE: Peggy Kalb, "San Francisco Brokerage Creates Own Internet Order System," *Securities Industry Daily* (October 9, 1995).

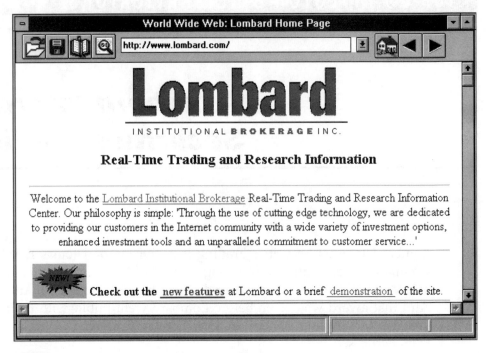

15.1 Lombard: real-time trading and research information.

Then, a few days after ramping up on the Web in September, the Netscape Communications Corporation issued a press release acknowledging a flaw in its browser's encryption method. This forced Lombard—and every other commercial user of the Netscape browser—into a holding pattern.

To its credit, Lombard took its new system offline while Netscape's problem was being corrected—a decision that won the respect of its customers and the Internet community worldwide. Today, Lombard is confident that all trades are executed in a totally secure transactions environment.

TODAY'S INTERNET TRADING IS TOTALLY SECURE

Shortly after Lombard was back online and on the Net with its system, its success was convincing enough to justify rapid expansion to a new level with an upgrade in the format and content of its Lombard Internet Securities Trading (LIST).

Here's what Lombard now provides for the cyberspace investor:

❑ **Lombard Investment Center:**   For active Lombard accounts, a gateway to place orders to buy and sell stocks, options, and mutual funds.

❑ **Real-time Quote Server:**   Track your favorite stocks. Enter symbols and get real-time data on stocks, options, bonds, and funds.

❑ **Chart and Graph Server:**   Investors can chart real-time, delayed, and historic data on demand. Plot every tick for selected intervals, including intraday, daily, monthly, and yearly. The system covers 7,000 stocks, 61,000 options, and more.

❑ **Portfolio Management:**   Monitor your Lombard account in real time, including trading activities, open accounts, executions, holdings, dividends, and balances. Also includes account performance tools customized to your portfolio.

❑ **Public Access Center:**   Before you open an account you can still access information with Lombard. Free 15-minute delayed quotes as

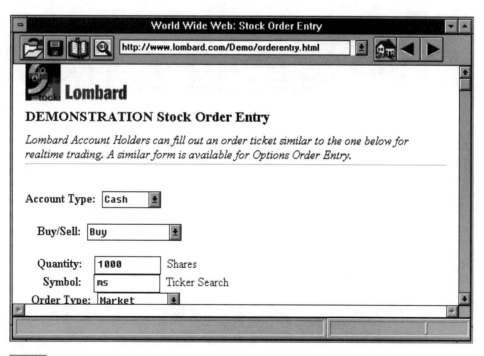

15.2 Lombard's demonstration stock order entry.

15.3 Unlimited real-time quote server.

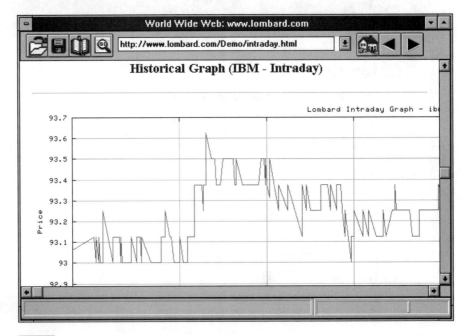

15.4 Sample intraday chart for IBM Corporation.

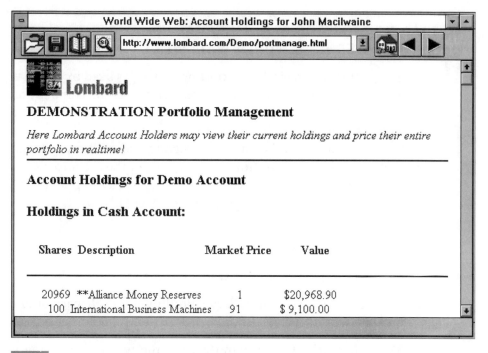

15.5 Lombard's portfolio management.

well as graphs and links to other investing tools. Tap into data on 7,000 companies.

❏ **Transaction Security:** Lombard's Internet transactions have several layers of encryption and authentication to prevent data leaking from their firewalls. They are convinced this technology creates the necessary protection, in spite of the fears that the ultraconservative Wall Street institutions claim are restraining them from online trading. Lombard's Internet clients vote in favor of its Internet trading system with each live trade.

Lombard Internet Security Trading is a solid-working NET*navigator for the new generation of cyberspace investors. You will need an account to enjoy the full benefits of the Website. However, the Lombard Public Access Center is open to everyone with a modem and an Internet provider. Take the Lombard NET*navigator out for a test run around the financial world.

TWO TRADING STRATEGIES: ONLINE/DIAL-UP
VERSUS THE INTERNET'S WORLD WIDE WEB

Note the difference in electronic trading strategies used by the various brokerage firms reviewed throughout this section. As the competition among brokers unfolds, their approaches to the cyberspace market show differing perceptions of the individual investor.

Following are several primary marketing and delivery strategies. Keep in mind that this field is so fluid that any one of these competitors is likely to switch gears and either move to or—as is in fact happening in several cases—add another delivery system to its arsenal.

❐ **Internet:**   Lombard, Aufhauser, Schwab, and PAWWS.

❐ **Dial-up Connections:**   Schwab, PCFN, and Quick & Reilly.

❐ **Online Services:**   CompuServe, Prodigy, and AOL each offer discount brokers, with PCFN, E*Trade, Quick & Reilly, and other brokers.

❐ **Multiple Options:**   AccuTrade gives the investor pick among seven systems, including standard fax and telephone, palmtops, online dial-up service, and the Internet. In this uncertain field, letting the client decide may be the best strategy.

At this point, you should also consider the key strategic differences between brokers using Reuters Money Network and those developing their own proprietary systems. Earlier we noted that Reuters is willing to take a back seat to brokers like Quick & Reilly, Schwab, and PCFN and others being added this year. Its subsidiary, Reuters Money Network, will customize the Money Network software package as an operating system for a particular broker, without emphasizing the Reuters brand name. This low-key strategy has been consistent with Reuters' approach to its market expansion.

By using a customized, private-label version of Reuters Money Network, a discount broker presents the identity and public image of a *full-service cyberspace broker,* rather than just another cyber-broker handling trades only. These systems are dial-up services, and Reuters still provides first-class technical support of each separate system.

NET*NAVIGATORS: PROPRIETARY SYSTEMS OR PRIVATE LABELS?

In contrast to brokers using customized, private-label versions of Reuters Money Network, brokers like Lombard and Aufhauser have taken a different strategy, electing instead to develop their own proprietary NET*navigators. The two strategies are also based on quite different perceptions of market trends. Reuters Money Network is currently a dial-up service only, although that is changing this year, while the proprietary systems are mainly Internet-based.

Also noteworthy is Reuters' strategic decision to remain in the background. This decision is in marked contrast to another key competitor in the NET*navigational field, the Quicken Investor Insight, which is offered by many commercial banks. Intuit maintains its brand-identity, rather than playing a behind-the-scenes role of developing operating systems for a particular bank to operate as its own.

Aside from the fact that the Lombard system targets the *Internet* investor—as opposed to the *dial-up* strategies of Schwab, PCFN, and Quick & Reilly—Lombard is also convinced that this strategy gives it firmer control of its destiny, *plus* genuine marketing distinction compared to being a Reuters groupie.

In fact, the cyberspace financial information market is so enormous that there'll be more than enough room for all of them, just as there is for Honda, Kia, Rolls Royce, and Saturn in the automotive world. AccuTrade probably has the best strategy: Give the customer a lot of alternatives to choose from.

On top of all this, Reuters is now planning an Internet Web alternative as well. Initially each of the services will be unbundled, including quotes, company research, and trading. That way, an investor will be able to pick and choose (and pay) cafeteria-style. And eventually, we definitely anticipate the option of using the complete Reuters Money Network package on the Internet, much as Reuters Instinet now exists as a private exchange or IntraNet—*then any and every broker could hook into Reuters Money Network, as a full-service cyberspace broker.*

BOTTOM LINE: LOMBARD IS "YOUR SEAT ON THE EXCHANGE"

No matter what happens in this highly competitive field of cyber-brokerage, whatever Reuters, or Schwab, or Intuit, or any other power player does to capture new accounts, the cyberspace investors themselves are controlling the shots, and they are moving onto the Web.

The fact is that brokers like Lombard and others were *out there* on the Internet pioneering for the *individual* investor light-years ahead of the traditional Wall Street firms. For that, Lombard deserves a 21-gun salute and a solid recommendation as an investor's NET*navigator. Lombard Internet Securities Trading is "your seat on the exchange," the new global cyberspace exchange. You'll find them on the Net 24 hours a day.

The Next Generation of Power Players

Online Commercial Banking:
The Quicken Alliance

Welcome to the wonderful world of online banking, also known as home banking, another hot new gateway to the world of electronic commerce and securities trading. That's right, your *commercial bank* could soon become your primary NET∗navigator, your gateway to Wall Street cyberspace, even your discount broker, as well as paying your bills and everything else promised by the online bankers—all wrapped into a one-stop/total-service system for all your financial needs.

INFORMATION REVOLUTION IS TRANSFORMING BANKING

"Representative Richard Baker, who chairs a key banking subcommittee, believes a telecommunications revolution will soon transform banking, whether Congress likes it or not. . . . Banking is coming to the Internet, he says, and companies like Microsoft and Intuit will figure out a way to electronically capture deposits, make loans, and sell securities."

SOURCE: James Glassman, "Goodbye, Glass-Steagall," *Worth* (January 1996).

Absurd? Not really. With tools such as Quicken, with their enormous technological budgets, and without the Glass-Steagall Act separating commercial banks and the investment firms, the banks are likely to get even more aggressive in pursuing the cyberspace investors as primary customers—even handling all their trading and managing their portfolios. You can expect the commercial banks to end-run the big retail brokerage

16.1 Security First Network Bank: first publicly held cyberspace bank.

COMMERCIAL BANKS ENTERING CYBERSPACE AT WARP SPEED

"Last October, Eric Walter, a 27-year-old single guy from Atlanta, became the first customer of Security First Network Bank, the only bank born and raised exclusively on the Internet. He is what you might consider an anomaly: a happy banking customer. Why? He can now look up his balances, transfer funds between accounts, download real-time account statements, and pay his bills electronically—24-hours a day, seven days a week.

"While online services and private dial-up solutions have been met with overall success, the Internet may turn out the winner. Already, IBM counts more than 300 institutions on the Web; the company also estimates the number of bank Internet sites about doubles every 60 days. At that rate, more than 5,000 banks will have a Web presence by mid-1996."

SOURCE: Chris Costanzo, "Easy Money," *NetGuide* (February 1996).

institutions, just as the discount brokers have been doing online in recent years. And the banks are using some familiar, proven online tools—such as Quicken, Microsoft's Money, and Kiplinger's Simply Money—as their inroad to the cyberspace investor.

Practically speaking, Glass-Steagall is no obstacle; it's a paper tiger. It has been de facto repealed by the World Wide Web's new global marketplace. So the commercial banks are now making a massive assault into financial cyberspace. With access to virtually every investor through checking accounts, the banking industry is clearly in a perfect position to compete with the brokerage industry and every other vendor of NET*investing navigators.

16.2 Online banking is here: Wells Fargo master directory.

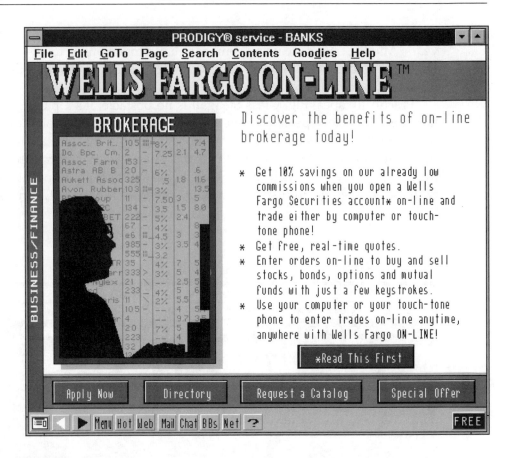

16.3   Wells Fargo Bank: competing as an online discount broker.

ONLINE BANKING REVOLUTION: QUICKEN VERSUS MICROSOFT

No wonder Microsoft desperately wanted to acquire Intuit. With 70 percent of the market for personal financial software, Intuit's Quicken could eventually dominate the whole online banking field, like Netscape currently dominates the Web browser field. Microsoft's own personal finance package, Money, was a distant second, along with Kiplinger's Simply Money.

For many customers, Quicken is the gateway of choice into their bank. Online banking customers using it have expanded Quicken's 70 percent market share to over 10 million users, and it's destined to grow even more rapidly as the commercial banks encourage customers to convert to online banking.

QUICKEN: TOTAL FINANCIAL PLANNING PLUS ONLINE BANKING

"To take your banking on-line, start by choosing the software that is best for you. Both Intuit and Microsoft are rolling out souped up editions of their software. . . . Of the pair, Quicken is the more comprehensive, with special features that help you anticipate your tax bill and select mutual funds, among other things. . . . With electronic banking, your branch need never be further than your keyboard."

SOURCE: Peter Keating, "Good News: Cheap Electronic Banking Is Coming Soon," *Money* (September 1995).

The banks are also gearing up for massive growth in online banking, while the customer avoids going to branches. One online banking expert projects an increase of more than 500 percent in online banking in the next year, to more than six million users. And like most estimates here, this is probably too conservative. In 1996, new encryption software will open the

---

ONLINE BANKING . . . ROCKET FUEL FOR THE REVOLUTION!

"The banking industry is moving quickly to develop its own electronic banking plans in an attempt to control the new wave of customer relationships. . . . Currently, about 800,000 customers bank by computer, barely 1% of the entire U.S. banking customer base . . .

"But all that's beginning to change as interest in electronic banking and electronic commerce grows. 'We projected that [online banking] would be 6% by 1997, but it seems to be growing at a faster rate than that now,' says Mayer [Andrew Mayer, senior manager of financial services, Ernst & Young].

"*If that growth continues, electronic banking has the potential to become the first great wave in the evolution of electronic commerce . . . The possibility that home banking could drive the information technology market is one reason banks, software companies, credit-card companies, online services, and others are racing to establish and lock in electronic commerce connections . . .*

"At one time, Gates called banks 'dinosaurs.' Today, U.S. banks are determined to use technology to prove that their time has not passed, and that they will be the ones to forge the path into a new era of electronic commerce."

SOURCE: Joseph Panettieri and John Swenson, "Bank Shot," *Information Week* (December 18, 1995).

floodgates to online commercial transactions of all kinds—not just online banking and online shopping, but online stock trading, online mutual fund investing, and online everything.

The commercial banking industry is hungry for a piece of the action. In fact, banks may want *all* the action. Last year Bill Gates referred to the banks as "dinosaurs." That upset the banking world, triggering a Jurassic Park–like revival of this dormant giant. When the Justice Department blocked Microsoft's merger with Intuit, a consortium of 23 of America's largest banks joined with Intuit to offer Quicken to their customers. Banks became aggressive and the online banking revolution was on!

Of course, Microsoft will continue to be a major, aggressive contender in this wide-open field. It already has a deal with Smith Barney, the second-largest retail broker, which is offering Microsoft's Money as well as Quicken Deluxe. In addition, many of the banks continue developing their own proprietary online banking software products.

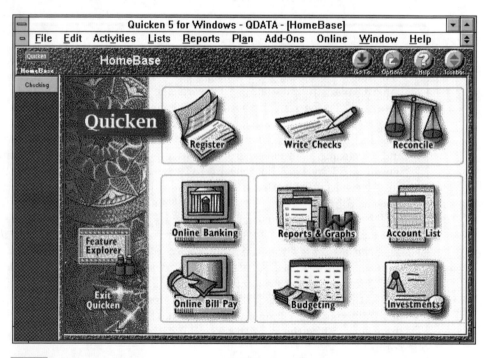

16.4 Quicken Deluxe for personal financial planning: Master Menu.

THE REVOLUTION PITS BANKS AGAINST CYBER-BROKERS

The emerging bottom line is patently clear: Online banking is rapidly becoming a crucial force in the Wall Street cyberspace revolution and the whole securities industry. The reason is simple. Online banking is a natural gateway to investors' finances—their money, their accounts, and their portfolios.

And this *banking* gateway is also an obvious location for an *investing* gateway, which is just what Quicken is doing. The commercial banks know this and are going after this online opportunity with a vengeance. That's where Intuit and Quicken have a huge advantage.

With the online banking revolution paralleling the Wall Street cyberspace revolution—and poised for takeoff—it doesn't take a genius to see that any one of the IS power hitters can easily target enormous technological and economic resources in the emerging *financial cyberspace.* Several players are already in the game big time—Fidelity Investments, Dow Jones News/Retrieval, and Reuters Money Network, for example.

However, any one of these companies is likely to lead the way in the new Wall Street cyberspace. Moreover, another major alternative on the list could emerge rapidly and unexpectedly, surprising every competitor. For example, Charles Schwab & Company's budget wasn't even in the *Information Week* list. Yet Schwab's StreetSmart and other products have been a major factor in advancing the information revolution more than the Establishment firms. Schwab's IS budget is over $130 million with a staff of 700. In other words, size alone is rarely the key to technological leadership. So it is hard to detect where the real competitors are on this unpredictable battlefield.

Along the way, the giants are likely to gobble up more and more of the smaller financial information companies as they expand their power bases—as Microsoft attempted with Intuit. This field is changing so rapidly, the giants can't grow from within fast enough.

Reuters created Reuters Money Network through acquisition. Dow Jones/Telerate and Knight-Ridder's Dialog came about in similar fashion. So you can bet there'll be many more mergers and acquisitions as the online banking and Wall Street cyberspace revolutions heat up. The big institutions are going to have to make up for lost ground fast. Investors should expect a lot of exciting action and also some excellent trading opportunities.

POWER HITTERS IN THE FINANCIAL INFORMATION GAME

Information Week magazine, the leading magazine in the field, publishes an annual directory of the 500 biggest spenders on "information systems" (IS), the corporate buzzword for computer professionals and their information technology game.

As you might expect, AT&T leads all companies, with $4 billion of its total 1994 revenues of $75 billion on information systems. This year it finally created an online service, the AT&T Business Network, shortly after writing off an investment of $50 million in Interchange, the service it acquired from Ziff-Davis.

Budgets of hundreds of millions of dollars are common even for the "smaller" giants. For example, Fidelity Funds manages almost a half trillion dollars in assets, spends $350 million on information systems.

That's right—Fidelity spends more on information technology than the total funds under management by many individual mutual funds.

Here is a sampler of the Information Systems power of the giants of financial cyberspace—the banks, funds, brokers, and data/news services:

Institution	IS Budget (millions)	IS Employees
Citibank	$1,547	9,000
Merrill Lynch	$925	3,400
BankAmerica	$808	3,719
J. P. Morgan & Co.	$680	3,200
Chase Manhattan	$600	2,300
Dean Witter	$387	1,032
Fidelity Funds	$350	1,400
PaineWebber	$261	837
Bear Sterns	$227	763
Time Warner	$101	577
Dun & Bradstreet	$67	382
Knight-Ridder	$35	207
McGraw-Hill	$38	215
Dow Jones	$29	500

SOURCE: "The Biggest & Best Corporate Users of Information Technology," IW 500 Annual Directory Issue, *Information Week* (September 18, 1995).

QUICKEN: TOTAL SUPPORT SYSTEMS FOR FINANCIAL INDEPENDENCE

Intuit has been helping individuals, families, and businesses with financial planning software since Quicken was first released in 1984. As a testament to the contribution this special software has made in automating the financial planning field, *Inc.* magazine jointly awarded Intuit founders, Scott Cook and Tom Proulx, the *Inc.* Entrepreneur of the Year Award a couple of years ago.

According to Cook, "Our goal is to lift the burden of financial hassles from individuals and small businesses. Our products organize users' financial matters and help them understand their personal financial trends with the click of a mouse. We're working toward the day when users will receive and act on all financial matters electronically—without paper transactions."

Today Intuit is achieving this goal by creating "electronic links," as they call them, between the major players in the financial market: banks, customers, and companies that bill customers, and more recently, the securities markets. In the past year or so since the Microsoft merger was called off, Intuit has made several major moves that are clearly positioning it as a more desirable tool for the cyberspace investor. These various software packages include:

❏ **Quicken Deluxe/financial software:** This provides online banking, bill paying, check writing, budgeting, financial statements, an Internet connection, mutual funds, portfolio tracking, and more.

❏ **StreetSmart/Reuters Money Network:** Cyberspace investors already using Quicken can also seamlessly interface with two more of the hottest NET*investing navigational tools on the market—Schwab's StreetSmart and Reuters Money Network—thus linking into the Quicken investing process everything essential for NET*investing, including brokerage.

❏ **Personal Financial Planner software:** This is one of the simplest and best personal financial planners designed to help investors plan for successful retirements. This planning software ranks with the best and is definitely in a class with Schwab's FundMap and Reuters WealthBuilder.

❏ **Your Mutual Fund Selector:** Using the comprehensive Morningstar mutual funds databank, you can screen through 4,400 mutual funds to build a successful investment portfolio.

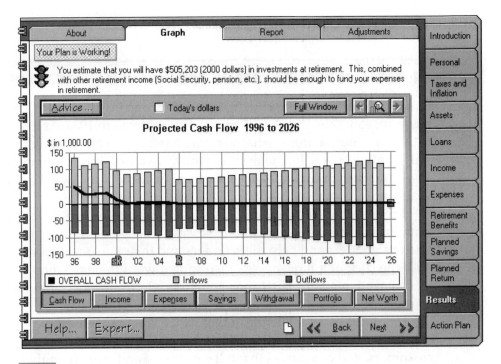

16.5 Quicken: cash flow projections through retirement.

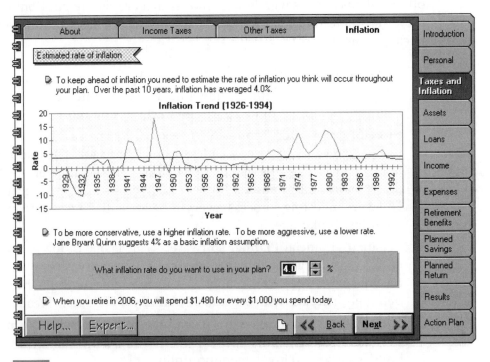

16.6 Quicken: historic inflation trends for comparison.

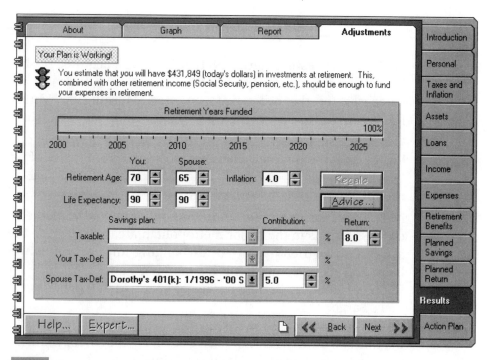

16.7 Quicken: adjusting data inputs to test alternatives.

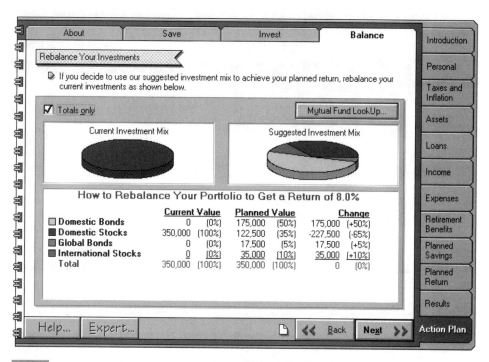

16.8 Quicken: recommended strategies for portfolio balancing.

❏ **NETworth Investor Internet Network:**   Intuit acquired the NETworth Website, a major cyberspace location for two of the most important databases for the cyberspace investor: Morningstar Mutual Fund Research and Disclosure Incorporated for company research.

❏ **Quicken Financial Network on the Web:**   Intuit recently opened for business on the Internet. Plans are to expand from topics of interest to Quicken users to a broad range of personal financial planning resources, for investors and others.

❏ **Network of major banks:**   Intuit is now partnered with over 20 financial institutions in the major metropolitan areas, to provide them with a secure, user-friendly way of exchanging information between each bank and its customers. Intuit's banking partners include American Express and Smith Barney, as well as Chase Manhattan, Chemical, and Wells Fargo.

In addition, Intuit has an extensive collection of other products and services for individuals, families, and small businesses. Taken as a whole, all

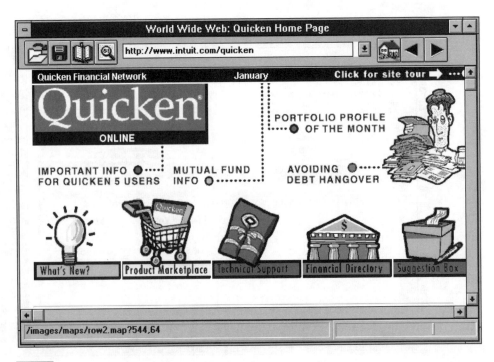

16.9   Quicken Financial Network on the World Wide Web.

of these electronic tools are part of the integrated system just waiting to support the cyberspace investor in achieving their goals of financial independence, economic freedom, and self-sufficiency. Intuit's system includes:

❏ **QuickBooks Pro** accounting software for small businesses, entrepreneurs, telecommuters, and self-confident independent cyberspace investors

❏ **PocketQuicken** financial management for mobile users operating from autos and airports, from laptops, modems, and cellular phones

❏ **Family Lawyer,** which helps you protect your family and your assets

❏ **Expend*Able,*** which helps track business and personal expenses when you are on the run

❏ **TurboTax** software for the NET*investor's annual filings

And there's a lot more to come from Intuit, a company that obviously understands the depth and needs of their customers. Intuit also offers a *Parent's Guide to Money,* to help young investors plan for the future while raising children through school and beyond to retirement.

THE COMPETITION FOR PERSONAL FINANCE SOFTWARE

"Tracking Investments. One of Quicken's strengths is that it can help the most basic user, but also can grow with you as you get more adept at handling your finances.

"While Quicken may dominate the personal finance software market, it isn't the only player in the game. Other titles have made a name for themselves with easy-to-use and unique features."

❏ *Managing Your Money:*   MECA Software's product is the closest competitor with a 15 percent marketshare (800-288-6322).
❏ *Microsoft's Money:*   Has almost 5 percent of the market according to Dataquest (800-426-9400).
❏ *Kiplinger's Simply Money:*   Also has 5 percent of the market (800-225-5225).
❏ *Quicken's Software:*   Contact Intuit (800-964-1040).

SOURCE: "Working at Home: Quicken, the Quick Fix for Your Finances," *PC Novice* (February 1996).

Intuit is one of the most impressive organizations in the cyberspace financial information world today. It has been a part of the computer revolution since the early 1980s with the first generation of PCs. Even its name fits its mission: The company has an *intuitive* understanding of the financial needs of today's independent-minded computer user, as well as the ability to develop products that work well with the kind of *intuitive* thinking used by computer users. And nowhere is this more apparent than in Intuit's new services for the cyberspace investor.

INVESTOR INSIGHT: QUICKEN'S POWERFUL NEW NET*NAVIGATOR

Since the early days of the personal computer, the Quicken products have been the software of choice for computerized personal financial management. Now Intuit is also targeting the computerized investor, the independent investor, and the cyberspace investor with an impressive collection of databases. With its dominance in the market, marketing power with the banking consortium, and long-term track record of qual-

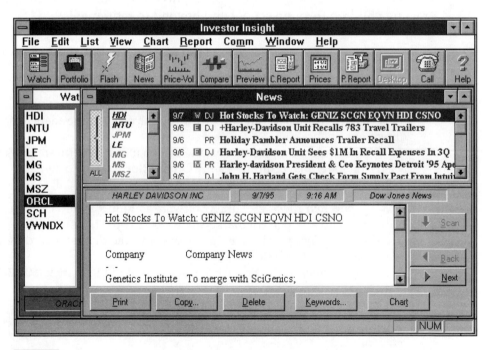

16.10   Investor Insight: specific company news.

ity products, Intuit is virtually guaranteed to emerge in a dominant position as an investor's Net*navigator.

Last year Intuit created Investor Insight as an add-on to the Quicken Deluxe package and with it came a wealth of investor resources:

- ❏ **Market news and analysis:** Dow Jones News/Retrieval and *The Wall Street Journal.*
- ❏ **Analysts' recommendations:** With ratings, market, and industry trends.
- ❏ **Company research reports:** From the best, Standard & Poor's.
- ❏ **Business press releases:** The Business Wire and PR Newswire.
- ❏ **Current stock quotes:** From the major national exchanges.
- ❏ **Price/volume charts:** QuickZoom tracks market-moving news and stocks.
- ❏ **Major indexes:** Dow Jones Industrials, S&P 500, AMEX, and NASDAQ.

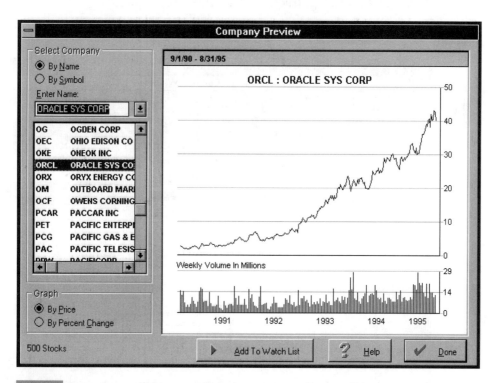

16.11 Company preview: fundamentals from the S&P database.

❏ **Historical information:**   Download five years of data on stocks and funds.

❏ **Mutual fund lookup:**   Tap into the Morningstar research database.

❏ **Analytical tools:**   Set up your criteria, screen and analyze charts.

❏ **Portfolio tracking:**   On-demand data updates of your favorite stocks.

❏ **Internet Web access:**   Through a Netscape browser to other data-bases.

Intuit has a solid NET*navigational system for the cyberspace investor that is potentially competitive with anything else on the market.

   In addition, as part of the basic Quicken Deluxe program, there is a host of other powerful tools all integrated into one operating platform and controlled by the click of the mouse, all of which are available to support an investor's unique decision-making processes and smooth the way to financial independence:

❏ **Online banking,** tracking accounts, credit cards

❏ **Financial planning,** cash-flow analysis, budgeting

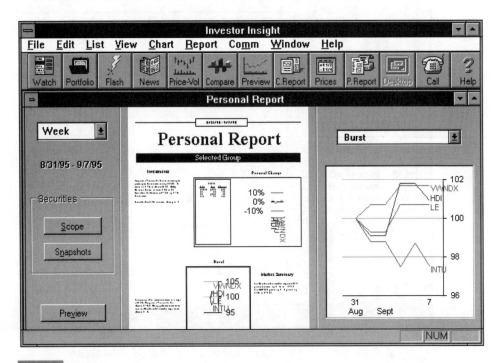

16.12 Printed reports for sectors and companies.

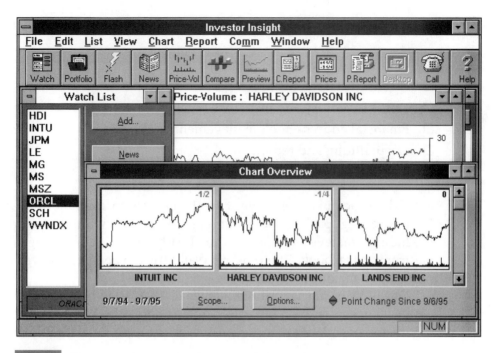

16.13 Chart overview: comparing several alternatives.

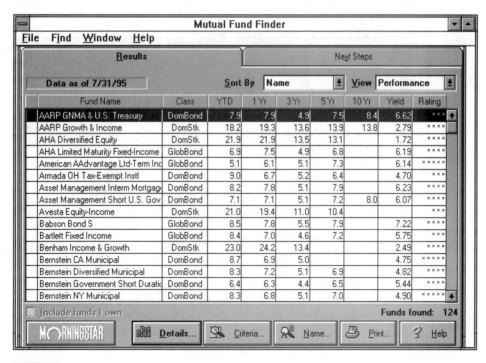

16.14 Quicken Mutual Fund Finder: screening funds.

❑ **Online bill paying** and loan tracking

❑ **Financial statements** and reports

❑ **Home inventory** and insurance review

❑ **Financial address book** management

❑ **Tax planning** and reports

❑ **Basic printing** of checks, labels, envelopes, reports

Cyberspace investors owe it to themselves to examine the Quicken NET*investing package and compare it closely with the alternatives (including whatever system they're already using). It's no longer just an electronic checkbook. The old-line Wall Street cyberspace power players now have a major new competitor.

One of its primary attributes is the fact that, as an investor's NET*navigator, Quicken is evolving into a totally integrated system that brings together in one place a comprehensive, easy-to-use set of tools to make not

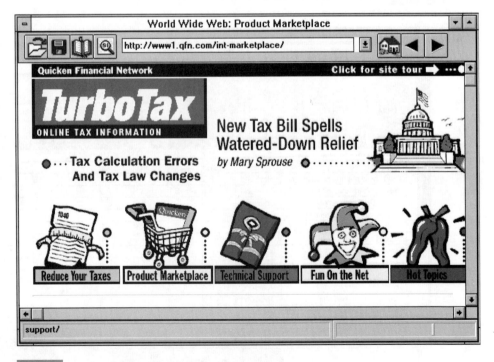

16.15   Intuit's TurboTax: online tax information.

QUICKEN'S NEW INVESTOR INSIGHT: "THE TOTAL PACKAGE"
AFTER A 30-DAY TRIAL OFFER. . . . YOU'LL NEVER GO BACK

"Tucked away in the Quicken Deluxe Version 5 is a powerful and time-saving module called Investor Insight. Intuit will let you sample it for free for a month, but investors beware: Investor Insight is highly addictive.

"It features stock quotes, Dow Jones News, and company information from Standard & Poor's. You'll be amazed after spending a month familiarizing yourself with Investor Insight's fluid sorting, charting, and reporting. Factor in Quicken's formidable portfolio management tools, and you won't likely go back to whatever you were using before."

SOURCE: Wayne Harris, "The Total Package," *Individual Investor* (March 1996).

---

only investing but the overall financial planning and budgeting process quick and painless.

QUICKEN: THE SAME INFORMATION AS YOUR BROKER

Intuit's new Investor Insight package is indeed impressive. Intuit's stated goal is to give the cyberspace investor the "same information Wall Street professionals use," and the company is delivering on its promise. This powerhouse of resources, databases, content providers, and financial services is now included with the basic Quicken Deluxe package.

Moreover, Investor's Insight is definitely competitive with other packages for a monthly fee of $10. Given the quality of the package, it's a real bargain. Investor Insight is powerful and easy to use. Just as Quicken has become the personal finance system of choice, Investor Insight could very possibly become one of the NET*navigators of choice for cyberspace investors.

It's obvious why a consortium of over 20 major money center banks would agree on Quicken as the primary operating system of choice for their next round of aggressive expansion in online banking. With all due respect to Microsoft, Quicken has little competition; it's the people's choice.

Less obvious, but in our opinion much more significant, is the common front—the bank alliance synergistically coupled with the power of the new Quicken Investor Insight package that's designed to give the banks

QUICKEN'S NET*NAVIGATOR GETS HIGH MARKS

"Quicken, the world's best-selling financial software, just got swifter. In its latest upgrade . . . the program moves well beyond its familiar turf of checkbook balancing and budget planning to become a creditable piece of investment software. To pull it off, Intuit, Quicken's manufacturer, has taken a leap into cyberspace—and developed a new on-line portfolio tracker for Quicken users, *Investor Insight* [and it's] not the only reason Quicken customers might consider upgrading. The new package also adds access to on-line banking, an Internet browser and a number of bells and whistles to its core banking and cash-flow monitors.

"*Investor Insight* . . . competes both with commercial on-line services like CompuServe, America Online and Prodigy, and full-fledged on-line investment databases like Reuters Money Network. . . . In my opinion, *Investor Insight* leads the pack in one basic task, keeping you up to date on your stock and fund investments.

"None of the competition matches *Investor Insight*'s facility at organizing the data into useful formats.

"One thing the Quicken package doesn't do particularly well is screen securities. The new program allows you to sift through a mutual fund database for funds that match certain criteria, but to get beyond that—or to screen stocks at all—you need more robust on-line investing programs, such as Reuters Money Network or Telescan. . . . And you can't use Quicken to trade stocks or funds—at least not yet."

SOURCE: Peter Keating, "Now Quicken Minds Your Portfolio Too," *Money* (December 1995).

a major, *direct* inroad to the cyberspace investor market, by providing the online banking customer an easy-to-use NET*navigator for building and managing an investment portfolio.

BOTTOM LINE: QUICKEN AND COMMERCIAL BANKS MAKING A STRATEGIC ASSAULT ON THE SECURITIES INDUSTRY

Intuit's Quicken is like a fighter pilot, a cocky maverick—one of the best of the best entering the top-gun school, where the flight trainers have call signs like Reuters, CompuServe, Dow Jones, and Schwab. Except Quicken comes in with the ground support troops of the money center bank divisions.

Very soon the Quicken squadron will be armed with the high-tech fire-power to target trades and score direct market hits for investors' portfolios. Quicken and the banks are like a deadly stealth fighter swooping into your Wall Street cyber-airspace, too, with smart bombs targeting the securities industry after a long reconnaissance mission conducted by the commercial banks.

Quicken *and the entire commercial banking industry* are in a perfect position for a quick and successful assault. In fact, both the full-service brokers and the discount brokers may be in trouble, with Quicken and the banks now on the attack.

Armed with Investor Insight, Quicken is a powerful force to be reckoned with—definitely a major contender to be one of the top-10 NET*investing navigators within the foreseeable future.

Corporate America:
DRIPs and No-Load Stocks

The editor of *MoneyPaper*, a newsletter dedicated to this field, is right on the money: DRIPs *are* "Wall Street's Best-Kept Secret." These company-sponsored dividend reinvestment plans (DRIPs), which also allow optional cash investments, may even be ahead of mutual funds as the perfect investment.

THE BIG SECRET WALL STREET AND THE SEC WON'T TALK ABOUT:
BUYING STOCKS DIRECT WITHOUT A BROKER

"Companies can't advertise these direct purchase programs. (The SEC forbids it.) Brokers hate them. These no-load stocks give you a revolutionary way to buy your first share and every share of stock without a broker's commission or mutual fund management fees."

SOURCE: Ad for Charles Carlson, *No-Load Stocks* (McGraw-Hill, 1995).

Also see "The Monthly Guide for the Self-Reliant Investor," in *Money-Paper*, a highly regarded newsletter that focuses on public companies offering direct stock purchase plans (*http://www.moneypaper.com*).

DRIPs are perfect for cyberspace investors—no brokers, no commissions, no funds, no exchanges. Just you and the corporation. No wonder the SEC restricts advertising here, and the brokers aren't going to mention it (although some are coming around). And no wonder this tool and the trend in general fits perfectly into the new Wall Street cyberspace, where the individual investor runs the show and calls the shots.

> **DO-IT-YOURSELF INVESTORS DISCOVER NO-LOAD STOCKS**
>
> "The evolution of no-load stocks has been greatly impacted by the growth of the do-it-yourself investor. . . . Individuals are more sophisticated now about stocks and investing than they've been in the history of the stock market. . . .
>
> "With computers and inexpensive software and databases, even individuals with modest means have the ability to store, analyze, and manipulate huge amounts of data to improve investment decision making. . . .
>
> "The end result is a more informed investor who wants to call his or her own investment shots while saving money in the process."
>
> SOURCE: Charles Carlson, *No-Load Stocks* (McGraw-Hill, 1995).

Wall Street cyberspace is rapidly becoming a single global securities market, which transcends all boundaries between the segments. Microsoft's Bill Gates was right: The information superhighway is eliminating distance—and increasing the power of the individual.

NO-LOAD STOCKS: NO BROKERS AND NO COMMISSIONS

As Wall Street transforms, old ways of operating are being destroyed and new ones replace them. Using all the new high-tech tools, the NET*investor is now able to pick and choose among many options including:

- ❏ No-frills discount brokerage while the investors do their own research
- ❏ Large networks of mutual funds for no-load performance funds
- ❏ Direct, no-commission, no-load investments in Corporate America

It should be obvious by now that in Wall Street cyberspace the individual investor is gaining vast new power. We saw it first in the explosive growth of the discount brokerage business, where independent investors who don't need any advice from a full-service broker are now turning to the basic electronic tools of the discount brokers—after doing the research and analysis on their computers.

Today the new NET*investor can go one giant step farther. Now independent investors can bypass *not just the traditional full-service retail brokers, but all brokers, including the discount brokers—and the exchanges.* Obviously,

---

HOW TO BUY NO-LOAD STOCKS: AS SIMPLE AS NO-LOAD FUNDS

Starting a portfolio of DRIPs is almost too simple. You become a shareholder in a company. Then the company reinvests your dividends while you regularly purchase additional shares and watch your portfolio grow. Charles Carlson tells you how simple it is to start this kind of investment program:

"The process of buying no-load stocks is the same as buying no-load mutual funds:

"**Call for information** . . . application form and a plan prospectus . . .

"**Fill out the application form** . . . read the prospectus and fill out the application form . . .

"**Cut a check.** To make your initial investment, make out a check to the company or its transfer agent . . .

"**Mail it to the company.** Put your check and the application form in an envelope and return it to the company . . .

"**And that's it!**

"In most cases, your initial investment will automatically enroll you in the company's dividend reinvestment plan and/or stock purchase plan."

SOURCE: Charles Carlson, *No-Load Stocks* (McGraw-Hill, 1995).

You might also check out Carlson's other books, *Buying Stocks Without A Broker,* and *Free Lunch on Wall Street.*

---

investing directly in the corporation is one more tool supporting the NET*investor's goals of financial independence and economic freedom. In other words, direct investing is another potent example of the growing power of the individual investor. Over 1,000 major American companies invite investors to buy securities directly from the company.

This trend is guaranteed to explode as more investors, armed with the new computer and telecommunications technologies, move into the world of financial cyberspace. And conversely, the needs of independent investors will be synergistically reinforced as the companies also continue moving into cyberspace. Companies are likely to seize this golden opportunity and more aggressively go after this new breed of cyberspace investor.

It's unlikely that no-load stocks will become a serious threat to the NYSE. They recently spent $125 million upgrading the NYSE information systems; they were having trouble handling heavy trading volumes. Now, however, they're even ready for another 1987-type meltdown. And besides, you may need the NYSE if you ever have to sell the stock.

The AMEX and other futures-oriented exchanges are also retooling their information systems with more than a side glance at the exploding cyberspace expansion. Yet, direct buying in Corporate America with DRIPs is definitely one solid alternative for the independent investor in Wall Street cyberspace.

CYBERSPACE: A NEW ROAD TO BUYING CORPORATE AMERICA

There are several excellent cyberspace resources for the NET*investor who fully appreciates the enormous potential of building an investment portfolio of America's top-performing companies. You can reach these valuable electronic resources in financial cyberspace both online and on the Internet's Web. Here are some of the best resources to date:

❑ *DRIP Investor* **Newsletter and DRIP Directory:**   Charles Carlson is the CFA and editor of two highly respected financial advisory newsletters, *DRIP Investor* and *Dow Theory Forecasts*. Both are first class. In addition to the newsletters, Carlson has written a book on DRIPs, called *No-Load Stocks* (McGraw-Hill, 1995). Full of how-to basics, Carlson's book may even inspire you to build your entire investment portfolio through direct purchase and reinvestment, avoiding brokers completely. Carlson has also published a directory of DRIPs, plus a few other books on investing.

❑ *MoneyPaper* **Newsletter and DRIP Directory:**   Here is another great newsletter for the cyberspace investor. Check out their Website for a quick education on dividend reinvestment plans and direct stock purchasing. Notice the subheading on the logo: "for the Self-Reliant Investor." For just $50 you get an annual subscription to the print newsletter plus the complete *MoneyPaper* guide to companies with DRIPs. *MoneyPaper* also supplies the investor with a valuable, time-saving rating system to help pinpoint the best DRIPs, providing solid facts and educational materials. It's a real bargain. Read it, then go directly to their Websites for more details, prospectuses, and financials—more data than you'll need for a thorough analysis.

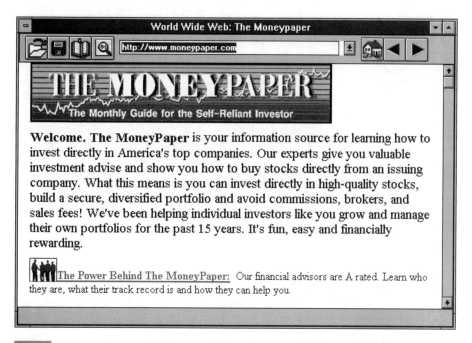

17.1 *MoneyPaper* for the "self-reliant investor."

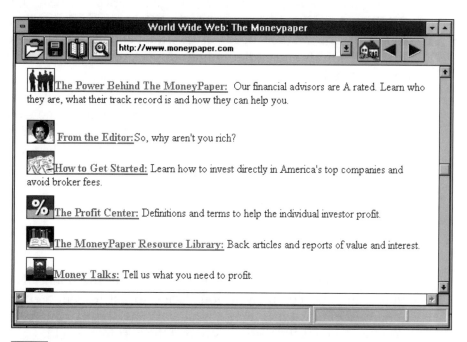

17.2 Master menu for the *MoneyPaper* Website.

CYBER-GATEWAYS TO INVESTING IN CORPORATE AMERICA

American Association of Individual Investors	800-428-2244
DRIP Investor (newsletter/directory)	219-931-6480
MoneyPaper (newsletter/directory)	800-388-9993
National Association of Investors Corp.	810-583-6242
S&P's *Directory of DRIPs*	800-852-1641
Carnegie-Mellon University DRIPs Website	*jdg@cs.cmu.edu*

You can jump to all of these resources from either *http://www.yahoo.com* or *http://www.cpcug.org/user/invest*, two of the best Web directories for investors. Reach AAII through America Online until its new Website is active.

☐ **American Association of Individual Investors:** The AAII posts a complete list of public companies offering DRIPs to investors. All of them are available as part of the AOL fee. The whole cost of AOL is justified just to get AAII materials on DRIPs online. In addition, there are several educational articles on DRIPs.

Right now AAII is accessible through America Online and the Web. AAII has 175,000 members and is definitely one of the major sources for all the information needs of the independent investor, including print periodicals and books, online support, offline software, and local meetings and seminars.

☐ **National Association of Investors Corporation:** NAIC is another organization with 300,000 individual investor members. For some time NAIC has been helping investors get into DRIPs as a way of building solid, long-term investment portfolios. Check out its Website as well as the many services, a newsletter, books, offline analytic software, and local investment clubs.

☐ **Standard & Poor's *Directory of Dividend Reinvestment Plans:*** Everyone's heard of the Standard & Poor's 500 market index. This McGraw-Hill company is unquestionably one of the most respected names in the field of financial information (note that they also publish Carlson's books). If you want reliable data on the financial markets, you're in good company if you decide to get it from S&P, which is where the professional money managers have been going for decades. And the *S&P DRIP Directory* is one of the best in the field.

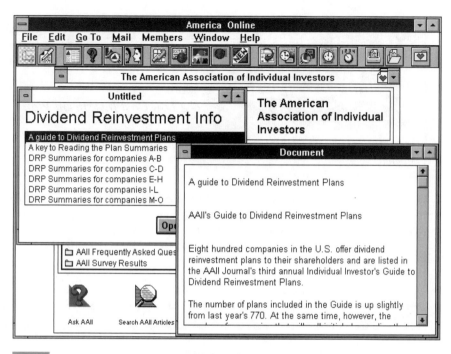

17.3 DRIPs: American Association of Individual Investors.

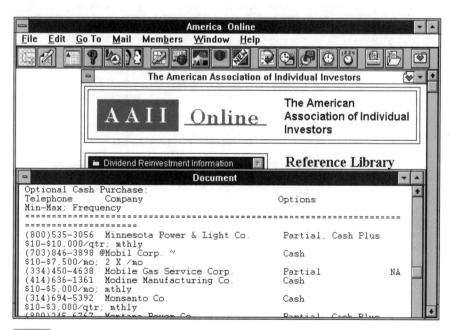

17.4 AAII: page from DRIP directory at America Online.

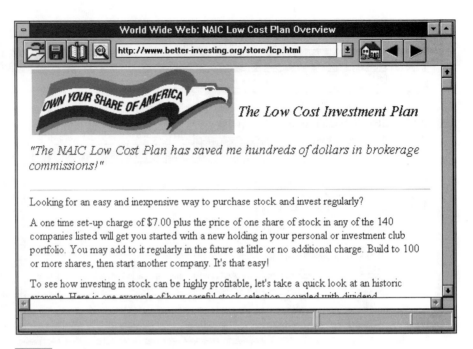

http://www.better-investing.org/store/lcp.html

OWN YOUR SHARE OF AMERICA

The Low Cost Investment Plan

"The NAIC Low Cost Plan has saved me hundreds of dollars in brokerage commissions!"

Looking for an easy and inexpensive way to purchase stock and invest regularly?

A one time set-up charge of $7.00 plus the price of one share of stock in any of the 140 companies listed will get you started with a new holding in your personal or investment club portfolio. You may add to it regularly in the future at little or no additional charge. Build to 100 or more shares, then start another company. It's that easy!

To see how investing in stock can be highly profitable, let's take a quick look at an historic example. Here is one example of how careful stock selection, coupled with dividend

17.5 NAIC's DRIP plan for small investors.

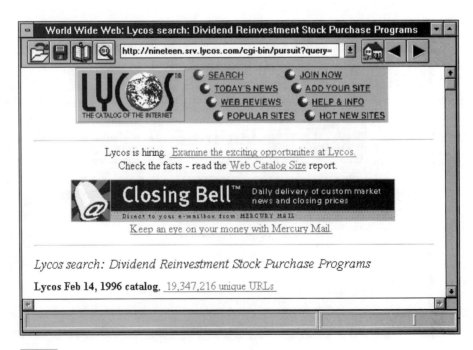

http://nineteen.srv.lycos.com/cgi-bin/pursuit?query=

LYCOS
THE CATALOG OF THE INTERNET

- SEARCH
- TODAY'S NEWS
- WEB REVIEWS
- POPULAR SITES
- JOIN NOW
- ADD YOUR SITE
- HELP & INFO
- HOT NEW SITES

Lycos is hiring. Examine the exciting opportunities at Lycos.
Check the facts - read the Web Catalog Size report.

Closing Bell™ Daily delivery of custom market news and closing prices
Direct to your e-mailbox from MERCURY MAIL
Keep an eye on your money with Mercury Mail.

Lycos search: Dividend Reinvestment Stock Purchase Programs

Lycos Feb 14, 1996 catalog, 19,347,216 unique URLs

17.6 Lycos search engine: tracking DRIP resources.

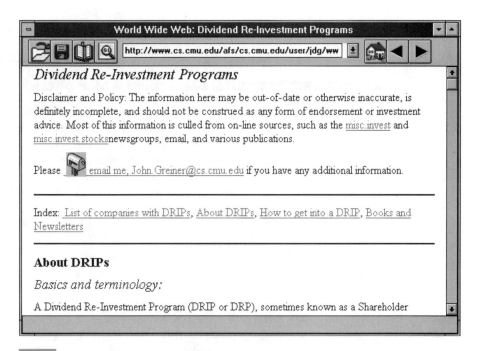

17.7 DRIP Website at Carnegie-Mellon University.

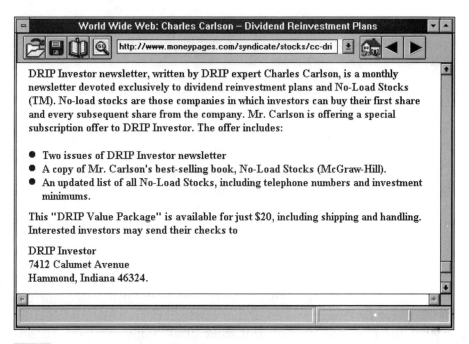

17.8 DRIP Investor Newsletter: Website information.

A MODEL DRIP PORTFOLIO: S&P'S "DREAM DRIP DOZEN"

"DRPs themselves are soaring. . . . With so many to choose from now, it's possible to build a thoroughly diversified portfolio of such stocks—creating, as Vita Nelson [*MoneyPaper* editor] points out, 'your own mutual fund.' Actually it's better than a fund because there are no annual expenses: Using Morningstar Inc.'s estimate of an average 1.4 percent expense ratio for a diversified stock fund, you can save at least $1,400 a year on a six-figure hoard.

"Scholars disagree about the number of different stocks you need for a well-diversified portfolio, but Joseph Tigue, editor of Standard & Poor's *Directory of Dividend Reinvestment Plans*, says even a dozen can do the job, if they balance each other properly. 'As a long-term investor, you want different types of companies in different industries, so the portfolio itself will do well in all the different economic and interest-rate cycles.'

"Tigue and other experts say the key to success with DRPs is reinvesting dividends and making new contributions on a regular basis. Over time, that can help you build real wealth."

SOURCE: Timothy Middleton, "The Best Commission-Free Stocks," *Your Money* (January 1996).

Tigue's "Dream DRIP Dozen" included: Abbott, Chubb, Coke, CPC, Du Pont, Exxon, GE, Gillette, Johnson & Johnson, Motorola, Old Kent Financial, and V.F. Corp.

❑ **Web directories and search tools:** An enterprising grad student at Carnegie-Mellon University also maintains a free Website on DRIPs—everything from a list of companies and the mechanics of how to buy in to information on the topic and key books and newsletters. The Webmaster, John Greiner, should be complimented for his initiative and for maintaining this growing information bank that is exposing *the best-kept secret in Wall Street cyberspace.*

You should also check out Yahoo and other master Web directories, and use Internet search engines, such as Lycos at Carnegie-Mellon, to track down other cyberspace resources on DRIPs. Recognize, however, that any one of these searches can lead to very incomplete databases. In the end, one of the print directories—*MoneyPaper, DRIP Investor,* or Standard & Poor's, or the AAII directory at AOL—may be more complete than the Web directories and search engines.

MODEL PORTFOLIOS FOR INVESTING IN CORPORATE AMERICA

Before you invest a lot of time and money in superpowered, high-tech NET*investing software and cyberspace hookups, do yourself a favor and read a couple of the new books on DRIPs that are now on the market. In particular, take special note of the suggested Model DRIP Portfolios in Charles Carlson's first book, *How to Buy Stocks Without a Broker.* In chapter seven he includes several: Starter, Golden Years, Bluest-of-the-Blue-Chips, Conservative Growth, and other model portfolios. In his second book, *No-Load Stocks,* Carlson adds several model portfolios, including Stock Index, Sector, and portfolios for the Financially Challenged.

NO-LOAD STOCKS = LOWER STRESS + MORE PEACE OF MIND

"Many people get burned as investors. They buy at the top and sell at the bottom. That's because emotions play such a large part in investment decisions. To overcome the effect of emotions, we suggest investors establish a widely diversified portfolio and buy shares on a dollar cost averaging basis.

"This will accomplish two things. When some stocks are lagging, others will be gaining. That way you won't feel so much pressure to sell the laggards. . . . And dollar-cost averaging imposes discipline on your investing. You decide how many dollars you intend to invest on an investment schedule you set up in advance."

SOURCE: Vita Nelson (ed.), *Guide to Dividend Reinvestment Plans* (Temper of The Times Communications, 1995).

Add this book to your library along with one of Carlson's.

Before you adopt a lifelong DRIP-only portfolio strategy, take heed of Carlson's warnings about diversification concerns, slower buy/sell executions, and record-keeping headaches. Generally, however, the pluses of DRIPs outweigh the minuses.

Is a DRIP strategy for you? All independent investors must answer that question for themselves. The answer is highly personal, a function of risk tolerance and other factors that would be addressed in personal financial planning, asset allocation research, and the like. But at least check out this simple alternative, along with the other NET*navigators identified here. Do some homework and find out for yourself.

Consider this: If you do get into a DRIP strategy, your Internet, cyberspace, and high-tech needs may be less taxing, and you may be able to enjoy prosperity and the things you really value in your life with more peace of mind than the day-traders who must obsessively follow every tick on the tape. Then you can go Web surfing and experience the rare beauty of the Net's art museums, literature, games, humor, and entertainment. And have some fun.

BOTTOM LINE: DRIPS ARE THE PERFECT TOOL FOR CYBERSPACE INVESTORS

Every independent investor cruising cyberspace for opportunities, wondering whether to buy this or that newfangled, high-tech, online NET*investing system, is strongly urged to spend a little time reviewing the DRIP strategic alternative first.

DO-IT-YOURSELF INVESTORS AND AGGRESSIVE COMPANIES ARE MAKING DRIPS POPULAR

"DRPs have grown increasingly popular with individual investors.... The SEC has made it much easier and far less costly for a company to offer a direct purchase program . . . and many more will be seen before long as companies jump on the bandwagon.... For the long-term investor, DRPs offer a convenient and low-cost way to build a stock portfolio.... Brokers go broke. A big attraction of DRPs is the commission you save on brokers."

SOURCE: Joe Tigue (ed.), "DRPs More Popular Than Ever," *Dividend Reinvestment Plans* (Standard & Poor's, 1995).

DRIPs may be the perfect solution for all your needs as a cyber-investor. Forget all the other fancy, supercharged mega-databases with high-tech analytics. If the real key is a matter of committing to regular savings, then why not just send your checks to buy some of America's top-performing companies?

Of course, you'll need some basic tools for fundamental analysis to help you pick the right companies, including the ones discussed here. So use AAII at AOL until you find something else. You'll even be able to ask

Charles Carlson specific questions at AAII's regular discussion forum on DRIPs, as well as have all the other valuable AOL resources on stocks, companies, mutual funds, and much more. But most important, you will eventually develop the confidence of a self-reliant investor who trusts his or her own gut instincts when making the final decision of picking solid companies for the long haul.

Telecommunications: AT&T Business Network

The AT&T Business Network has the potential to become the ultimate Internet service. After all, here's a company with over $50 billion in annual revenues (even after the latest split-up). AT&T is so big it was able to take its $50-million investment in the Interchange Network (an online service acquired from Ziff-Davis publishing company) and write it off while bringing the AT&T Business Network online.

WEB POWER: AT&T, APPLE, AND MICROSOFT PUSHED OFFLINE

"The retirement of Interchange, AT&T's proprietary online publishing and information delivery platform, marked the latest casualty of the non-Web-based information services.

"AT&T's decision last month to abandon Interchange in favor of a Web-based service by year's end follows Apple's recent announcement that its e-World service would migrate to the Web, and Microsoft's surprisingly quick decision, just three months after launching The Microsoft Network, to recast its online service as an 'Internet online service.'

"AT&T, which purchased Interchange from Ziff-Davis Publishing Co. for an estimated $50 million in December 1994, had tried in recent months to redo its service. . . .

"By the middle of the year, AT&T Business Network will move to the Web. . . . AT&T is planning to use both a subscriber model and an advertising model to generate revenue."

SOURCE: Ellis Booker, "AT&T Abandons Interchange for the Web," *Web Week* (February 1996).

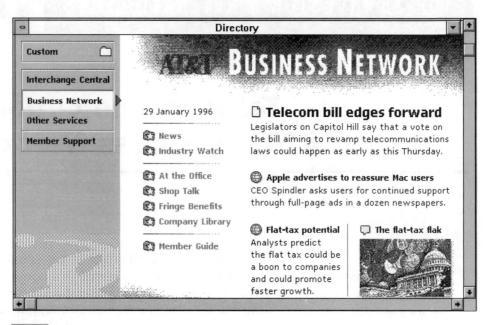

18.1   AT&T Business Network: master directory.

Fortunately, it looks like AT&T has learned something from Interchange. It's on a comeback trail with the AT&T Business Network and looking much stronger than before.

Journalists are fond of taking potshots at the big firms, convinced that they're aging and slow. That may be true, but AT&T reminds me of old George Foreman—you better stay out of the ring with this boxer.

The first thought that came to mind when AT&T announced the AT&T Business Network was, "Hey, they own the railroad; it's a winner. Don't bet against it." And the new telecommunications law is likely to reinforce its position. AT&T can't lose—or, at least, the cyberspace investor won't lose as this competition heats up.

There's an even bigger reason to believe AT&T Business Network will become one of the major NET*navigators for cyberspace investors: *content.* Like the railroads of the past, AT&T can easily hook up an incredibly powerful inventory of informational resources along its tracks and sidings.

THE ULTIMATE YELLOW PAGES ARE NOW IN CYBERSPACE

Before taking a peek at the extensive inventory already evolving on the new online AT&T Business Network, imagine the potential of this gargantuan system. It could ultimately become the new universal yellow pages. Think of what it'd be like if your telephone book's yellow pages were actually on a CD-ROM, or better, if it took up a few megs on your hard drive, *plus* each entry actually included a *direct link* (online dial-up or Internet connection) to the respective company in the yellow pages. Even better, imagine having *nothing* at your workstation—no CD-ROM that might be outdated, no bytes on your hard drive. Instead, you just dial your friendly electronic operator via your modem—you just reach out and search someone through the AT&T global yellow pages. In addition, you get all the Website links you need to Wall Street cyberspace.

Suddenly, your yellow pages come alive: They are no longer just raw information, but direct and interactive communication links. It's enough to

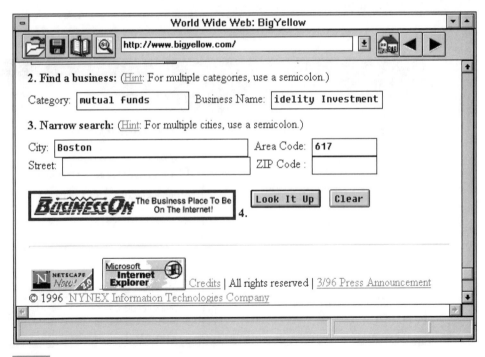

18.2 NYNEX: Big Yellow directory to business world.

make you buy more phone company stock, even if you don't subscribe to the AT&T Business Network. Frankly, this new network could be the beginning of something really big, assuming AT&T learned its lessons well with the Interchange writeoff.

THE WORLD'S BIGGEST BUSINESS AND FINANCIAL NETWORK

Let's take an overview look at the 2,500 key information resources already linked along the sidings of this cyber-railroad (notice that many of these appear regularly on virtually every key investor's NET*navigator):

❐   **Financial and Business News**
    Dow Jones Business Information Systems
    Reuters NewMedia real-time business news
    Knight-Ridder Financial News from CNNfn
    PC Quote stock quote server

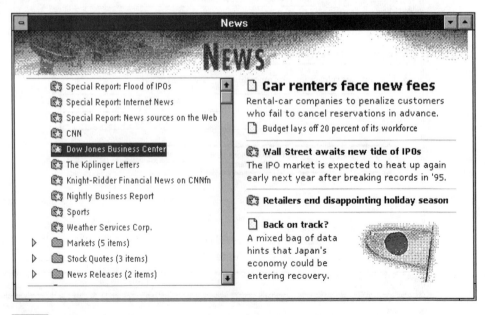

18.3   AT&T Business Network: business and financial news.

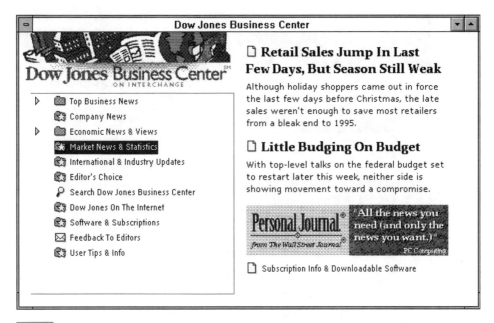

18.4 Dow Jones Business Center on the AT&T Network.

    Nightly Business Report

    PR Newswire for company news releases

    Kiplinger's five newsletters

    Individual customized business news

❏ **Industry Watch**

    Investext analysts industry reports

    Entrepreneur magazine

    Information access from 1,000 industry periodicals

❏ **Company Library**

    Dun & Bradstreet for company research

    Standard & Poor's company profiles

    Thomas Register of American manufacturers

    TRW credit and marketing information

❏ **Business Support Services**

    Guerrilla Marketing

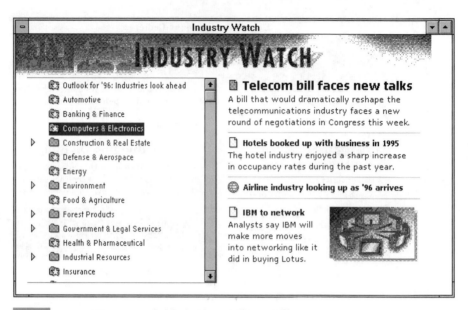

18.5 Knight-Ridder Financial News from CNNfn.

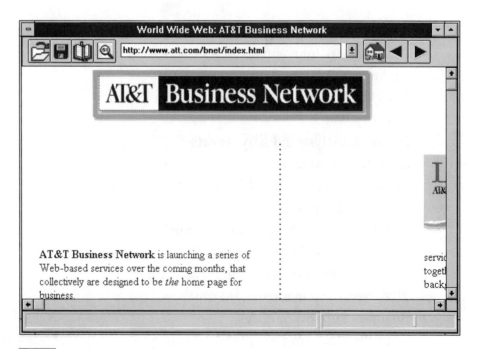

18.6 AT&T Business Network moves to the Web.

Business Travel News

Weather Services

INSO Business Almanac

BNA Employment Issues

Other resources

The AT&T Business Network is already looking like the ultimate yellow pages for cyberspace investors. Yahoo and the other pseudo–yellow pages on the World Wide Web could be in serious trouble if AT&T decides to toss another $50 million ante on the table here, which it is almost sure to do, to save face after the blow it took with Interchange. And this is just the opening round.

Expect a good fight from this contender. With AT&T and the other phone companies controlling the telephone land-line-based systems for the information superhighway, plus their long-distance satellite links, you have to expect that eventually—and *probably very soon*—AT&T should be

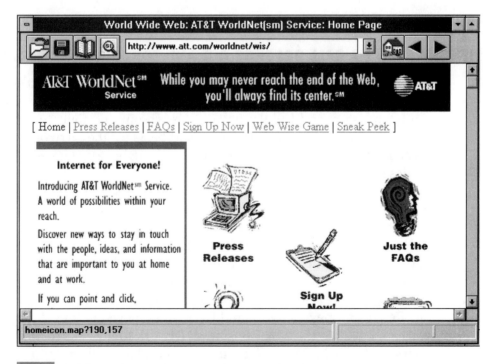

18.7   AT&T WorldNet: prototype Web service for all phone companies.

AT&T GORILLA AWAKENS, RATTLING THE INTERNET CAGE

"For more than a year, AT&T was the gorilla in the corner that nobody in the Internet business wanted to acknowledge. . . . Indeed, since the company had flubbed its attempt at launching a proprietary commercial online service . . . some competitors wrote AT&T off. Big mistake. . . .

"Five hours a month on WorldNet, its Internet access service, free— for 12 months. . . . The offer includes access via an 800 number, a free copy of the popular Netscape browser, unlimited customer assistance. . . .

"And when you factor in the software and frills, such as AT&T's offer to cover the cost of any credit-card fraud when WorldNet members use AT&T Universal Card on the Net, even the $19.95 regular price beats other low-cost Internet services."

SOURCE: Paul Eng, "Surfing's Biggest Splash," *BusinessWeek* (March 4, 1996).

able to link virtually every financial information business up to its own master yellow page directory in cyberspace.

BOTTOM LINE: MA BELL REACHES OUT AND TOUCHES THE WORLD

AT&T is in an enviable position with considerable leverage as a result of its linkage to individual investors through the existing telephone system. It can ID investors and has the power to reach out and touch every one of them. Let's hope it learned its lesson and beefs up the Network's menus, specifically targeting more of the needs of the cyberspace investor, as well as those of the business community.

There are a few services missing from AT&T's package, which would be quite essential for the company to compete effectively against Dow Jones News/Retrieval, CompuServe, or Reuters Money Network. In particular, AT&T should provide cyberspace investors with some resources for portfolio management and more links to some of the big discount brokers, such as PCFN, Schwab, E*Trade, and QuickWay.

However, the price is definitely in line with the competition—for example, Reuters Money Network and Dow Jones News/Retrieval. Right now you can hook into the AT&T Business Network for just $25 monthly for 10 hours, and only half that if you use the necessary tools to minimize your online time, such as offline analytics and news readers. For other Web research and surfing, you can always hold your cost down by using a separate Internet access provider for under $20 a month of unlimited use.

Bottom line: AT&T Business Network has the potential to become the ultimate World Wide Web yellow pages. You can count on them to expand rapidly now that they've moved from a dial-up online service to an Internet Web service. They have the technology to serve the cyberspace investor.

Electronic Publishers: Pathfinders in Cyberspace

The publishing world has been quicker on the draw than the broadcast industry in taking advantage of the many new opportunities offered by the exploding Internet market. One of the early standouts—Enews, The Electronic Newsstand—jumped in shortly after the Internet became really popular in early 1994.

Enews was the brainchild of the publisher of *The New Republic* magazine, and it quickly became the cyber-newsstand for a couple of hundred periodicals. Today it continues as an electronic version of the corner newsstand—in fact, its opening Webpage even displays a quaint picture of one, rather than flashing high-tech interactive Webpages like Time Warner's classy Pathfinder.

Loaded with content at a time when ad revenues were falling for many publications, the print news media simply saw the Internet as electronic publishing for paperless versions of their news periodicals, edited and digested enough to avoid giving away the publication free. Increased circulation was the attraction. And the World Wide Web would open a whole new and very big market for them.

MONEY MAGAZINE PARTNERS WITH COMPUSERVE'S FINANCE CENTER

Call it clout, chutzpah, pizazz, power, or whatever—*Money* magazine has it and is using it to aggressively go after the new cyberspace investor. When *Money* took over CompuServe's financial section, you knew that this move would put the magazine just one short step away from much bigger things down the information superhighway. That gut feeling was further reinforced by the recent upgrading of the bold, award-winning Internet Website, Pathfinder. *Money* and its parent Time Warner are obviously on the prowl, making aggressive plays for the financial cyberspace information market.

MONEY MAGAZINE: PATHFINDER GOES DEEP INTO CYBERSPACE

While *Money* was taking over CompuServe's financial section, *Money*'s parent, publishing-industry giant Time Warner, was beefing up its Pathfinder Website, a flashy cyberspace version of MTV and the Vegas Strip, featuring not just *Money* and *Fortune* but all the other popular Time Warner resources. This was an impressive strategic business move. Dow Jones, CompuServe, Reuters, Bloomberg, and other Wall Street cyberspace info-giants are likely to retaliate with new competitive offerings to one-up *Money* and Time Warner.

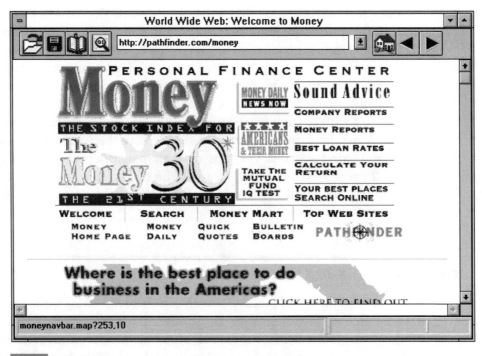

19.1 *Money* Personal Finance Center on the Web.

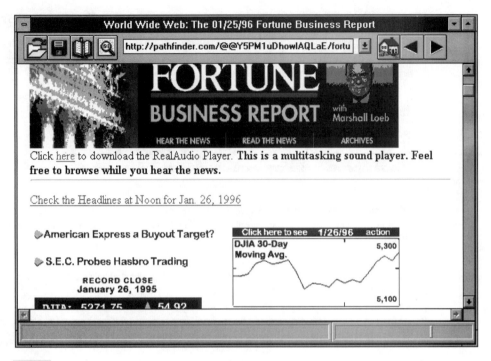

19.2 *Fortune* Business Report on Pathfinder.

With *Money* now controlling the CompuServe Personal Finance Center *Money* has a great opportunity to glean everything CompuServe has learned in the last 25 years and virtually download all their knowledge database into the development of their Pathfinder Website. More power to them if that's the path to carving out a niche among the top NET*navigators for cyberspace investors.

Here's what you will discover when you log on to *Money* magazine and Pathfinder's showbiz-style Website:

❏ Headline news and detailed analysis
❏ *Fortune* magazine business reports
❏ Daily Money, free on the Web and by E-mail
❏ Hoover's company financial reports
❏ Quick quotes on the stock market
❏ Major market index updates

World Wide Web: Hoover's Online

http://pathfinder.com/@@Y5PM1uDhowlAQLaE/path

The Hoover's Online database on Pathfinder provides profiles of over 400 of the America's best-known companies. Company profiles are updated annually and revised when major events affect their content.

Click on the appropriate letter to jump to that section of this alphabetical selection of Hoover's Company Profiles. (Or go to the industry listing.)

19.3 Hoover's Online: company fundamentals on Pathfinder.

- ❏ Calculator for your returns
- ❏ Best market loan rates
- ❏ Web and online search engine
- ❏ Links to top Internet and Websites
- ❏ Bulletin boards for serious investors

There's a lot here, especially when you realize that this is the work of a print magazine. Perhaps you won't have as many alternative databases to tap into as you do on Dow Jones News/Retrieval or CompuServe, but this is a solid start for the new cyberspace investing arena. And given the fact that many investors really aren't looking for a lot of alternatives, a *limited menu* of choices probably works best for them. Also, compare the content noted here with those in the earlier section on CompuServe's NET*naviga-tion system for overlap between these two alternatives for cyberspace investing resources.

CYBERSPACE INVESTORS' STRATEGY: SOLID, LIMITED MENU

Let's face it, today's cyberspace investors are so inundated with information and confronted with so many choices, that they're likely to throw up their hands and go to the sidelines. Or, as we have here, they'll welcome with open arms a resource that makes a lot of the decisions for them in advance and presents a limited menu of choices. Cyberspace investors want solid but focused menus, plus some color and action.

Money, like AOL and other similar services, probably has the right strategy for appealing to the new cyberspace investors. They want to be entertained with something that will spice up their diet of dull-tasting facts. This is the MTV generation; they were raised on sophisticated graphics, as well as high-tech analytic power. For them, morphing cyborgs and commercials that solve all their problems in 30 seconds flat are *real*. Pathfinder understands this audience, and the graphics of the *Money* Personal Finance Center clearly reflect it.

INVESTOR'S BUSINESS DAILY: "FOR IMPORTANT DECISION MAKERS"

A couple of other less dramatic—yet perhaps equally significant—conversions from the print financial media into cyberspace are the new Web versions of *Investor's Business Daily* and the *USA Today* Money section.

Investor's Business Daily brashly claims to be "America's fastest-growing newspaper." It is certainly one of the most respected sources of financial news. *Investor's Business Daily* is definitely not new to financial cyberspace. It has had an outstanding news section on America Online for some time. And, of course, its famous CANSLIM stock-picking formula is used as a screening tool on CompuServe and other online systems.

Investor's Business Daily's electronic version includes its special brand of reporting on events and their impact on the market, companies, and securities, plus its unique daily graphs used to select top-performing stocks.

USA Today's Money pages include the bare-bones basics. Great graphics, some basic market information. It offers quotes, too, but they don't mean much anymore, now that everybody's giving them away. As a NET*navigator for cyberspace investors, *USA Today* may present little serious competition for the major NET*navigator, but *Investor's Business Daily* could if it goes beyond the image of a newspaper reporting news.

19.4 The newspaper for important decision makers.

In order to do that, *Investor's Business Daily* would probably have to beef up its analytic tools more and add portfolio management capabilities, so that the investor has everything in this one NET*navigator.

BOTTOM LINE: FINANCIAL CYBERSPACE OSCARS AND GOLDEN GLOBES

As you will recall, we have already covered the cyberspace activities of the major publishing power players dealing with financial information. Those four power players—Dow Jones News/Retrieval, Reuters Money Network, Knight-Ridder, and Bloomberg—have been competing in Wall Street cyberspace for a long time. In combination, their total revenues exceed $10 billion.

In varying degrees, these four info-giants understand *and serve* both the institutional and *individual* investor. And as we've already seen, more and more they are targeting the individual investor market.

19.5   *USA Today*'s Money section: headline news.

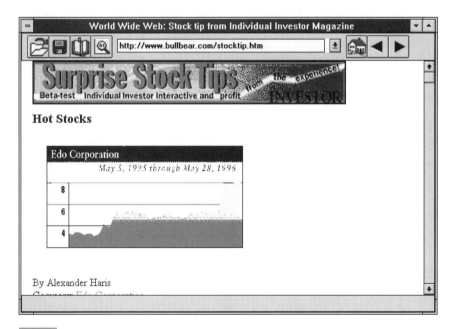

19.6   Bull & Bear Website: *Individual Investor* Magazine.

Across the board they seem to grasp the total needs of the individual investor—from news and quotes, research and analytics, to brokerage and portfolio management. Moreover, they seem to have a strong grasp of the essential need to *integrate* content with a solid NET*navigation system, putting this process into one single package.

In the competition for the top spots among NET*investor's navigators, the four publishing superpowers are likely to remain among the top ten. They will get the Oscars.

When it comes to the Golden Globes and People's Choice Awards in financial cyberspace, however, you can count on them going to *Investor's Business Daily, Money* magazine, *Individual Investor,* America Online, and their peers. They are the ones that will capture the *hearts* of the voters, with *facts plus flash.*

Television Broadcasters:
CNBC and CNNfn

Bill Gates tells us "the highway metaphor isn't quite right." He calls the Net "the ultimate marketplace. Markets from trading floors to malls are fundamental to human society." *The Net eliminates distance—and time.* Eventually the Net could have all the drama and intimacy of rubbing with traders in the pits of the Chicago Merc or on the floor of the AMEX—with all the chaos, noise, hand signals, voices, smells, colors, flashing lights. *And you'll be right in the middle of it.*

Gates' distinction *between a highway that distances and a marketplace that centralizes* is crucial as the next generation of NET∗navigators is developed by our financial institutions. The successful ones already get it and are using that knowledge and awareness to satisfy the needs of the new cyberspace investor.

BROADCASTERS IN POWER PLAY TO CONTROL WIRELESS SKYWAYS

So far, most financial institutions are still caught in the highway metaphor. Consequently, they are trapped into believing it's enough to just put up a "billboard" along the information superhighway, and investors will flock to your vaults. Today, however, many on Wall Street are waking up to the fact that that won't work in the next generation. As the Internet explodes, adding 100 to 200 million connections in the next few years, you'll need something more like MTV than a highway billboard to get any traffic to make a pit stop. There was a day when "owning the railroad" bestowed great power and control. But as we've already seen, owning the telephone system hasn't even given AT&T any special powers in financial cyberspace.

Today, the power is not in "owning the railroad," nor even in owning the highway's tollroads; power is in owning the airways, the skyways, the network. Remember Ted Turner. Remember the cellular phone industry. As the Net expands, distance will be further eliminated by the use of wireless, over-air broadcasting. Even more significantly, satellite transmissions may even be eliminating, or at least minimizing, the need for *all* land-based telephone and cable connections. Fiber optics may soon become an obsolete technology.

NEW "SKY-NET" BROADCASTING WILL REPLACE INTERNET BY 2005

Craig McCaw "has decided to create a celestial counterpart to the Internet, the burgeoning network of networks that carries even greater streams of digital data and sound and pictures around the globe. The hunger for that kind of exchange seems certain to grow, overwhelming the ability of communications companies to bury fiber beneath the streets of the world's cities and throughout the neglected but populous hinterlands.

"McCaw would put this power to interact within the reach of everyone on earth within a decade, and satisfy the world's craving for communication. He would remove the penalty from location. McCaw hopes to achieve this by creating a constellation of 840 satellites that will gird the planet."

SOURCE: Andrew Kupfer, "Craig McCaw Sees an Internet in the Sky," *Fortune* (May 27, 1996).

Let's face it, the use of land-lines for telephones and cable television better fits the *highway* analogy than the *marketplace* analogy. Consequently, land-lines are likely to diminish, as the era of cellular phones and the world of minidisk Direct TV expands. Point-to-point and disk-to-disk broadcasting will soon dominate Wall Street cyberspace, too. We already see it with, for example, Data Broadcasting Corporation's Signal and QuoTrek. *Bottom line:* All broadcasters are in an enviable position to become major power players.

ONLINE BROADCASTERS: MORE THAN THE LATEST HEADLINES

Television broadcasters have been one of the great eliminators of distance. CNN brings Bosnia and Tokyo right into your home, live, every hour. And the broadcasters are now in a perfect position to continue the tradition in this explosive transition from Wall Street NYC to Wall Street cyberspace.

However, the specific question for Wall Street cyberspace is whether the financial news industry can make the transition from instant dissemination of widely disbursed current news information to become a workable *navigator* for the cyberspace investor. The odds may be against them. The competition is getting fierce, primarily because cyberspace also gives the print publishers, such as Dow and Reuters, the opportunity to broadcast without the old restrictions of the static paper version, delivering a paper edition once a day. Broadcasters might be more successful just broadcasting news.

Currently several of the top financial news broadcasters are making some excellent strides in the right direction:

❑ **CNBC-TV: Financial and Business Television.** Since the original Financial News Network merged into CNBC in 1991, CNBC has risen from a "fledgling network with a barebones budget, a paucity of big-name stars, viewing numbers so low that they often barely register on the Neilsens . . . to create a near-cult following among the nation's investors . . . the CNBC generation," as Dow Jones' *Smart Money* magazine called it.

CNBC is now making the transition from a first-generation billboard on the Net, using its Website primarily to present its daily schedule. Perhaps even more important from a strategic perspective, CNBC's parent, NBC, is now in a joint venture with Microsoft.

The mission of this dynamic duo is to create both a 24-hour news channel to compete with CNN, as well as an online/cyberspace component. Microsoft will also be adding the technology for live broadcasting on the Internet—*which may render text-only service obsolete very soon, at least for the broadcasters.*

❑ **CNNfn: new 24-hour financial channel.** Another bold move from Ted Turner. Whether he can compete as effectively with CNBC in the financial news arena as he has with the major news networks remains to be seen. We hope so—the cyberspace investor will be the winner in that contest.

Although a late entry on the racecard, it looks like CNNfn is trying to upstage CNBC with its Internet news broadcasting. CNBC's first effort was an old-style billboard. In contrast, CNNfn came out in a typical Turner flash and dash. Its Internet Website immediately included an impressive collection of major areas of content, in addition to plain old TV news. In fact, CNNfn's Website suggests a strategy of creating a total-service NET*navigator for the cyberspace investor, as other products are added. Their Website already includes:

THE CNBC GENERATION IS REPLACING THE MTV GENERATION

"What's CNBC's appeal? For John A. Yurko, a New Jersey resident with substantial holdings in overseas investments, it's the fact that each morning he can get market reports from the London, Frankfurt, Paris and Tokyo exchanges. 'Otherwise, I'd have to go into CompuServe to Global Reports. At prime time, that costs $60 an hour.'

"For Peggy Krist, who watches the channel from her home office in New Jersey, it's that she can get regular insights into the direction of the precious-metals prices and long-term interest rates, two key factors in the value of her gold fund.

"For Jamie and Bill Krasnow, who live in Charleston, Mass., it's the chance to see such mutual fund heavyweights as Mario Gabelli and Peter Lynch talk at length on the nightly program, 'Mutual Fund Investor.' 'I don't expect them to tell me anything earth shattering,' says Jamie. 'But it's fun to listen to what their hot tip might be.'

"The programming is designed to satisfy everyone from the person who wants to know the best mutual fund for his or her retirement money to the market junkie who has to know—immediately, and not in tomorrow's paper—what's happening to the price of corn futures. . . .

CNBC "has clearly found a niche. 'I need CNBC,' says one New York money manager who has a reason for requesting anonymity. 'If customers call me, and I'm watching, I can repeat the last couple sentences that I heard on the air and sound smart and up to date.' "

SOURCE: Jean Chatzky, "The CNBC Generation," *Smart Money* (January 1995).

—Knight-Ridder Financial's World News

—S&P ComStock Resource Center with Market Scope, etc.

—Quotes including indexes, stocks, and mutual funds

—Market data on currencies, commodities, securities

—Hoover's search database of 9,600 companies for summaries

—CNNfn Almanac: upcoming government stats, earnings reports, etc.

—Official company Websites with direct links

—Weblinks to key financial resources: retirement planning, tax information, global exchanges, government resources

—Transcripts of on-air material you missed

—Glossary of business and financial terms

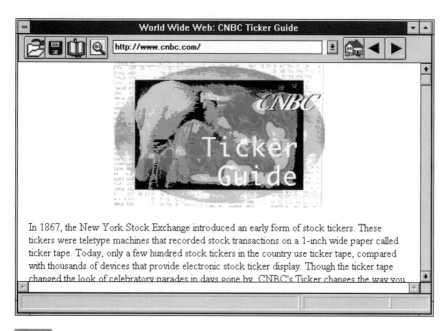

20.1 CNBC-TV: first in financial television.

20.2 CNNfn News: U.S. stock market indices.

For a first-time online effort from a new financial television broadcaster, this is very impressive. In fact, the collection of content providers here is almost as powerful as the other online NET*navigators previously reviewed.

Cyberspace investors should take special note of CNNfn's strategy here: obviously, it is aggressively targeting the online NET*investor right up front. CNNfn may be looking down the superhighway, which could explain why it appears to be more interested in competing head to head with CNBC for this new audience than for the more traditional broadcasting markets. In that case, CNNfn's strategy strongly suggests that the individual investor operating in cyberspace should consider CNNfn's Website as another major contender for one of the top spots among NET*navigators.

❑ **Bloomberg Online, newswire and broadcaster.** Bloomberg is the Avis of the financial cyberspace information providers, growing so rapidly that, in size, Bloomberg may soon be larger than any one of its three main cyberspace competitors, Dow Jones, Reuters, and Knight-Ridder—if not through internal growth, then through acquisitions.

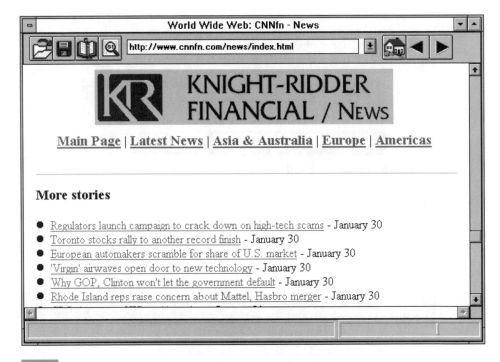

20.3 Knight-Ridder Financial: global news on CNNfn.

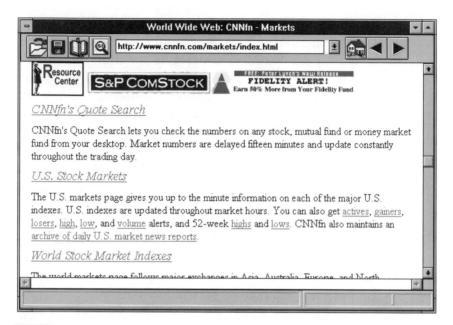

20.4 S&P ComStock: market resource center on CNNfn.

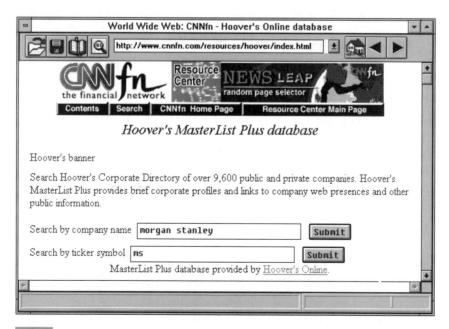

20.5 Hoover's directory: searching 9,600 companies.

Actually Bloomberg television is a relatively small part of Bloomberg's huge financial information empire, which also includes print publications and a complete array of information services for institutional investors. However, when it comes to serving the individual investor (in contrast to the institutional investor), the new Bloomberg Online service seems to fit more appropriately in this category of broadcasters, for the next generation.

In fact, we would anticipate that Bloomberg will soon make an acquisition or offer a new service that would allow it to quickly expand from an excessively *institutional* client market to the low-cost *individual* investor products. Reuters did it with the Money Network and Dow Jones with its News/Retrieval, both with a base price under $30 monthly. In short, if Bloomberg is to stay competitive, expect it to expand into the individual investor market soon with a new high-powered system rather than a basic-news-on-the-Web strategy.

❏ **Regional financial networks.**   One of the top regional television stations devoted entirely to financial news is KWHY-TV, Channel 22, the

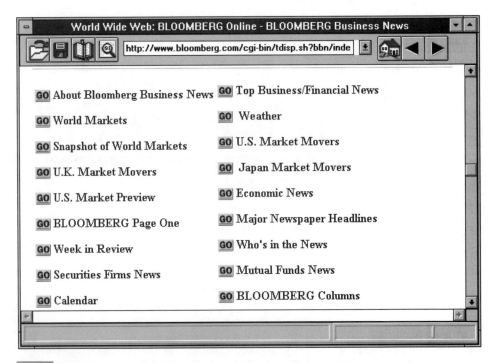

20.6 Bloomberg Online: first-class financial news.

business channel in Southern California. Originally KWHY announced that it was joining the talent on the Microsoft Network. Then, as Microsoft altered its strategies with MSN, KWHY put this move on the back burner. However, investors should fully expect them, and other regional financial broadcasting stations such as Chicago's WCIU-26, to take advantage of the global reach of the Internet, probably by the turn of the century.

WEB BROADCASTING: IDEAL MEDIUM FOR FINANCIAL TELEVISION

When it comes to getting financial news *out there* to a cyberspace audience, the analogy that most accurately fits the Web is broadcasting, not publishing. I've been in both fields, as an editor with a metropolitan newspaper and as head of the Financial News Network, and *cyberspace is broadcasting*, pure and simple.

The publishing analogy implies print-on-paper periodicals, just as the information superhighway analogy implies stationary billboards. Slow and static. In contrast, the term *broadcasting* suggests action and emotional reactions, crowds milling around, traders screaming in the pits. Live television broadcasting best captures the feel of marketplace. If a picture is worth a thousand words, a television clip is worth a book.

Financial news is broadcast news, from all corners of the world, filtered and edited by skilled broadcasters, and delivered instantly—*or as close to the event as possible*—to the investor, especially the individual cyberspace investor. There's no waiting at a newsstand for delivery of the latest edition.

The broadcasting analogy fits because financial news is filled with late-breaking stories—hot news that pushes everything else aside. We've grown to expect the urgent, and the broadcasters give hot news a preferred position throughout their day-long programming schedules. You can wait for the late-night news. But thanks to CNN, news is available all day long. Next, it's 24-hour financial news, from stations all over the globe.

BOTTOM LINE: BROADCASTERS JUMP AHEAD OF NEW TECHNOLOGIES

Paradoxically, the print publishers are the ones that understand the *broadcasting* analogy so far, although often their advertising copy still compares their paperless electronic editions with print delivery to your doorstep in the morning. For example, ads for *The Wall Street Journal*'s Personal Journal contrast the delivery of the print version once a day to the round-the-clock updates of the electronic editions.

Fortunately, the financial television industry is now also getting the message, as evidenced by all their snappy new Websites. The real potential for broadcasters on the Net is not likely to be realized until the *third generation* of technology kicks in. That is, Internet technology will progress through at least three generations, and right now the broadcasters are still playing in the *second generation*.

First generation: billboards along the superhighway

Second generation: comprehensive databases controlled by NET*navigators

Third generation: interactive video/audio (mingling CNNfn, MTV, and Nintendo)

In other words, given the current state of the Internet's technology, the broadcasters are actually at a competitive disadvantage in this transition from the first to the second generation. There are already so many other successful NET*navigators available that fit the needs of the cyberspace investor, within the current technological limits.

The maximum potential of television broadcasters on the Net cannot be achieved until the technology advances to the *third generation*. Then the broadcasters will go live—*with interactive audio and video*—on the Internet and the entire World Wide Web, and reach five billion people with instant financial news.

When that happens, *text-based* Websites will suddenly become outdated technologies for the television broadcasters—about as absurd as putting up the information seen on an anchor's teleprompter. And it would limit broadcasters to what amounts to an electronic version of a two-dimensional newspaper.

If the broadcasters are in fact anticipating this third generation—as some apparently are—then we also anticipate that those looking ahead to the future will be ignoring or minimizing their development of text-only online services. Furthermore, since this trend is already in process and some *live television is already on the Web,* it's probably unrealistic to expect that financial broadcasters will rush to follow CNNfn's lead in developing their own text-based NET*navigational systems for the new cyberspace investor.

Quote and Market Data Vendors

Before Netscape and Mosiac, before commercialism took over the World Wide Web in 1994, the Internet was the peaceful domain of pipe-smoking university professors, government scientists, and the military. In fact, for 25 years everyone with a computer linked to the Internet knew that everyone else *out there* on the Net was just another explorer, *freely sharing information.* Then the Internet went commercial, and the old guard went into culture shock.

WEB COMMERCIALISM: TODAY THE COST OF FREE INFORMATION IS VERY HIGH

For many of the Internet old-timers, the new commercial Net—with advertisements, shopping malls, credit cards, stock trading, and its newer policies of paying for information—was a source of considerable grieving. It was as if a close friend had died. For them, information was not a saleable commodity—at least not like it is today. *Today, information is the purist of commodities,* more precious than oil, gold, or any other commodity.

Fortunately, since 1994, many of the successful *commercial* Websites have continued this tradition of at least partially giving away information. Network television, for example, gives you *Star Trek* in order to get you to watch a McDonald's ad. In the same vein, "free quotes" is now a common advertising teaser that attracts the attention of the media and Websurfers alike, even though it's of minimal value in the decisions of a serious cyberspace investor. Another popular Web teaser is an offer of ten or so innocu-

341

ous news headlines. Both of these teasers—free quotes and headlines—are fairly inexpensive and of limited value to the serious investor.

But in this relatively new medium, capturing Websurfers is important in justifying the expenditure of ad dollars. So as part of the ad game, some Websites began reporting hundreds of thousands of visitors monthly. Although no one really knows, many of the visitors are probably analogous to rubberneckers who slow down as they drive past a highway accident, or to college kids cutting classes. But so what? It's a new medium, and we're all inching our way down the highway, trying to avoid costly accidents.

FREE QUOTES: DECISION-MAKING TOOLS OR MERE TEASER ADS?

Today there are so many Websites in financial cyberspace offering "free quotes" that it often appears that investors will no longer have to pay for stock quotations. In fact, investors could probably get individual free quotes on every single S&P 500 company one at a time, if they had all day and nothing else to do. Serious investors know that quotes by themselves are useless. Yet today, free quotes are commonplace because they create the illusion of action, interactivity, and interest in the customer. On the other hand, giving away free quotes no longer distinguishes one Website from another. It seems like everybody's got them.

So what's new? What's next? Now that we're back to the basic task, what do you do with those quotes? That's the real bottom line of the cyberspace investor. How do you convert *raw data* into valuable information and *successful trades?* These questions are the context surrounding the transition impacting the pure quote servers now operating in financial cyberspace.

Actually it's very interesting to see what some of the early leaders in the basic quote-server business are already doing to further distinguish their Websites in the now-jaded era of free quotes. Let's take a look at some of these major Internet quote servers which could emerge as NET*navigators for investors:

Quote.Com on the Web

This veritable patriarch of Internet quote servers got smart early on. It nailed down the Internet name "quote.com." What a license! Now nobody else can use the term "quote" in their Internet domain name.

It's odd that the Internet powers-that-be would, in effect, give someone full ownership of a generic term, when the U.S. and international trade-

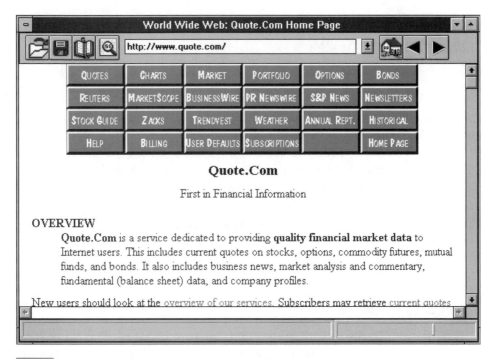

21.1 Quote.Com: pioneer Internet quote server goes full service.

mark agencies might reject granting ownership to such a commonly used term as "quote." But that's their policy, and they did just that. In any event, Quote.Com owns the name.

Fortunately, they deliver quite a lot. In fact, Quote.Com offers the cyberspace investor much more than market quotes and mere raw data, including:

❏ Stock charts
❏ Market updates
❏ Portfolio monitoring
❏ Option and bond data
❏ Reuters News
❏ S&P MarketScope
❏ Business and PR newswires
❏ Newsletters
❏ Zacks Estimated Earnings
❏ Trendvest

❐ Stock guides

❐ Annual reports

❐ Historical data

Moreover, Quote.Com does a surprisingly credible job for an entrepreneurial start-up on the Net, offering a NET*navigational system comparable to those of some of the other systems.

Given the pressing need of larger, slower companies to expand fast on the Internet, which triggered a wave of mergers and acquisitions, it's surprising that Quote.Com has lasted this long as an independent, without being bought out by some larger organization. It happened to Reuters Money Network and NETworth Website. It'll probably happen to Quote.Com soon. These guys are good; and they're ready to go to the next level in developing a high-powered NET*navigator.

InterQuote on the Web

Enter the next generation, with real-time quotes. In a bold move that apparently one-upped Quote.Com and just about every other quote vendor in America, the InterQuote team developed quote-server software that offers cyberspace investors *real-time* quote data delivered right on the Internet browser. Not only that, it also offers some basic market statistics.

In addition, you can download the operating software right onto your hard drive. You can get real-time quotes for as low as $35 a month. This may be the bargain of the century, when you consider that you may be paying several times that for quotes from the traditional sources. These guys will succeed in one of two things: driving the competition to lower prices (which is happening) or getting bought out by an old-time Wall Streeter who needs to expand fast on the Net. Either way, the individual cyberspace investor wins.

Data Broadcasting Corporation's Signal: New Power on the Web

There are many, many commercial sources for quotes and market data as we detailed in our earlier book. Here is one of the best real-time data services for the professional trader, a spin-off company created when the Financial News Network was sold to CNBC-TV. DBC is now on the Internet offering a slimmed-down, low-end package for the individual investor.

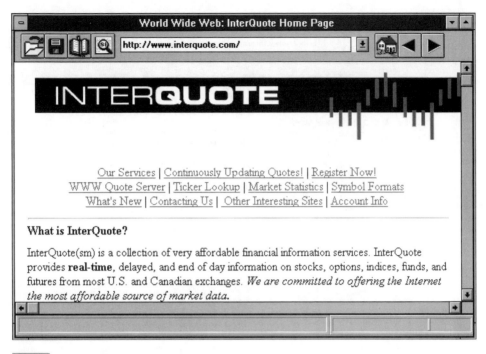

21.2 InterQuote: real-time quotes at a discount.

And if you find the Internet too slow—*which it is all too often*—DBC has several other alternative cyberspace delivery systems to pick and choose from; FM radio broadcasting, cable network connections, satellite delivery, handheld portable units, and SignalCard, a receiver the size of a credit card that plugs into your laptop computer.

The DBC team has been around Wall Street cyberspace for a long time and has built a solid reputation in the process. DBC is rapidly proving a powerful competitor and is likely to set the standard for the other quote servers already on the Internet. In addition, DBC offers a fine collection of other services: headlines and analysis from newswires, institutional research reports, and advisory newsletters, all of which are essential to developing a one-stop, integrated package for cyberspace investors.

As with other quote servers that are scurrying to include more than the standard five free quotes, you can also purchase extra services from DBC, supplied by top organizations such as Dow Jones News/Retrieval, Option News Exchange, and Futures World News. Moreover, DBC covers every U.S. and foreign market—national and regional stocks, commodity

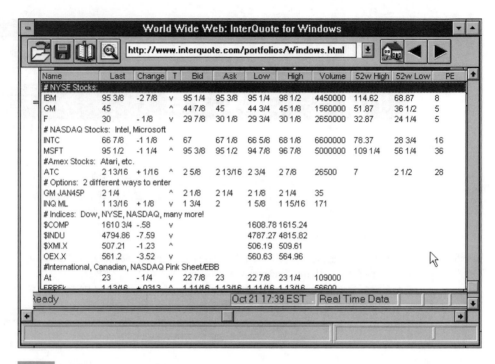

21.3 InterQuote: Website demo for real-time data.

DBC "PRIVATE LABELS" STOCK QUOTES WORLDWIDE

"*U.S. News & World Report* ... joins *USA Today* Online, Microsoft's MSN ... Data Broadcasting, America's leading provider of real-time financial data to individuals, is now providing more than one million quotes a day through nearly 30 partners on four continents through its newly formed Brand Labeled Quotes business.

"If a customer requests a stock quote on the *USA Today* Online site (www.usatoday.com), that customer is automatically routed to the DBC server, which in turn displays the quote in a format prescribed by *USA Today* especially for its customers. The customer sees the *USA Today* graphics and mapping and is easily guided back to *USA Today* Online."

SOURCE: Press release, Data Broadcasting Corporation (February 15, 1996).

21.4   Data Broadcasting Corporation: full service and real-time quotes.

futures, stock and currency options, mutual funds, plus market indexes and statistics. And their real-time quote service is only $29.95 a month.

BOTTOM LINE: QUOTE SERVERS EVOLVING INTO TOTAL SYSTEMS

The entry of Data Broadcasting Corporation, along with IDD, PC Quote and, most likely, other publicly held quote-server organizations will definitely heat up the competition on the Net. Many of the old standbys in the quote-server arena have already been hovering behind the scenes, wholesaling quotes to retail server organizations such as Quote.Com.

PC Quote, for example, supplier to such power players as Schwab, AOL, and CompuServe, now has a Website. And more are likely to come out of the closet and into the Web limelight. In order to be competitive, here are a some essential ingredients:

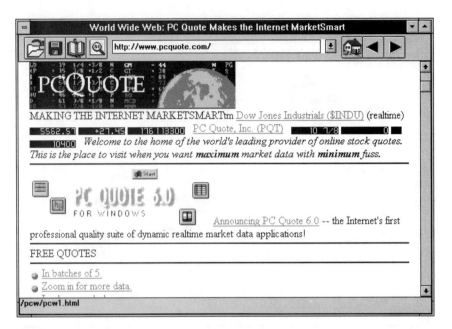

21.5 PC Quote: reliable and respected quote leader.

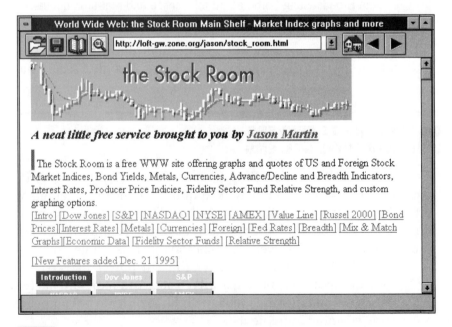

21.6 The Stock Room: some free data are still *out there*.

❏ **Full-service navigators:** In the future, quote servers will have to offer a much more comprehensive menu, more than even *unlimited* free quotes. They are old hat to an audience of cyberspace investors now quite sophisticated in the new technologies on the Internet.

❏ **Brand-name identity:** Perhaps more significantly, in this new arena, any new names on the block will also have to create brand-name identity against familiar names like CompuServe and Reuters, which are established, and offer solid analytics and navigational power.

As a result, most quote servers will probably be seriously handicapped in the competitive race for recognition and commercial success as a preferred NET*navigator for cyberspace investors. With the rare exception of DBC—which is actually more of a broadcaster in the tradition of CNBC and CNNfn and actually provides analytic technology—the best strategy for a new face here may well be to stay in the shadows as a behind-the-scenes wholesaler of quotes and market data. Otherwise, they should come prepared for heavy-duty competition that is already armed with *full-service* systems and tested on the Internet battlefield.

World Wide Web Directories:
Classified Yellow Pages

When the World Wide Web began developing commercially, several Web-site directories surfaced that were loaded with valuable content on investing. Our initial assessment was that they would eventually evolve into investors' NET*navigators. As the Web developed further, however, and as other services—such as Telescan, Reuters Money Network, and Compu-Serve—began offering their more sophisticated NET*investing systems, some distinctions emerged. In particular, there is a fundamental difference between Web directories that simply offer large numbers of links to other Websites and the new, emerging NET*navigators reviewed in this book. That distinction is made between the following:

❐ **Internet Web Directories: yellow pages and classified ads.** In most cases these Websites serve the same function as the yellow-page directories in a telephone book or the classified ads in a newspaper. They provide the cyberspace investor a centralized platform from which to point, click, and jump to other commercial sites, most of which are advertisements with limited usable content for the investment decision-making process—until you become a paid subscriber for the additional services offered. However, these yellow pages still serve an invaluable function by pointing investors to fee-based vendors of essential services.

❐ **NET*navigators: integrated content plus a navigator**. These NET* navigators actually provide you with access to content or information resources for all steps in the investment decision-making process—from quotes and analytics to trading and portfolio management, and they attempt, in some degree, to integrate everything into a whole working package for the individual investor.

Whether they're free or fee-based, these NET*navigators are now attempting to go beyond the role of being simply yellow-page directories or classified ads. The AT&T Business Network is one obvious example. Here the telephone company itself is, in effect, taking its own yellow pages and elevating them to the level of a cyberspace NET*navigator for investors. And so far they're succeeding in this strategy, with more to come.

This distinction between directories and NET*navigators is also important primarily as a way to avoid adopting a mind-set that one or more of the major Website directories alone will be enough for success as a cyberspace investor. After a while, every Websurfer discovers that it's time to come off the Internet beach (no matter how much fun you're having Websurfing) and get down to the real, serious steps and processes of making investment decisions—in order to achieve the goal of financial independence.

WEB DIRECTORIES: CLASSIFIED YELLOW PAGES OR INVESTOR'S NET*NAVIGATORS?

There are several important Web directories that have evolved in the past few years that specifically focused on helping the individual investor find necessary cyberspace resources. One big word of caution: Be skeptical—most are very incomplete. Even the best of these directories only covers a small percentage of the resources in any specific categories.

Having seen many other Web directories for investors, knowing what's actually out there in cyberspace, and being aware that many Web directories are kept by volunteers, amateurs, or part-timers and are much like free classifieds in community weekly newspapers, we can recognize the limitations as well as the tremendous value of these evolving cyberspace resources.

As a result, investors should keep in mind that it's usually *not what's in these directories, but what's missing* that may be most important. So make sure you maintain a healthy skepticism and check out *several* Web directories periodically.

Some of the better ones for cyberspace investors are:

❑ **American Association of Individual Investors:**   The ultimate cyberspace investment club, with almost 200,000 members. Chock-full of resources on AOL and on the Web.

INDIVIDUAL INVESTOR MAGAZINE RATES AAII AND NAIC TOPS

"Most broadly informative. . . . It's not as flashy, amusing or interactive as Motley Fool, not as stylistically impeccable as the offerings of *Fortune* or *BusinessWeek,* but the American Association of Individual Investors forum on AOL offers a slew of practical information and advice. . . .

  "Honorable mention in this category goes to the National Association of Investors Corporation . . . on CompuServe."

SOURCE: Wayne Harris, "The Best of the Commercial On-line Services: And the Winner Is . . ." *Individual Investor* (August 1995).

Note that *Individual Investor* is referring to the online services of the AAII and NAIC. Their Websites are even better.

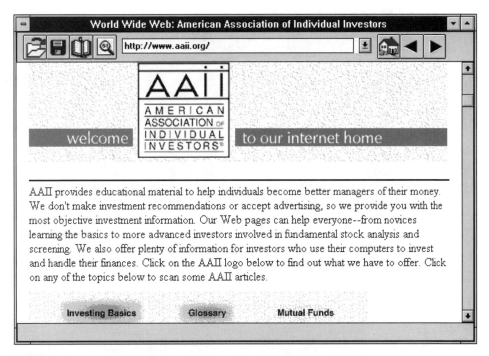

22.1 American Association of Individual Investors on the Web.

❏ **Financial Data Finder:**   From Ohio State University, a solid directory.

❏ **Excite from Architext:**   Yahoo's new rival Web directory, with some unique advanced search technology, backed by the team behind Netscape.

❏ **FINWeb:**   One of the original academic directories, at the University of Texas, with many resources for the bottom line–focused investor.

❏ **InvestSIG:**   The Capital PC Users Special Interest Group has a Web directory that's clearly one of the best *out there.*

❏ **Innovation:**   International finance from a location in the Netherlands.

❏ **National Association of Investors Corporation:**   On CompuServe, with almost 400,000 members, this is one of the best resources for setting up local investment clubs and many other key resources for the cyberspace investor. Also on the Web.

❏ **NetMoney:**   The *NetGuide* series of books is one of the most comprehensive sets of *print* directories on the Internet. The NetMoney system is great for all phases of personal finance, and they are also in cyberspace as a Web directory.

22.2 Excite: Web directory for Money & Investing.

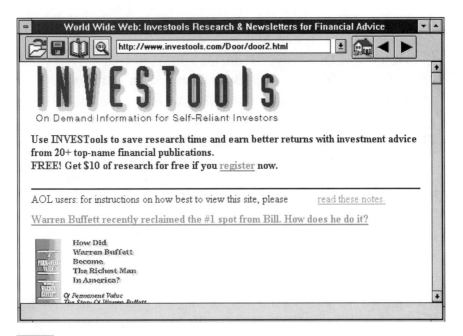

22.3   INVESTools: yellow pages to financial periodicals.

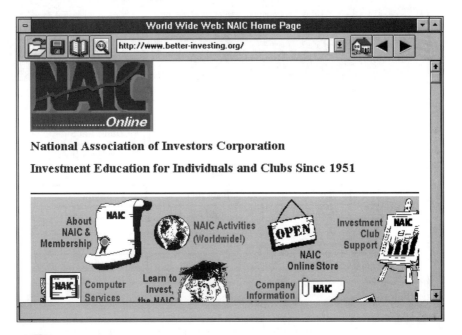

22.4   National Association of Investors Corporation.

❏ **Personal Finance Center:**   Available from the Global Network Navigator (GNN), now an AOL subsidiary.

❏ **Wall Street Directory:**   From the editors of *Wall Street Software Digest,* with over 2,500 links, especially designed for active market traders.

❏ **Wall Street Direct International:**   Another super Web directory from the publishers of the *Trader's Catalog and Resource Guide.*

❏ **Yahoo Business and Investing Pages:**   Yahoo has one of the largest collections of pages on all topics, including investing, markets, and business. Yahoo is the AT&T yellow pages of the Internet, and everyone knows it, so almost everyone submits their directory listings to Yahoo.

Most of these early Internet directories are actually quite helpful, in spite of the randomness of the World Wide Web. Moreover, once you get the hang of it and start bookmarking favorite sites on your own browser, you'll wind up with your *own personalized Web directory.*

Perhaps more important, the commercial potential here is so huge that future directories are likely to be handled by commercial organizations like

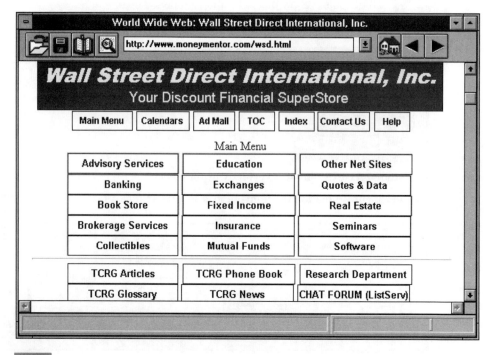

22.5 Wall Street Direct: See their National Financial Yellow Pages.

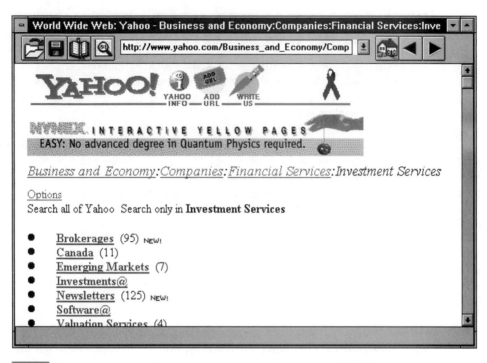

22.6 Yahoo's yellow pages for investing, business, and the economy.

the telephone companies who are experienced at building and maintaining *commercial* yellow pages. This is especially true in the financial services field, where AT&T itself is now attacking the Web, with the AT&T Business Network, the ultimate yellow pages.

BOTTOM LINE: WEB DIRECTORIES CHALLENGE NET*NAVIGATORS

Some final words of caution about using the Web directories: Websurfing can be an addictive form of entertainment. It's easy to enjoy touring the nation and the world, zipping from one location to another, because there really is virtually zero distance between locations in cyberspace. However, please keep in mind that while these investors' Web directories may be extremely valuable in pointing you to important resources, many of the better tools you'll need are either not on the Internet or are not listed on the particular directory you're logged onto.

THE WEB: A NEW BIBLE OR PLAIN OLD YELLOW PAGES?

"When will we come to our senses? The World Wide Web is inefficient and overhyped. . . . Have we completely lost our minds regarding its incredible inefficiency and the fact that 95 percent of the pages served up on the web are useless garbage? . . .

"Many of the favorite Web sites are nothing more than lists of other sites. It's as if the entire Web were modeled after a pyramid scheme or a chain letter. Saying that Yahoo or Lycos is your favorite site is like saying the Yellow Pages is your favorite book. . . .

"Put the Web in its proper place—right next to the Yellow Pages, not next to the Holy Bible."

SOURCE: John Dvorak, "Web Schmeb," *PC Computing* (March 1996).

Dvorak is a highly regarded Internet guru and curmudgeon who frequently challenges sacred cows blocking the information superhighway.

In short, the technology underlying Web directories and search engines is imperfect, incomplete, time-consuming, and probably too unreliable and risky for serious investment decision making, which is why a reputable NET*navigator is essential—because one of its functions is to serve as an information resource *integrator* for cyberspace investors.

Software Developers: The Road Ahead

When Microsoft introduced the Microsoft Network, the computer world staged a major counterattack. Everyone from CompuServe, Prodigy, and America Online to Netscape, Sun, and IBM participated. The U.S. Attorney General even tossed in a few grenades.

The opposing team fought Microsoft hard and fast, not only in the legal and political arenas, but also by taking advantage of all the publicity in the public marketplace. All of us were deluged with free online installation disks stuffed in just about every consumer and technical magazine sold. Sun savored Java. And Netscape went ballistic on Wall Street.

HOW MICROSOFT MISSED THE FORK IN THE ROAD AHEAD

"Gates' description of the current Internet, for example, leaves the impression that we're still back in the dawn of the new era, back before the world discovered the World Wide Web and started building a new computer industry there—without waiting for Microsoft to lead the way.... The name Netscape doesn't appear in the book....

"You can't blame Gates for such wishful thinking. But the Web and companies such as Netscape and the new Internet technologies such as Sun Microsystems Inc.'s Java programming language (also not mentioned) are changing the rules of the software industry. That has investors questioning Microsoft's future—and Gates' applying his talents to a broad range of Web initiatives."

SOURCE: Geoff Lewis, "Heavy Fog on the I-Way," review of Gates' autobiography, *The Road Ahead, BusinessWeek* (December 4, 1995).

Moreover, the competitive pressures exerted by Microsoft's massive $100-million marketing campaign forced the commercial online services to make substantial upgrades in the services offered. They added Internet connections and Web browsers, as well as new content and formats. Acquisitions became commonplace. Entry to the Internet world came quickly as CompuServe bought SPRY and America Online bought WebCrawler—just a few examples in the unfolding drama.

Net result? The online services actually grew larger and became *much stronger competitors* as a result of their responses to the *mere threat* from the Microsoft Network. Meanwhile, MSN was unable to meet expectations, having misjudged the Internet market.

As Microsoft was being attacked from all sides, there must have been many days when Gates wished he'd simply concentrated on the new Windows, without having distracting himself with Intuit, the Microsoft Network, and that biography all at the same time. The wake-up call came when Netscape scored a grand slam.

MICROSOFT NETWORK: VINTAGE BUS IN PIT STOP FOR AN OVERHAUL

For all practical purposes, when the Microsoft Network decided to convert from a subscription-based online service to a Website, it was a wise decision, the sign of the turnaround. At that point the content available to investors was not even in competition with that of the average free Web directories. Moreover, better resources were available elsewhere in much larger, more interactive doses with the online services, such as CompuServe.

In addition to misgauging the Internet, Microsoft also made a major strategic marketing error, by limiting MSN exclusively to Windows 95. Even traveling in a reliable, vintage bus like Microsoft's Windows 3.1 wasn't good enough to allow a curious Websurfer an opportunity to sample MSN's content.

When MSN was axed a few months after launching, it had less than 100 content providers in the business area. By comparison, the free Website, such as Wall Street Directory, has 2,500 links to resources, and CompuServe has a total of 3,000 providers. MSN had no more than perhaps 15 selections of some value to the cyberspace investor—and virtually every one was already available on the Web, and without Windows 95.

23.1 Microsoft Network: on a long bus ride to the central marketplace.

MICROSOFT DECLARES WAR: THE SLEEPING GIANT AWAKENS

"On December 7, 1995, Microsoft invited analysts and journalists to an all-day briefing in Seattle to hear CEO Bill Gates and other top company executives divulge its Internet strategy. Pointing out that it was Pearl Harbor Day, Gates in his opening remarks quoted a U.S. admiral who had said Japan's attack on the United States had 'awakened a sleeping giant' [and] had been riled into action and would, like the United States in World War II, triumph in the Internet arena. . . .

"In a well-orchestrated show of force, Gates and his lieutenants sought to reverse the tide by demonstrating a strong Internet strategy and a commitment to winning the market. . . . Thus the stage is set for a battle of titans—with Gates pitted against Netscape's Jim Clark and Marc Andreessen, Sun's Scott McNealy, AOL's Case, IBM's Gerstner, and a galaxy of other opponents. It is now a fight for market share and mindshare."

SOURCE: Michael Neubarth, "Microsoft Declares War," *Internet World* (March 1996).

According to Microsoft, the main reason for this current situation is the fact that Microsoft changed its Internet strategy shortly after launching MSN. Now, Microsoft is finally committed to the Internet and has shifted its focus from an online service to a Web-based service.

Instead of providing MSN by subscription (like AOL, for example) and doing it *exclusively* on Microsoft products—Windows 95, Microsoft's browser, and its Web publishing software—MSN will now be open to *any* browser, *any* publishing, and *any* programming technology available on the Web. As a result, all this fuss over MSN's problems now appears to be little more than a footnote to Microsoft's corporate history.

NEW CORPORATE STRATEGY: A FORMULA 500 RACING TEAM

Microsoft Network is included here among the top competitors principally because of Microsoft's *potential power rather than actual performance*, at least in the financial cyberspace arena. Clearly Microsoft now has a strong commitment to the Internet. But more important—much like the other *potential* next-generation giants such as AT&T, Data Broadcasting, CNBC, and Time Warner—Microsoft has enormous financial and technological resources that could be brought to bear rapidly, if it chooses.

Microsoft may not have been able to merge Intuit into the fold, but the move showed it had a clear understanding of the strategic role Intuit and Quicken are destined to play as the commercial banks invade a game that the discounters, retail brokers, and investment bankers thought belonged to them. In addition, Microsoft Network could suddenly buy a Telescan, DBC, or Mutual Funds Online, for example. Such a merger or acquisition would get it back in the content game quickly, by adding some hefty, industrial-strength information resources for the individual investors. However, that's an unlikely strategy.

From another perspective—*the long-range, corporate, strategic view*—MSN is now a minor part in the larger drama. Microsoft appears to be tackling bigger financial priorities—strategic corporate issues that will eventually benefit Microsoft's own investors and, hopefully, the cyberspace investor in the near future. Some of these financial areas are:

❐ **Internet Credit Card Payment Systems:** The competition is with IBM and MasterCard to create the industry standard and another lock on another essential Internet technology.

- ❐ **Online Banking:** Microsoft missed with Intuit, but it is still a preferred software offered by most banks as an alternative to other electronic banking services to customers.

- ❐ **Telecommunications Partnerships:** Early this year, Microsoft committed to a joint venture with MCI, the telecommunications giant.

- ❐ **Online News Broadcasting:** Recently Microsoft inked a deal with General Electric's NBC to create both a 24-hour cable news channel and an online news service, in direct competition with CNN and CNNfn.

- ❐ **Interactive TV and Video Servers:** Microsoft is testing interactive television with cable systems around the world, as well as digital storage and delivery of film and television programming on demand.

- ❐ **Wireless Communications:** Microsoft has also invested in various companies and technologies for over-air, destination-to-destination delivery of E-mail, messaging, and data information.

- ❐ **Unrestricted Software Usage:** Recently, Microsoft decided to let content providers use any Net publishing and browser software, including Java and Netscape, rather than restrict them to Windows 95 and Microsoft's Web browser.

- ❐ **Entertainment and the Dream Team:** Gates is now an investor in the entertainment Dream Team, with producers Stephen Spielberg, Jeffrey Katzenberg, and David Geffen. In fact, *Wired* magazine says Microsoft "is morphing into a media company for the new millenium."

Gates is again showing the spirit of Indiana Jones and the drive of the Terminator. Should he be worried about all the potshots taken at him? Hardly. Expect him to have the last laugh. All this reminds us of the comment a rock star once made when somebody asked him about a potentially damaging article about him in the *National Enquirer.* All he wanted to know was, "Did they spell my name right?" Gates has a similar confidence. Watch out: There's nothing more dangerous than a wounded dinosaur.

Forget about writing the Microsoft Network's obituary. They played a good defensive game. Now watch them run the ball. As quarterback, Gates is obviously more focused on a broader strategic positioning for the long run and on the investment community, rather than on the specific content for an MSN Website.

Gates' war is being fought on a highly unpredictable playing field. Gates is not alone; he has coaches, investment bankers, and in-house corporate strategists helping him scope out the road ahead. The MSN arsenal is limited now, but it would be a serious mistake to count Gates out of this market for investors' NET*navigators.

BOTTOM LINE: NEW TECHNOLOGIES ACCELERATING THE CYPERSPACE REVOLUTION

Software developers are the brains driving the Net technology revolution. And just as Intuit and its banking consortium is a strong contender to become a dominant force in Wall Street cyberspace, Netscape's browser and Sun Microsystems' Java also have as much of a chance as the MSN has right now. They are revolutionaries on the cutting edge of Net technology with broad customer bases.

SUN'S HOT JAVA: REVOLUTIONARY NEW SOFTWARE

"What is this thing called Java? And how might it revolutionize the Internet, if not the entire software business?

"Java is a computer language that Sun Microsystems Inc. designed just for network computing. A program written in Java can run in any computer or digital device. . . .

"There's vast potential in this computer-within-a-computer scheme: It can let millions of otherwise incompatible computers all use the same Java software.

"More important, though, Java's ability to hide incompatibilities could rewrite the rules of the software industry—on and off the Net. With Java everywhere, software companies would no longer have to create unique versions of their products for machines running Microsoft Windows, Macintosh, and Unix workstations. They could be sure of compatibility even with computers not yet invented . . . as Sun says it, 'Write once, run anywhere.'

"And not just on computers. The virtual machine program is small—only 64,000 bytes—so it may even get used in cellular phones and TV sets. . . .

"Most critically, Java looks like it will play a key role in bringing additional functions to the Internet itself. . . . The effect would be to greatly accelerate the Internet's already frenetic evolution."

SOURCE: John Verity, "Meet Java, the Invisible Computer," in "The Software Revolution, the Web Changes Everything," *BusinessWeek* (December 4, 1995).

For example, Netscape and some sharp financial information providers could retrofit the Netscape browser into a perfect, customized operating platform specifically designed for cyberspace investors, armed with all the necessary content and analytics for investment decision making. Most likely, Netscape is already doing this for its private IntraNet clients.

And Sun's Java is so flexible, you don't need any special hardware or software. *None. You'll simply download all applications when and as needed,* through any one of the currently popular browsers and navigators. That's right—download not just demos, but complete working systems that an investor can use in managing a portfolio and making new investments.

Think of it. Your online commercial bank, or your discount broker, or one of those new cyberspace financial resources will be able to send you all the necessary data—plus, temporarily install all the new software you need to use that data. Java acts like a mini–stealth bomber in cyberspace. Small wonder experts predict Java will revolutionize cyberspace.

Technological alternatives remain wide open. Netscape has dramatically and decisively proven that all software developers, regardless of size

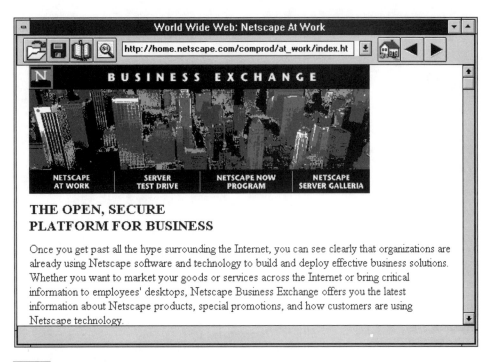

23.2 Netscape's Business Exchange: bottom-line solutions.

and incorporation date, are on equal footing with Microsoft, Sun, and IBM. *The playing field is leveling for software developers, as well as for investors. So expect the unexpected as the revolution rapidly unfolds—especially some new power players.*

Bottom line: It's virtually guaranteed that the *independent investor* will come up the winner, regardless of which one of these software developers comes out on top of *the* competitive struggle. The Wall Street cyberspace revolution is being controlled from Main Street, not Wall Street. On Main Street the power of the individual investor is exercised with each new online connection to the Internet, to an IntraNet, or to some exciting new software technology. This revolution cannot be stopped.

New Securities Exchanges: World Wide on the Web

The exchanges are less likely to take a leading role in developing effective NET∗navigators for investors. The discount brokers, the commercial online banks, the investment banks, and the companies themselves, through direct buying and other means, are all way ahead of the exchanges. They have more of a commercial incentive and are already *into action*.

Nevertheless, since the exchanges have started developing some rather extensive Websites in the past year, it's certainly conceivable that in the near future they, too—like other quasi-public utilities, such as the telephone companies, broadcasters, and publishers—may start playing a bigger role in helping the cyberspace investor navigate through the investment decision-making waters.

NEW COMPETITION: FUTURES EXCHANGES VERSUS STOCK EXCHANGES

We know all too well that financial cyberspace is eliminating distance—in particular, the distance between the new cyberspace shareholders and the company issuing the security. For example, most of the write-ups on the benefit of DRIPs emphasize the fact that this is a perfect way of cutting out the big bad brokers and their big bad commissions. Not just full-service brokers, *but all brokers including the discounters.*

Carried to its logical extreme—eliminating distance between investor and issuing company, and providing the new NET∗investor with the right content, technology, and analytic power—financial cyberspace could also reduce the role of the exchanges themselves.

THE SEC IS LEVELING THE PLAYING FIELD FOR SMALL INVESTORS

"The SEC plans a radical overhaul to give the little guy a fair shake.

"When the new NASDAQ Stock Market opened for business in 1971, it was heralded as the market of the future. Instead of face-to-face haggling at the existing exchanges, it featured a new electronic stock-quote system. Since then, NASDAQ has grown astronomically to become the world's second largest market, after the NYSE. . . . As the market evolved, it has tilted further away from the small investor in favor of brokerage firms, who make huge trading profits, often at the little guy's expense. . . .

"Not any longer, if Arthur Levitt Jr. has his way. The SEC chairman is personally overseeing a revolutionary overhaul that could drastically change and improve the way NASDAQ does business. . . . The SEC chief says his plan to 'level the playing field' for the small investors will attract more players. . . . Small investors will have access to the same stock prices as the professionals. . . ."

SOURCE: Michael Shredder and Amy Barrett, "NASDAQ: Power to the People?" *BusinessWeek* (March 4, 1996).

The Stock Exchanges

The more tradition-bound stock exchanges could face declining importance. For example, as more and more investors shift to cyberspace funds and DRIPs and get in the habit of purchasing their stocks directly from the OneSources and the corporations, the stock exchanges may have to shift their focus to accommodate the new trend toward long-term buy-and-hold strategies.

Obviously, there are many contrary factors that clearly show that the NYSE and other exchanges are already near the maximum with increased trading volumes, at times bordering on another Black Monday meltdown. It is probably enough so that they actually welcome more DRIPs, rather than worry about the loss of traffic.

Besides, every shareholder—even if a very long term buy-and-hold nontrader—eventually needs an exchange to create a marketplace for his or her securities. And that may explain, in part, why the stock exchanges are slow in developing Websites. They have enough to focus on elsewhere.

Futures, Options, and Derivatives Exchanges

The exchanges dealing with futures, options, and derivatives are thriving in cyberspace; they love the glitz. Moreover, they've been experiencing increasing trading volumes as more and more investors are drawn to these exchanges. Besides, corporate issuers don't offer derivatives, so DRIPs aren't competing directly in the same markets as the more exotic securities.

Barron's Guide to Making Investment Decisions is probably correct in observing that, "the futures market might be described as people selling what they don't have [such as 5,000 bushels of corn] to people who don't want it anyhow." However, it's where the action is.

The high-flying, hotshot derivatives business, which used to be just a game of insurance side-bets played by farmers and ranchers up to 50 years ago, is becoming competition for Las Vegas, the lottery, and the race track—at least psychologically. Today, speculators are more dominant than farmers and ranchers in this contest.

For many speculators, these exchanges are no different from betting on the Super Bowl. It's a sport, it's a game, and it's exciting. Psychologically, the thrill pays off more for investors than the money does. Moreover, making money in futures is infinitely more predictable *for the professional* who systematically applies a trading method.

FLASHY FUTURES UPSTAGE STAID STOCK EXCHANGES

The exchanges have a vast amount of specific content concentrated in one spot. And when you consider that the portfolios of many *individual* investors may have just a dozen or two stocks and funds to follow, any one exchange could evolve into the focal point or navigational center for an investor, if it chose to. Of course, the exchanges would have to offer a few more analytic tools to perform as a NET*navigator. But it is clear that they already grasp the power of the World Wide Web as a *marketing* vehicle in reaching the new NET*investor.

Now that these futures exchanges are taking full advantage of its enormous marketing potentials, it would be a short step to add more complete navigational power. For example, if the commercial banks can offer customers Quicken with Investor Insight and discount trading, perhaps stop the exchanges might try something quite similar.

TOP-10 FUTURES, OPTIONS, AND DERIVATIVES EXCHANGES

- ❑ **CBOE:** Chicago Board of Options Exchange
- ❑ **CBOT:** Chicago Board of Trade
- ❑ **CME:** Chicago Mercantile Exchange
- ❑ **DTB:** Deutsche Terminboese
- ❑ **LIFFE:** London Int'l Financial Futures and Options Exchange
- ❑ **MATIF:** Marche a Terme Int'l de France
- ❑ **MEFF:** Renta Fija
- ❑ **SFE:** Sydney Futures Exchange
- ❑ **SOFFEX:** Swiss Options and Financial Futures Exchange
- ❑ **TOCOM:** Tokyo Commodities Exchange

SOURCE: Investment News Online at *http://www.ino.com*

Unfortunately, the major stock exchanges, like the full-service brokerage firms, have been slow in ramping onto the new financial cyberspace, perhaps because they are unsure of their direction and how they fit in the global cyberspace competition for the investor's trading action. Instead, the exchanges showing the strongest interest in the Web are those in the high-risk futures business, which may be of less value to the average investor building a solid, long-term investment portfolio. Besides, the data they display is too late for successful futures day-trading.

Some of the important exchanges that are up and running include:

❑ **Chicago Mercantile Exchange:**   The biggest futures exchange worldwide, with trading not just in fluid milk, soy beans, and pork bellies in the central United States, but it includes the Mexico 30 Stock Index, Brazilian Real, Asian, European, and other exotic global securities. The classy Merc opening projects a United Nations of financial cyberspace. Its Website is updated and upgraded on a regular basis and, in the near future, could even begin including some analytic tools to help make it more of a navigator.

❑ **Chicago Board of Trade:**   The Merc's main competitor, this is a rival with almost the same volume of business in the commodity futures and derivatives markets. Check out its pages; there are loads of educational and current trading data here. The opening page tries to capture the electric spirit of the trading pit, with a waving hand in your face.

24.1 Chicago Merc: a United Nations for futures trading.

☐ **American Stock Exchange:** This Website tells you that AMEX is the "Smarter Place To Be," with "800 innovative, growing companies . . . serving financial markets worldwide." Its interest in financial cyberspace is obvious with its featured "Inter@ctive Week Internet Index," a composite of the major cyberspace companies tracked by *Inter@ctive Week,* a major computer industry magazine.

☐ **Philadelphia Stock Exchange:** Although this Website is still under development, one thing stands out like a sore thumb. Here we have the oldest and most respected exchange in America *hustling* Websurfers with a "Success Kit" showing a cartoon of a juggler tossing around AT&T, GE, Coke, and other major companies.

The imagery may be more suited to Vegas and MTV than distinguished American exchanges, yet it is probably in line with *what's to come: more entertainment value on financial Websites to capture the new cyberspace investor, with a short attention span and high-tech sophistication.* In all fairness to the Philadelphia Exchange, more than anything else this kind of inconsistent

24.2 Chicago Board: trading action in the pits.

24.3 AMEX: "The Smarter Place to Be" in cyberspace.

SEC APPROVES NEW CYBERSPACE STOCK EXCHANGE ON NET

"Spring Street Brewing Co., the firm that pioneered the initial public offering over the World Wide Web, is now taking on Wall Street with plans to arrange Internet IPOs for other companies *and set up an online stock exchange.* . . . A new firm, Wit Capital Corp . . . will compete with underwriters for new issue business and allow investors to buy shares on the Web and trade them without using a broker. . . .

"The Securities and Exchange Commission welcomed the innovative move, but NASDAQ, a potential competitor, was more reserved and said there are regulatory issues to be resolved." The brewery "went public over the Internet in 1995 and *is not listed on an exchange.*"

SOURCE: "Spring Street Brewing Plans to Start an Internet-based Stock Exchange," Reuters newswire, *Los Angeles Times* (April 3, 1996).

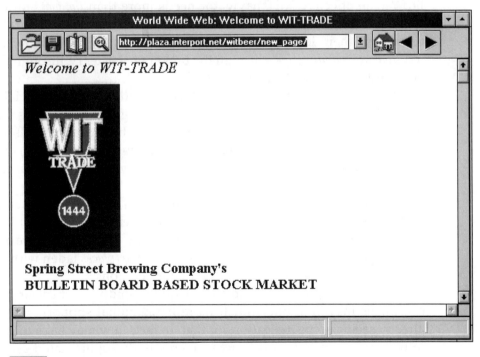

24.4 WIT-TRADE: first Web-based stock market of future.

imagery shows the uncertainty and confusion many organizations have when they initially move into cyberspace and, in the process, misjudge their own identity and the intelligence of their audience.

If you are seriously interested in the higher-risk derivative securities, then you might start with one of the better independent Websites for exchange information, such as Investment News Online (I-NO), "the Website Center for Futures & Options."

However, caution is again advised. For most independent cyberspace investors, derivative securities are a small part of a long-term portfolio. Or if they do invest, it's likely to be a minor allocation of high-risk money they're prepared to lose completely, like the attitude most people have about cash taken to Las Vegas.

BOTTOM LINE: GLITZY BILLBOARDS FOR HIGH-RISK SECURITIES

Data, information, content—all are essential to building a winning portfolio. Yet, an effective NET*navigator needs more than *the facts* to work. In spite of the enormous power base and the interest the exchanges have in controlling their destiny, the exchanges historically work with the individual investor—*indirectly*—through the brokerage industry, through the data vendors, and through corporations.

After observing the exchanges develop and grow in financial cyberspace for a couple of years now and recognizing that anything is possible, it remains highly unlikely that in the near term the exchanges will compete either directly or indirectly with Dow Jones, Reuters, Bloomberg, Quicken, Telescan, CompuServe, or the others actively working on their own NET*navigators for cyberspace investors.

For the present, the securities exchanges—in particular, the derivatives exchanges—appear satisfied with using their Websites more like billboards along a superhighway headed toward the glitzy casinos. They are a way to whet appetites rather than true cyberspace *marketplaces* laden with content and tools to support successful investment decisions.

Nevertheless, all that could change quite rapidly. By the year 2000, the exchanges may well offer much more navigational support, and we are already seeing some indications of that. In fact, they may have to get more into the game, in order to attract an increasingly sophisticated cyberspace investor in an increasingly sophisticated Internet marketplace.

THE EMERGING NEW GLOBAL CYBERSPACE SUPER-EXCHANGE

Back in 1992, the editor-in-chief of *Wall Street & Technology* asked, "Could the NYSE floor become a museum devoted to vintage technology?" Fortunately, since then the magazine has reported a major overhaul, as the "NYSE Heads Off A Crash." The cost of creating this new high-tech system was $125 million, a large sum for an organization with a mere $180 million in annual revenues at the time.

Notwithstanding the NYSE's upgrade, the cyberspace revolution continues to be driven by uncontrollable and unpredictable *external* forces that leave open and unresolved the *destiny of not only NYSE but every individual exchange throughout the world* that continues operating under the old myth that it exists as a separate entity.

For example, the following are a few powerful offshoots of a revolution that is creating many new kinds of *private exchanges*—privately run networks, IntraNets, or NET*exchanges—capable of operating *independently* of and/or parallel to the *traditional* financial exchanges, especially in a single global stock market network:

❐ **Private exchanges on IntraNets:**
   Dow Jones/Telerate: generates almost a $1 billion in revenues
   Reuters Instinet: a network already installed in over 30 counties
   Bloomberg Network: new billion-dollar financial info company
   Every major national and international corporation has an IntraNet

❐ **The Internet, a universal global exchange:**   An instant global network linking all investors anywhere with every exchange, plus huge databases, new analytics, new online computer technology, instant news, portfolio management tools, and more; forcing more competition and cooperation *between* the exchanges.

❐ **Emerging mutual fund trading systems:**
   Schwab's OneSource: accessing 150 mutual funds outside the
      Schwab family of funds
   Fidelity's FundNetwork: linking a few hundred non-Fidelity funds
   Fidelity's Fund Switching Options: although they must make even
      internal swaps on the NYSE, the trend is still there

❐ **Electronic discount brokerage:**   Today your phone company may be doing more than your broker, and probably soon will be much more involved in content and transactions as well as basic connections and delivery.

(Continued) ▶

▶ *(Continued)*

❑ **Buying direct from Corporate America:** Direct stock and dividend reinvestment purchase plans; no brokers and no commissions when you buy direct; a growing trend as we get a whole new breed of better-informed individual investors, who are sharper than most brokers.

And this is just the beginning. The dimensions of this emerging new financial cyberspace are staggering. Any exchange or, for that matter, any major company or institutional investor that assumes it has a lock on the individual investor as a customer may be in serious trouble just for making that assumption—not unlike IBM was back when it struck a deal with the young William Gates.

Wall Street Investment Bankers: The Establishment versus Rocket Scientists

The traditional Wall Street institutions, especially the investment banks and full-service brokerage houses, have been noticeably absent from the new financial cyberspace. They created financial cyberspace in the 1970s. However, in the 1990s many have openly refused to help the *independent* investor in cyberspace.

Their strategic avoidance of the new online and Internet technologies is at first puzzling, and yet, as you'll see on further investigation, it makes perfect sense. Wall Street has been defending the established order, the old paradigm, on survival instincts.

Consider the recent history: A couple of years ago, about the time the discount brokers were jumping online and on the Internet with their new Websites, an aggressive branch office broker with PaineWebber also saw opportunities in cyberspace.

Acting on his own initiative, this local broker created an impressive Website, loaded with content, interactive and multidimensional. When the Wall Street leadership heard of his efforts, they actually put his Website out of business. Other branch office efforts were similarly shut down. Paine-Webber offered this simple explanation: The regulatory agencies had not set up appropriate rules. As a result, one of Wall Street's largest and most respected names decided not to risk pioneering in this new cyberspace technology. Instead, they took a safer, slow lane on the information super-highway.

WHY WALL STREET'S ESTABLISHMENT FEARS THE INTERNET

"Matthew Long *was* a pioneering sort of broker. *Was* is the correct word, because this PaineWebber broker's popular site on the Internet's World Wide Web—the part of the Internet that's graphical, interactive and growing in leaps and bounds—was shut down . . . on the orders of the firm's compliance officers.

"The firm's feeling is that 'as the Internet is a relatively new media without rules and regulations as yet defined by the NASD or the SEC, PaineWebber feels it must take a conservative posture with its 6,000-plus investment executives until the parameters are set by those regulatory agencies,' says spokesperson Peter Casey."

SOURCE: Rosalyn Retkwa, "Broker Automation: On & Off the Info Highway," *Registered Representative* (June 1995).

However, the lack of regulations didn't stop the discount brokers. They didn't even slow down. Apparently thriving on this new freedom, they've been roaring around the cyberspace racetrack, waving the checkered flag. Meanwhile, the big Wall Street race cars stalled out, sidetracked in a long pit stop.

Aside from pointing the finger at the regulatory agencies, there are at least four fundamental and strategic reasons why the big institutions are reluctant to take full advantage of the competitive opportunities offered by the Internet. A review of these four reasons may give you some perspective

---

WALL STREET'S BILLBOARDS ALONG THE SUPERHIGHWAY

"Financial service firms are salivating at the idea of being able to do business over the Internet. But what products and services the denizens of cyberspace will be willing to pay for remains an open question.

"Wall Street's presence on the Net thus far has been confined to little more than advertising, with some exceptions. Many of the firms with Web pages offer only information on their products, background on the company and some basic data on the market."

SOURCE: Dean Tomasula, "Gravity Pulls Wall Street into the Net," *Wall Street & Technology* (October 1995).

in evaluating whether independent investors will get any help from traditional Wall Street institutions in cyberspace.

1. INSTITUTIONAL CONSERVATISM WINS OVER INNOVATION

In reporting on the impact of the cyberspace revolution in business, *Forbes* magazine recently noted the tendency of larger institutions to hold back, letting the smaller entrepreneurs pioneer new technologies and pave the advance. Conservative institutions normally avoid or minimize these risks, because, as the saying goes, pioneers often wind up with arrows in their backs.

The positive side of this wait-and-see tendency is that when *and if* the giants do move, they can move swiftly, with the resources, effectiveness, and speed of a Desert Storm attack. And that may well be their conscious or unconscious strategy on the Internet battlefield: Hold back, then quickly climb over the backs of the fallen pioneers and race triumphantly to the target.

2. DEMOGRAPHICS: AN AGING CUSTOMER BASE

An officer of another of these Wall Street top-ten giants explained that the cyberspace investor simply did not fit its profile of a targeted client. Web-surfers and cyberspace investors are considered too young, with relatively small portfolios. As a result, they can't afford to pay hefty fees for Wall Street's advice.

In contrast, the profile of the ideal customer for the large Wall Street firm is a wealthy 57-year-old who needs professional help with an investment portfolio. And most important, this client can afford the substantial advisory fees.

Of course, this Wall Street brokerage executive was ignoring the fact that someday the 27-year-old he's avoiding will be 57 with a sizeable portfolio—and by then, quite used to the do-it-yourself independence of cyberspace investing.

Wall Street is in a double bind, because if it does help its clients do it themselves, the fear is that eventually the client won't need them. Still, it

---

LOCAL BROKER: "WALL STREET DOESN'T SEE WHAT'S HAPPENING"

A Texas broker e-mailed this response to an online passage from my first book describing the Wall Street cyberspace revolution.

"Regarding the Cyberspace Revolution, I have been a broker for over 30 years with several New York Stock Exchange member firms. There really has not been that much change in the industry as far as the large member firms' approach to the investor. Most of the changes have occurred in the area of technology to process order flow and back office flow.

"What amazes me is the total indifference the full service brokerage firms have toward this changing environment. The last 4 to 5 years have been a revolution, and they just don't see it happening right before their very eyes. . . .

"There are only two things full service brokerage firms have to market: service and information. Service is important, but to be informed is critical.

"Now, any investor with any computer knowledge can go outside the halls of Wall Street and gather information and act on that information. Many of the regional firms don't seem to acknowledge this revolution is taking place.

"The next generation of investors will approach the markets totally different than all previous generations. The dynamics of capitalism will prosper, but at a different level."

is short-sighted to ignore this scenario. A similar mind-set preceded Microsoft's difficulties with the Internet, Sun, and Netscape.

3. REVOLUTIONARY NEW CYBERSPACE TECHNOLOGIES

As the Internet explodes from 25 million to many more than 100 million computers connected by 2000, this vast *public* network of computer systems is likely to begin choking on its own success and size. More than one experienced Internet guru has already commented on the coming slowdown. Obviously higher-speed transmission systems and over-air broadcasting technologies, like McCaw's Sky-Net, will reduce the impact. But the fact is that the Internet's becoming a common carrier like the Greyhound bus. In contrast, most travelers in the financial community prefer a more exclusive, private-club-car atmosphere in which to conduct their transactions.

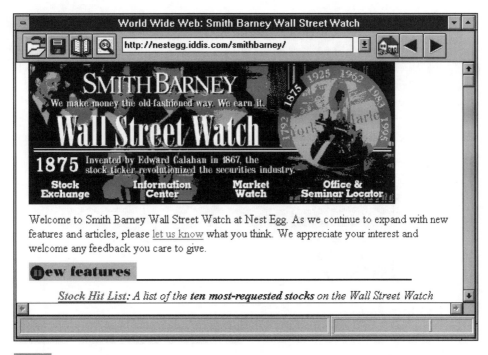

25.1 Wall Street Watch from Smith Barney.

As a result, in the midst of all this drama about the Internet and the Web, we are also seeing a parallel explosion of *private networks* for financial services: IntraNets. Several of the elite IntraNets have been around for decades and even created financial cyberspace in the 1970s—such as Reuter's Instinet, Dow Jones/Telerate, and, more recently, Bloomberg's international network. A *Wired* magazine editor referred to them as "toll roads," an appropriate term, given the increased traffic, the overload clogging the main highway, and the fact that you're charged for each mile of data or time spent.

Typically, these IntraNets are not on the Internet, although by definition they are still part of the larger, emerging information superhighway. Or if they are connected to the Internet, there are security firewalls preventing leaks. Another example of a working IntraNet is the global telecommunications network that is the backbone of CompuServe's incredible success, with private links throughout Europe and the Asia/Pacific Rim, as well as throughout the Americas.

Very few people know about or understand how critically important these emerging new IntraNets are becoming. Moreover, as the Internet

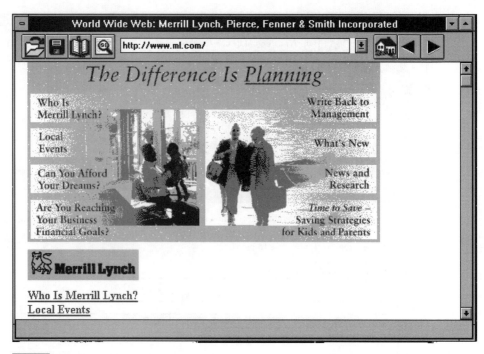

25.2　Merrill Lynch: The Difference Is Planning . . . for wealthy clients.

expands, *these IntraNet toll roads will probably grow even faster than the Internet,* both to handle the overload and to meet security needs and the demands of many Wall Street cyberspace investors for higher quality.

Thus, it's entirely conceivable that Wall Street's conservative wait-and-see Internet strategy may pay off. Why? Because Wall Street's top guns are already hooked into the major financial IntraNets in cyberspace.

4. FEAR OF COMPETING DIRECTLY WITH DISCOUNT BROKERS

When you set aside all the other reasons and excuses, the fact remains that ever since the SEC mandated *negotiated* commissions in 1974, the full-service Wall Street firms have had a hard time competing *directly* with the discount brokers and their cut-rate commissions. In fact, they've conceded, *and decided not to compete in the price arena.* In other words, this is not simply a new '90s issue about the Internet and online brokerage. Brokerage firms have been fighting this battle on Main Street for over 20 years.

WALL STREET LEADER DISAGREES: "DO-IT-YOURSELF INVESTING IS *NOT* A VIABLE CONCEPT IN THE 1990S"

In order to compete effectively with operations like Schwab's OneSource, Smith Barney will offer a deluxe service that will include no-load fund transactions on mutual funds, stocks, and bonds; access to mutual fund and other investment research; and personal investment advice.

One traditional brokerage firm says, "Wheat First's FundSource requires a minimum of $35,000; customers also pay an annual fee based on assets, starting at 1.5% on the minimum account. Smith Barney's program will be structured similarly. The brokers are betting that by acting as middlemen for the no-load funds they can please affluent investors who value—and are willing to pay for—personal service.

"Says Jay Mandelbaum, executive vice president at Smith Barney: 'Do-it-yourself investing is not a viable concept in the 1990s.' "

SOURCE: Bethany McLean, "A Better Way to Buy No-Load Mutual Funds," *Fortune* (December 25, 1995).

Obviously, *discount* brokers disagree with Smith Barney. So, too, do the growing numbers of computer-savvy individual investors. Smith Barney's position that do-it-yourself investing is not a viable alternative today is rapidly becoming a minority position. Nevertheless, that position is fiercely defended by many traditionalists who do not yet fully comprehend the inevitability of the Wall Street cyberspace revolution.

One major Wall Street firm, Donaldson Lufkin Jenrette, got smart early on. DLJ's answer was simple. They acquired a wholly owned subsidiary to handle bare-bones discount brokerage. And their PCFN subsidiary's done quite well marketing and delivering through commercial online services like AOL. But Morgan, Merrill, Lehman, Smith Barney, and the other old-line establishment institutions haven't followed DLJ's lead.

The big firms are between a rock and a hard place. Merrill and the others believe they are in a no-win situation if they compete head to head with the discounters. Meanwhile, the discount brokers are now offering new cyberspace technologies that allow them to provide not only bare-bones, do-it-yourself trades, but discounters are now also giving the cyberspace investor many new high-tech alternatives to the previously exclusive advice that was supplied by the large full-service brokers, as well as teaching the next generation of investors to think for themselves and to make independent investment decisions using these powerful new technologies.

WALL STREET'S STRATEGIC TARGET:
THE WELL-TO-DO ELITE, NOT THE DO-IT-YOURSELF MASSES

"Merrill is the world's largest underwriter, and it boasts the largest sales force in the business, blanketing America with 13,000 brokers serving 4.5 million households.

"By the year 2000, Tully [the CEO] wants $1 trillion in client assets, up over 42% from the current $703 billion, and enough to generate fees that would cover every dime in fixed costs. . . .

"Merrill 'will never compete with a Schwab on price. Merrill Lynch supports not only an expensive branch network, but a $200 million budget for research as well.

"By contrast, the discounters are stripped-down outfits that sell mainly through 800 numbers and don't employ analysts. Hence, they can sell stocks and bonds for a lot less than Merrill.

"But Merrill is striving to create a one-stop shop that untangles a well-to-do client's scrambled financial profile from retirement savings to mortgages, then provides an array of mutual funds, insurance products, trust accounts, and loans to put the picture in order.

"The advice and planning . . . will enable Merrill to keep charging rich prices for its products.

"There's already a measure of competition offering similar services. But for its Cadillac service, Merrill isn't courting the masses. Instead, it's aiming at a narrow segment, the wealthy and near-wealthy. The target is 'priority households' with $250,000 to $5 million in liquid assets: families headed by executives, doctors, lawyers, entrepreneurs, all too busy making money to manage it—or retirees who'd rather fish and travel than pick mutual funds.

"Its 534,000 priority households—20% of its total customers—generate 80% of its brokerage revenues. The big money is in the hands of people over 50. Fortunate for Merrill, 36 million baby-boomers lugging a trove of savings will cross that milestone by 2005."

SOURCE: Shawn Tully, "Merrill Lynch Bulls Ahead," *Fortune* (February 19, 1995).

Unfortunately, many of the Wall Street old-timers fail to see this new generation of do-it-yourself investors as sufficiently important, let alone consider that the technological revolution is having a profound impact on the next generation of investors.

The Wall Street establishment still believes that the simple trading-only technology is the prevailing cyberspace model. And that could be a fatal error, because:

❏ Today's cyberspace investors are quickly learning how to go online and on the Internet and do their own analysis quickly and efficiently, often for only $10 to $20 a month, or

❏ Investors will find some mutual funds network like OneSource or FundsNetwork to manage their portfolios in conjunction with an online service, or

❏ They can use Quicken's Investor Insight and their commercial bank for trading, as well as bill paying, planning, and budgeting, or

❏ They can go direct and buy stocks in hundreds of blue-chip companies now on the Net.

And the list goes on.

Moreover, these options are becoming technologically quite sophisticated. They're not just something like a Nintendo entertainment game package your kids want from CompUSA. In fact, the new NET*navigators for cyberspace investors are often more powerful than the ones used by your local branch office broker.

WALL STREET REVOLUTION IN THE AGE OF THE INDIVIDUAL

"The great unifying theme at the conclusion of the 20th century is the triumph of the individual. . . . The new source of power is not money in the hands of a few, but knowledge in the hands of many."

SOURCE: John Naisbitt, *Megatrends* (Warner, 1982); John Naisbitt and Patricia Aburdene, *Megatrends 2000* (Avon, 1990).

Furthermore, these cyberspace alternatives are endlessly proliferating, on a daily basis. And yet the big Wall Street firms haven't grasped the fundamental significance of the paradigm shift that is transforming Wall Street right under their noses.

WALL STREET'S OUTDATED STRATEGY . . . A DEPENDENT INVESTOR

Smith Barney is an excellent example of the current state of mind the traditional Wall Street institutions have about the emerging financial cyberspace revolution. Its position: "Do-it-yourself investing is not a viable concept in the 90s." This strategy clearly shows a denial of reality. Today's do-it-yourself investors are the core of the cyberspace investing revolution, and they are rapidly growing in numbers.

This focuses us on the fundamental issue here. *Bottom line:* Wall Street is *not* committed to the independent investor, quite the contrary. Wall Street's Establishment is locked in a basic belief system, convinced that *their survival is a direct function of keeping investors dependent on their advice.* As a result, their financial products and their entire marketing strategy is based on a form of organizational paternalism.

It does not matter that the belief system no longer fits the flood of new technologies and resources available to today's individual investor. *These institutions have unconsciously chosen to deny the significance of new technologies as well as the independence of the cyberspace investor.* This is unfortunate.

The titans are at war. There is obviously a major clash between two opposing paradigms here: Wall Street institutions are defending an old paradigm based on *dependency,* while the new individual investors are fighting for their *independence,* and their numbers are growing rapidly.

Ultimately, the Merrill Lynch and Smith Barney strategy will prove to be their Achilles heel. Hopefully, this questionable battle strategy will spur the next generation of Wall Street's leaders into action, *before it's too late.*

WALL STREET: DRIFTING OUT OF CONTROL INTO CYBERSPACE

Seen from another perspective, it's important to remember that today's Wall Street is no longer located in New York City. Physically yes, but that's irrelevant today. Wall Street is now located *out there* in global cyberspace, thanks to the technology revolution. This new reality is particularly unnerving for many in the traditional Wall Street institutions.

Why? Because Wall Street cyberspace is drifting beyond their control. In fact, it is beyond everyone's control—with a mind of its own, run by the awesome and unpredictable forces of technology. The traditional Wall Street power structure has lost control of its destiny in cyberspace, and that is extremely frustrating, forcing the Establishment to cling tenaciously to the old paradigm.

With a little luck, the old-line Wall Street institutions will soon take a cue from their siblings, the commercial banks, who responded aggressively to Bill Gates' remark that they were dinosaurs. Perhaps then they'll see that the new information technology is like a meteor about to disrupt the natural order of life on Wall Street.

Unfortunately, it may already be too late. Today's independent investor now has so many other incredible, new, high-tech resources—NET*investing navigators, electronically accessible databases, and other computerized power tools—replacing all that heretofore unique advice from the full-service Wall Street institutions.

CHALLENGE: BOLDLY GO WHERE NO ONE HAS GONE BEFORE

The discount brokers, the commercial banks, the mutual funds, the electronic information vendors, and so many other *new cyberspace information providers,* including the exchanges and the SEC itself, are already taking steps to satisfy the insatiable information demands of the new independent cyberspace investor.

The Wall Street Establishment would have to make some outrageously bold, swift, and unprecedented moves to recapture any semblance of leadership in the new Wall Street cyberspace. Meanwhile, Wall Street's traditional power players currently offer no competitive NET*navigators for consideration. Instead:

❏ Some traditional Wall Street institutions are focusing on global capital sources serving the emerging, independent nations, and

❏ Other traditional Wall Street institutions are focusing exclusively on the independently wealthy who presumably have neither the time nor the interest in becoming do-it-yourself investors.

By default, the *discount* brokers are the ones offering the new electronic tools to help the independent investor in cyberspace.

Arguably there's enough room for both markets—the wealthy and the masses—at least today. However, in the near future, the shift will continue toward more independence for the masses, and no amount of resistance or denial can stop it.

That one fact is inevitable. The thrust of the Wall Street cyberspace revolution is so powerful that in the very near future the sleeping giant is bound to awaken and come thundering forth. Thus, once again, the individual investors will wind up with even more power in the new world of global NET*investing.

BOTTOM LINE: NEW WALL STREET EMERGING
FROM THE REVOLUTION

If John Naisbitt's assertion in *Megatrends* is accurate that "the new source of power is not money in the hands of a few, but knowledge in the hands of many," it may well explain the paradigm shift in Wall Street cyberspace and why the traditional institutions must steadfastly deny or minimize the impact of technology on the wave of new do-it-yourself investors. And why the new Wall Street power players are likely to be high-tech rocket scientists such as D. E. Shaw & Co.—firms that are not locked into defending the established order.

Shaw's FarSight project will result in a new NET*navigator, which, if it meets its production goals, will be far more advanced than anything reviewed here, potentially combining the best features of the best systems. And in a major departure from the current denial of the cyberspace revolution, Shaw will be the first Wall Street firm to help the *independent* investor with cyberspace technology.

ROCKET SCIENTISTS ARE TRANSFORMING WALL STREET

"Way up atop a Manhattan skyscraper, inside the investment banking firm of D.E. Shaw & Co., is a tiny hexagonal room staffed by six people who look fresh out of college . . . utterly unimpressive—except for the fact that Shaw's trading volume is sometimes equal to 5% of the total trading volume on the New York Stock Exchange. . . .

"D.E. Shaw & Co. is the most intriguing and mysterious force on Wall Street today. It's the ultimate quant shop, a nest of mathematicians, computer scientists, and other devotees of quantitative analysis. . . . It's the answer you'll get if you ask the question, What's the most technologically sophisticated firm on the Street. . . .

"Now Shaw and his scientists and mathematicians are pursuing a hugely ambitious plan to venture far beyond Wall Street. If they succeed, anything but a sure thing—D.E. Shaw could become as well known as Charles Schwab, if not Bill Gates. . . . What he's aiming to do, he says, is 'to identify ways in which technology has the potential to fundamentally transform our world, and to play a significant role in bringing about that transformation.'"

SOURCE: James Aley, "Wall Street's King Quant," *Fortune* (February 5, 1996).

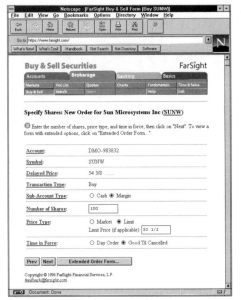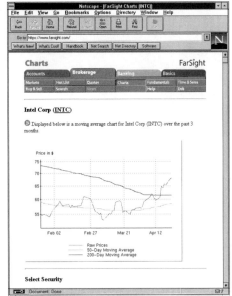

25.3 FarSight: Rocket Science transforming Wall Street.

Moreover, assuming FarSight achieves its goal of creating a supersystem, the individual investor will beat a path to Shaw's doorstep, demanding the FarSight service. Then watch out—because the sleeping giant, the *traditional* Wall Street institutions, will be *forced* to counterattack, as Microsoft did after being wounded by Netscape and like the commercial banks did after Bill Gates called them dinosaurs.

The individual investor wins the game at every competitive turn in this incredible Wall Street cyberspace revolution.

Cyberspace Revolution: A Power Shift from Wall Street to Do-It-Yourself Investors

Revolutions begin with rebels stockpiling arsenals with new weapons. The Wall Street Cyberspace Revolution is no different.

This conflict pits Wall Street institutions against Main Street investors—the "little guy," Beardstown Ladies and Generation Xers, Motley Fools and Market Wizards. They join the American Association of Individual Investors, not the New York Yacht Club.

The prize is freedom: The revolutionaries are fighting for the right to be *independent* investors. Meanwhile, the Wall Street Establishment is fighting to keep investors *dependent* on them. The opposing battle cries are loud and clear:

❒ **The Wall Street Power Establishment:** "Do-it-yourself investing is not a viable concept in the 1990s," asserted a Smith Barney executive vice president in *Fortune* magazine. In fact, many Establishment firms are now renaming their brokers "financial consultants," an obvious misnomer for firms that survive on charging sales commissions and keeping alive the illusion that investors are incapable of independent thinking and decision making.

❒ **Main Street Do-It-Yourself Investors:** "At Fidelity, we believe that, given the proper tools and information, individual investors like you make their own best investment decisions," asserts America's largest mutual fund manager. A similar battle cry echos loudly throughout the emerging new global financial cyberspace.

The Wall Street Establishment is losing the war. Like Bill Gates a year ago, Wall Street is trapped in denial. Distracted, Gates' radar failed to see Netscape on The Road Ahead . . . until Netscape made a preemptive strike, rocketing into Internet territory. Today, Wall Street is similarly off guard and vulnerable to the new weaponry arming the do-it-yourself rebels.

MAIN STREET INVESTORS NOW CONTROL FINANCIAL CYBERSPACE

Yes, Wall Street had a big head start in financial cyberspace. Created by institutional investors in the late 1970s (before Gates was even out of high school!), Wall Street's arsenal included powerful mainframes and analytic workstations, Quotron and CompuServe, Instinet and Telerate. Financial cyberspace was a private club, a playing field for members only, the Wall Street Establishment.

The little guy on Main Street had nothing. The PC didn't even exist until we were well into the 1980s. And by then, Bloomberg was supplying Wall Street institutions with heavy weapons and rocket science.

The 1990s have changed the rules of engagement. Information technology is now the new source of power, not capital. We have a new ball game, and the playing field is leveling. Wall Street is overconfident. And Main Street is relentless, quietly building its arsenal.

POWERFUL NEW WEAPONS FOR DO-IT-YOURSELF INVESTORS

The weaponry being stockpiled by the rebels is truly awesome, thanks to the rapid, accelerating transfer of new technologies into the hands of the individual investor. Their arsenals include many powerful new weapons that reflect the key trends in the sweeping transformation of Wall Street described throughout this book:

❏ **Supercharged personal computers** more powerful than mainframes of a short decade ago. Portable, intuitive, fast, cheap, and linked to a powerful global network.

❐ **Low-cost online services** developed and marketed specifically for do-it-yourself investors: Reuters Money Network, Telescan, Dow Jones News/Retrieval; even AOL, Prodigy, and CompuServe are beefing up their inventories of financial services. The Bloomberg at $1,595 a month versus Reuters Money Network for $25 a month? No contest!

❐ **New Internet and online access** to the best financial databases loaded with information on company fundamentals and mutual fund data; today, publishers such as Dow Jones, Hoovers, Holt, Morningstar, Disclosure, D&B, Lexis-Nexis, and S&P are all guilty of collaborating with the enemy.

❐ **Powerful analytical software** for both fundamental and technical analysis: StreetSmart, Metastock, Windows on WallStreet, and TradeStation.

❐ **Cyberspace investment clubs** are sharing valuable weapons information online and on the Net. These clubs include the American Association of Individual Investors, National Association Investors Corporation, and many local PC users groups specifically for computer-savvy investors.

❐ **Free quotes and news:** Delayed quotes are available free from countless cyberspace locations, plus real-time quotes and news at big discounts from the big info-gunners, Data Broadcasting Corp, DTN Wall Street, and PC Quote.

❐ **Electronic discount brokers** are fighting such a heated battle for online customers that Merrill Lynch and the major Wall Street firms have openly conceded the fight, focusing instead on the wealthy investor's need for "financial consultants," professional advisers to do your thinking for you. Meanwhile, Schwab, E*Trade, Quick & Reilly, PCFN, and other electronic discounters attract more new revolutionaries every day.

❐ **Mutual funds** are aggressively catering to the small investor in a big way, supplying the rebels with sophisticated software, online trading, and market and company information. The new multifund exchange networks such as Schwab's OneSource, Fidelity's FundsNetwork, AOL's Mutual Fund Center are there, too.

❐ **Online banking:** Commercial banks are now pushing discount brokerage, plus new electronic, do-it-yourself power tools from Quicken and other software developers—total one-stop electronic services, including financial planning, budgeting, tax preparation, and mutual fund management, specially designed for the new breed of *independent* investors.

❏ **New telecommunications laws,** mergers, and commercial opportunities are enticing giant telephone, television, and cable networks into the competition of delivering financial data to the new cyberspace investors; NYNEX and AT&T Business Network are becoming the ultimate yellow pages in cyberspace.

Today the SEC and federal agencies are also major allies, making it easier for do-it-yourself investors to take charge of their own financial destiny . . . and further undermining the power of the Wall Street Establishment.

SOON ALL INDEPENDENT INVESTORS WILL BE CYBERSPACE INVESTORS

Remarkably, virtually none of these cyberspace technologies were available to the individual investor until very recently. Wall Street institutions had *all* the power tools.

Today, institutional investors are on the defensive as more and more new technologies fall into the hands of the do-it-yourself rebels. Unfortunately, Wall Street continues seeing the *independent* investors as a threat to its very survival, primarily because they want discounts and no-loads.

Yet at the current rate new independent investors are going online and on the Net, by the year 2001 all 52 million shareholders will be in cyberspace.

This revolution won't go away. On the contrary, it's accelerating, while Wall Street continues denying the existence of the independent investor. Continue ignoring them, however, and soon it'll be too late. They'll continue defecting to Schwab, Reuters, Fidelity, Quicken, AOL, FarSight . . . and anyone else who says, "Yes, yes, I will help you," when this new breed of independent investor says, "*I demand to do it myself!*"

MAIN STREET DO-IT-YOURSELF INVESTORS ARE WINNING THE WALL STREET CYBERSPACE REVOLUTION

Bottom line: In this revolution, the do-it-yourself Main Street investor is not merely fighting for discount commissions and no-load securities—as the Wall Street Establishment believes—Main Street investors are fighting for freedom

. . . for the right to think independently and make independent investment decisions. That right is the ultimate prize being fought over in this Wall Street Cyberspace Revolution.

Fortunately, the individual investor is winning this battle, thanks to all these new weapons. Cyberspace technology is transferring enormous power to the individual investor, and in the process will totally transform Wall Street.

Soon the impact of the paradigm shift will be so overwhelming that Wall Street will no longer be able to deny the transformation and the new world order. It will then surrender and join forces with Main Street. And in the final analysis, the independent, do-it-yourself investor will emerge the clear winner in the Wall Street Cyberspace Revolution.

Cyberspace is the key to your financial independence.

Directory of World Wide Web Addresses for the Top-25 Investor's Navigators

COMMERCIAL ONLINE SERVICES

1. **America Online: Personal Finance Menu**
   <www.aol.com>
2. **CompuServe: Personal Financial Center**
   <www.compuserve.com>
3. **Prodigy: Informed Investor**
   <www.prodigy.com>
4. **Reuters Money Network**
   <www.moneynet.com> <www.rol.com>
5. **Dow Jones News/Retrieval**
   <www.dowjones.com>
6. **Telescan Investor Platform**
   <www.telescan.com> <www.wallstreetcity.com>

MUTUAL FUNDS IN CYBERSPACE

7. **Fidelity Investments**
   <www.fid-inv.com>
8. **Vanguard Group**
   <www.vanguard.com>

9. **NETworth Internet Investor Network**
   <www.networth.galt.com>
10. **Mutual Funds Magazine Online**
    <www.mfmag.com>

CYBERSPACE DISCOUNT BROKERS ONLINE

11. **The New Cyber-Brokers**
    <www.etrade.com> <www.quick-reilly.com>
12. **Charles Schwab & Company**
    <www.schwab.com>
13. **PAWWS Financial Network**
    <www.pawws.com>
14. **Aufhauser & Co.'s WealthWEB**
    <www.aufhauser.com>
15. **Lombard Internet Securities Trading**
    <www.lombard.com>

THE NEXT GENERATION OF NET*NAVIGATORS

16. **Commercial Banks: Quicken's Online Banking**
    <www.intuit.com/quicken> <www.sfnb.com>
17. **Corporate America: DRIPs and No-Load Stocks**
    <www.aaii.com> <www.moneypaper.com>
18. **Telecommunications: AT&T Business Network**
    <www.att.com> <www.bigyellow.com> <www.nynex.com>
19. **Electronic Publishers: Time Warner's Pathfinder**
    <www.pathfinder.com/money>
20. **Financial Television Broadcasters: CNBC and CNNfn**
    <www.cnbc.com> <www.cnnfn.com>
21. **Quote and Market Data Vendors: DBC, InterQuote, and Quote.com**
    <www.dbc.com> <www.interquote.com> <www.quote.com>
22. **World Wide Web Directories: Global Yellow Pages**
    <www.cpcug.org/user/invest> <www.cts.com/~wallst>
23. **Software Developers: Microsoft, Sun, and Netscape**
    <www.msn.com> <www.sun.com> <www.netscape.com>
24. **Securities Exchanges: U.S. and Global Financial Networks**
    <www.cme.com> <www.amex.com> <www.mbnet.mb.ca/~russell>
25. **Investment Bankers: Institutions and Rocket Scientists**
    <www.farsight.com> <www.prusec.com> <www.ml.com>

Index

Page numbers for illustrations (computer screen representations) are in italics. Page numbers for references to boxed text or quotations from magazines, newspapers, newsletters, and books are in boldface type